ISLANDS, PLANTS, AND POLYNESIANS

ISLANDS, PLANTS, AND POLYNESIANS

An Introduction to Polynesian Ethnobotany

Edited by
Paul Alan Cox
and
Sandra Anne Banack

Department of Botany and Range Science
Brigham Young University
Provo, Utah 84602

*Proceedings of a Symposium Sponsored by
the Institute of Polynesian Studies
Brigham Young University-Hawaii Campus
Laie, Hawaii*

DIOSCORIDES PRESS
Portland, Oregon

ISBN 0-931146-18-6
Printed in Hong Kong

DIOSCORIDES PRESS
Theodore R. Dudley, Ph.D., General Editor
9999 S.W. Wilshire
Portland, Oregon 97225

Library of Congress Cataloging-in-Publication Data

Islands, plants, and Polynesians : an introduction to Polynesian
  ethnobotany : proceedings of a symposium / sponsored by the
  Institute for Polynesian Studies, Brigham Young University--Hawaii
  Campus, Laie, Hawaii ; edited by Paul Alan Cox and Sandra Anne
  Banack.
      p.   cm. -- (Historical, ethno- & economic botany series ; v.
  5)
    Includes bibliographical references and indexes.
    ISBN 0-931146-18-6
    1. Polynesians--Ethnobotany--Congresses. 2. Ethnobotany-
  -Polynesia--Congresses. I. Cox, Paul Alan. II. Banack, Sandra
  Anne. III. Brigham Young University--Hawaii Campus. Institute for
  Polynesian Studies. IV. Series.
  GN670.I85 1991
  581.6'0996--dc20   90-19562
                                                          CIP

Contents

Preface

Ethnobotany, the study of the use of plants by indigenous peoples, has always been something of a scientific orphan. Any field dealing with plants must, of course, have some affinity with botany. Yet few botanists have acquired the specialized anthropological training and linguistic skills necessary to interview indigenous planters, healers, or weavers in remote areas of the world untouched by Western culture. Similarly, any field dealing with indigenous peoples must have some relationship with anthropology, yet few anthropologists are comfortable with the botanical entities about which their informants seem so knowledgeable. And any study of prehistoric uses of plants obviously impinges upon archaeology, yet again few archaeologists have the biological tools to recreate from limited plant remains the broad patterns of plant domestication and exploitation that allowed cultures to expand or decline. Even linguistic studies frequently involve traditional plant taxonomic systems, yet few linguists have the necessary botanical background to authoritatively discuss the changes in plant names over both space and time. As a result, ethnobotany has sometimes been viewed with a bit of a raised eyebrow by the academic community. All too frequently it has been seen as the domain of dilettantes and academic dabblers who have strayed a bit too far from their own discipline.

Yet, the importance of ethnobotanical research has never been greater. Today the traditional plant lore of indigenous peoples is vanishing even more rapidly than the tropical rain forests on which many of them depend. As a result, our generation may be the only one in which original ethnobotanical research can be done in non-Westernized societies, since the survival of both indigenous plant lore and primary rain forests for more than two decades at this moment appears to be unlikely.

Fortunately, the need for scholarly documentation of indigenous plant lore is being recognized, and indeed several recent developments have been heartening. Some scientific journals, such as *Economic Botany, Ethnobiology,* and *The Journal of Ethnopharmacology,* have chosen to focus largely on ethnobotany, and in 1990 two major international symposia, the Ciba-Foundation/Chulabhorn Institute Symposium on Bioactive Molecules from Plants (Bangkok, Thailand), and the First International Congress on Ethnopharmacology (Strasbourg, France), highlighted the importance of ethnobotanical research. Governmental interest in ethnobotany is also increasing. In the United States, the National Science Foundation and National Institutes of Health have slowly increased funding of ethnobotanical research, and in countries ranging from Mexico to Thailand, institutes of ethnobotany have been organized. Particularly encouraging has been the number of new courses in ethnobotany established at universities and colleges throughout the world, and the increased recognition that is being given to indigenous healers, weavers, and planters worldwide.

Perhaps some of the recent interest in ethnobotany has been fueled by the hope that new economically important products from plants, such as drugs, will be found through ethnobotanical research. But I also like to believe that academic interest in ethnobotany is increasing because the discipline in its broadest sense represents a unified approach to understanding the interaction between culture and environment in indigenous societies.

The importance of the interaction between culture and environment is particularly pronounced in the case of the Polynesians, who colonized one of the largest, most ecologically diverse and environmentally unpredictable areas on the surface of the earth. In an age when environmental problems loom large in public awareness and on societal agendas, we can learn much from the successes and occasional failures of this remarkable people who faced recurring environmental uncertainty and resource scarcity. From the construction of the large oceangoing rafts that carried them, to the crops and agricultural strategies they introduced to the islands they colonized, the Polynesians depended on plants for their food and shelter, used plants in their religious rituals and healing practices, and celebrated plants in their legends and oral traditions. To understand the development, expansion, and intensification of Polynesian cultures, an appreciation of Polynesian ethnobotany is not only desirable but necessary.

Each of the ten authors of this volume was invited to prepare a chapter on a selected topic with the goal of producing a broad overview of the interaction between plants and people in Polynesia. Though recruited from a variety of disciplines, including anthropology, botany, linguistics, and horticulture, the authors have met on the common ground of ethnobotany in an attempt to elucidate how plants have assisted and influenced the Polynesian people. Professionally the authors range from young, new researchers to mature scholars with many years of experience throughout the Pacific. Yet, as their chapters make clear, they are united in a deep respect for and admiration of the Polynesian people.

The contributions which appear in this volume are arranged roughly to follow the sequence of exploration, colonization, and intensification in Polynesian prehistory. Raymond Fosberg begins with an analysis of the island environments which the early Polynesian colonists faced when they arrived. Sandra Banack then discusses how plants were used in constructing and provisioning the seacraft the Polynesians travelled in on their prehistoric voyages of exploration and colonization. Arthur Whistler continues by examining the plants the Polynesians brought with them, both intentionally and unintentionally, in their long journeys. Next, Douglas Yen focuses on the crop plants the Polynesians introduced to the islands—where did these crops come from and how did they affect Polynesian settlement patterns?

The various agricultural strategies used to plant these crops are then examined by Patrick Kirch, who suggests that these strategies determined to a large part the later trajectories of Polynesian societies. The subsequent influence of plants and plant names in Polynesian languages is considered by Karl Rensch, who focuses on the names of one of the major Polynesian crops, the sweet potato. An examination of Polynesian foraging and the use of noncultivated plants, in this case, seaweeds, is then provided by Isabella Abbott.

The book concludes with three detailed examinations of specific uses of plants by Polynesians. I discuss the use of plants in Polynesian medicine, and present my views on whether Polynesian ethnopharmacology is an indigenous tradition or, as has been claimed by some, merely a practice introduced by the early European missionaries. Vincent Lebot provides a detailed, Pacific-wide look at *kava*—the Polynesian plant famed for its use in ritual—and presents compelling evidence that the chemical composition of various cultivars is the product of human selection. Finally, Diane Ragone concludes the volume by discussing the plant that not only drove the events leading to the mutiny on the *Bounty*, but continues to play a major role as a subsistence crop throughout the tropics—breadfruit.

I express my deep appreciation to each of the authors for accepting my invitation to participate in the symposium "Plants and Man in Polynesia" which was held at the Brigham Young University-Hawaii Campus, Laie, Hawaii, in December 1988. All the chapters in this volume stem from oral presentations given at that symposium. I am also grateful to the Institute for Polynesian Studies for their generous financial support of the symposium. The institute director, Jerry Loveland, the associate director, Lamoyne Garside, and the publications director, Dale Robertson, deserve particular thanks, as well as Brigham Young University-Hawaii campus and the Polynesian Cultural Center, for hosting the symposium participants. I also thank the National Science Foundation for a Presidential Young Investigator Award (BSR-8452090) that provided partial financial support for the symposium and, perhaps more importantly provided me the freedom to dream about a symposium in the first place. Finally, I thank my coeditor, former graduate student, colleague, and friend, Sandra Banack, for her encouragement and assistance throughout this project.

All of us are deeply indebted to the people of Polynesia who have been so hospitable to us throughout the years. It is my sincere hope that this volume may help younger Polynesians to appreciate the tremendous achievements of their ancestors. This volume is dedicated to them, and to Dr. Jacques Barrau, whose pioneering studies in Polynesian ethnobotany have been an inspiration to all.

Paul Alan Cox
Orewa, New Zealand
19 December 1989

CHAPTER 1

Polynesian Plant Environments

F. RAYMOND FOSBERG

U.S. National Herbarium
The Smithsonian Institution
Washington, DC 20560

I undertake in this chapter to give an idea of the nature and diversity of the oceanic island environment with emphasis on plants and on the environmental basis of insular ethnobotany. I speculate as to what was in the islands before the human period, what it was like during the Polynesian period, and the changes after the advent of Europeans until the present.

The Polynesian Plant Environment

For the benefit of those less familiar with the great diversity of Polynesian islands—both island to island, and within an island—some elementary Pacific geography seems appropriate. In an ethnological sense, Polynesia includes the islands scattered over a vast triangular area in the Pacific with Hawaii, Easter Island, and New Zealand as its apices, and with a scattering of outlying islands westward into Melanesia and Micronesia. All the islands are tropical or sub-tropical except New Zealand and its outlying islands and groups, which are temperate or even cold.

Topographically and geologically, again excepting New Zealand, the islands may be roughly separated into "high," mostly volcanic islands, and "low," coral limestone islands, mostly ringlike structures called "atolls" (see below). A few are intermediate, either elevated coral platforms or "almost atolls," small, dissected volcanic summits surrounded by lagoons bounded by barrier coral reefs with or without flat coral islets. In modern geographic theory—starting with the observations and writings of Charles Darwin, and amply substantiated by subsequent investigations, again excepting New Zealand—all or most oceanic islands are volcanoes which arose from fissures in the bottom of the sea and emerged above the sea as islands.

As these volcanoes, or groups of them, grew taller—up to as much as 4000 meters or more above sea level—and as much as 10,000 meters above the bottom of the sea, the masses of dense basaltic rock became so heavy that the earth's crust could no longer support them and so by isostatic adjustment slow subsidence began and continued. Organic reefs formed and grew around their shorelines (fringing reefs). As slow subsidence continued through geologic time, with faster growth on the turbulent peripheries, and as settling continued, the above-water part of the volcano became smaller, leaving a lagoon of shallow water between island and reef. The volcano during this time was being eroded and dissected. In advanced stages of subsidence, when the island became small in proportion to the total lagoon area, the term "almost atoll" became appropriate.

The penultimate stage was, or is, when the volcanic island disappeared beneath sea level, leaving the ring-shaped reef, usually with one to many above-water accumulations of "coral" limestone debris, loose or consolidated, called "islets" or in Polynesian, *motu* or *moku*. Minor fluctuations in sea level at times left more-or-less intact portions of reef rock exposed, also as islets. Limestone sand and gravel, dead skeletons and fragments of lime-secreting plants and animals, usually accumulated around these islets, which changed in shape and character with storms, wave action, and the growth and disappearance of vegetation. Terrestrial vegetation tends to fix and hold the sands and loose sediments and give semipermanence to these loose accumulations, and to bring about soil formation and development. The ultimate stage in this temporally vast geographic or geologic process is when the rate of subsidence exceeds that of reef growth and the whole structure disappears beneath the sea and becomes a "guyot" or flat-topped seamount (submerged mountain on the floor of the sea).

The islands in Polynesia, though widely scattered, are not distributed at random. With some exceptions, they are arranged in groups, or archipelagoes, usually in roughly linear sequences. The sequences start with the youngest, in several cases still active, volcanoes at one end and with gradually older areas along the line, followed by almost-atolls, then apparently ending in atolls, but sometimes continuing as a series of seamounts. Many of these chains, usually the older ones, run roughly southeast to northwest, but some are oriented differently. The reasons for this arrangement and orientation have become clear in the last few years, but are too involved to go into here. Some of the groups, such as Hawaii, illustrate very well the series of island types described above, namely, live volcanoes at one end, and seamounts at the other.

Since all stages in this scenario have existed presumably since the oceans assumed their present form, and are still occurring, the environmental diversity of and on oceanic islands is truly great. It is even greater because of the variation in geographic situations, wind and rainfall differences, and hurricane distribution and frequency.

New Zealand, large enough and diverse enough to be called a mini-continent, has a far more ancient origin, probably being originally, 80 or more million years ago, a part of the Australian, or possibly even Antarctic, continent. It has great geologic complexity, with sedimentary, metamorphic, and igneous rock formations and many extinct and some active volcanoes. Coral reefs, at least recent ones, are lacking, as the entire island group lies well south of the tropics, where reef-building organisms cannot contribute to land formation. Its biota is somewhat disharmonic (many families not represented) and, for its size and continental origin, impoverished. This is puzzling, but may be related to its relatively cool climate, or to its paleogeographic history. Many tropical groups are lacking.

Since the term and concept of "insularity" will occur many times in this volume, they may properly be introduced here, especially since the concept, though used largely by geographers, seems basically environmental and biotic in nature. The term is used to convey a complex of features: geographic, physical, biologic, sociologic—constraints, and advantages, due to which island phenomena are different from corresponding phenomena on continental areas and large "continental" islands. The term is not precisely definable, and its information content may differ with the context of the discussion in which it is used and with the nature and location of the island or islands being discussed. Some of the general features involved are isolation, being isolated by water barriers, climatic equability, resource limitation, environmental fragility or low resiliency, space limitation, and others often of a more intangible nature. Each author may have his or her own version of the above features or of the meaning of the term.

The Island Environment

Useful generalizations applying to all or most islands, even all Polynesian islands, are not easy to make and will inevitably be subject to exceptions. To attempt several such generalizations may invite interesting discussion.

In spite of the above introductory statements about diversity, compared with many familiar continental situations, impoverishment in many phenomena is prevalent—small floras, small faunas, limited diversity in rocks and soils, even limited ranges in temperature. Not only is the biotic diversity limited, but very often populations are small, or even very small, ranges of species are limited and consequently, with the high endemism of oceanic island biotas, extinction is frequent.

In an evolutionary context, adaptive radiation is prominent and founder-effect is important. Because "open habitats" are frequent and isolation by lava flows and erosional dissection is common, microspecies, subspecies, and varieties characterize the biotas. Loss of habitat leads to rarity or extinction. In an ethnobotanic context this leads to complete loss of useful plants, animals, minerals, and other commodities.

Though isolation is an obvious feature, on the plus side island people have been known to count water "barriers" between islands as an advantage because they make it easier to go by boat from one island to another.

Diversity of Physical Environments in the Islands

Class 1: Young, Active or Recently Active Volcanoes

Climatically these volcanoes are mostly tropical, though a few, such as the Kermadec and Chatham groups, are temperate. The high summits are temperate or cold, with snow on the highest peaks. The islands vary from dry to very wet, and in prevailing trade-wind belts, they vary from wet on the windward side to dry on the leeward side. Their surfaces are of hard lava flows (smooth or ropy called *pahoehoe*, or rough to very rough, *a'a*) or of ash, cinders, lapilli, clinker, or pumice, all forms of ejected, when molten, then solidified rock. This rock, in eastern Polynesian volcanoes, is practically always basaltic, a mixture of mostly iron and magnesium silicates, tending to be neutral in reaction. To the west, the rock tends to be andesitic, aluminum silicates and slightly more acidic. The topography in the east tends to be sloping and undissected, broadly dome-shaped; in the west, more conic and steeper. Soil is scanty—ash accumulation in pockets and crevices, and somewhat to considerably weathered areas, or kipukas, not covered by recent lava flows. Streams may occupy ravines on lower slopes.

Class 2: Older, Dissected Volcanic Islands

These differ from class 1 in being deeply weathered, rugged, and very dissected. Slopes tend to be steep and upper ridges sharp. Some islands are so eroded as to be called "skeletonized." Soils tend to be deep on gentler slopes and on broad, lower interfluves, but very leached, acidic, and bauxitic on wet windward sides of old islands. The rock, at least on high, wet slopes, tends to be rotten, and landslides are common on steep slopes. Permanent streams are frequent, especially on windward sides, and waterfalls are common, often spectacular. Much of the rainfall is orographic and in some middle-elevation islands, extremely high. The difference between windward and leeward sides is often striking, changing from saturated to desertlike terrain in a few kilometers' distance. On some windward sides the coasts have been greatly eroded by waves or, in some cases cut off by major faults, resulting in great cliffs which often have deep valleys cut in them. Chemical erosion has been a factor in forming fluted cliffs, with spectacular vertical ravines or valleys. The ground water, where it issues as springs or is pumped or collected in tunnels, is just under neutral in reaction. These older volcanic islands often have a narrow, flat, coastal strip, which is often backed by low cliffs or increasing slopes. The islands are usually surrounded by fringing or barrier coral reefs and, in the latter case, by shallow-water lagoons.

Class 3: Almost-atolls

The volcanic inner islands of almost-atolls are much like the islands of class 2, but more eroded and worn-down, lower, and often drier. In extreme cases like Clipperton and French Frigate Shoals, the volcanic island is a mere rock, steep and rugged.

Environmentally the islets on the barrier reefs do not differ much from the coral atoll islets to be described next as class 4. Those on the leeward side may be significantly drier if the volcano is high enough to cast a rain shadow by removing water from the wind orographically.

Class 4: Coral Atolls

A typical atoll is a roughly ring-shaped, coral reef, with one or usually more, often many, low, flat islets of coral limestone. This may be of loose coral sand and rubble, or partly or entirely consolidated into reef limestone. The reef usually encloses a shallow lagoon. Occasionally such structures are simply flat coral-limestone platforms with no lagoon or with only a small pond, either of salt or fresh water. The islets are entirely calcareous except for occasional pumice pebbles floated to them from nearby or faraway volcanoes. The islet surface shows little relief except peripheral beach ridges of coral sand and gravel, higher storm ridges of cobbles and boulders, and occasional low, to 10 m, dunes. Depressions here and there may reach the water table and contain fresh, or rarely brackish, water. The bottoms of these may be marl (calcareous mud) or, more rarely, smooth reef rock.

All Pacific atolls are tropical or subtropical and their rainfall varies from much and regular to very little and very irregular, depending on where in the ocean they are located. Belts of dry or variable climate extend east and west across the Pacific on both sides of the equator, and the atolls lying in these have dry or very uneven climates. Several atolls in the dry, central Pacific and several in the Tuamotu archipelago are very slightly elevated, with areas of very rough, eroded reef limestone a meter or two above the level of the loose sand or gravel of the rest of the islets.

Atoll lagoons provide a marine habitat of relatively quiet water, in strong contrast to the turbulent water on the reef flat and algal ridge on the outer periphery.

Class 5: Elevated Atolls

A very few atolls—three in Polynesia (Niue, Makatea, and Henderson) two Polynesian outliers (Rennell and Bellona in Melanesia), and the larger of the Tonga archipelago (and several in Micronesia)—are platforms of coral limestone raised 30–100 m above sea level. Presumably they are elevated atolls—they are highest around the periphery and somewhat lower in the interior. Some doubt has been cast on the theory that this topography is preserved from a lagoon surrounded by a reef (MacNeil 1950), but their atoll origin is still probable. Most such islands have been found to contain large deposits of calcium phosphate, and their topography has been drastically altered by mining of this fertilizer. Henderson, at least, in far eastern Polynesia, is still very much in its original state. Rennell contains a sizable fresh water lake in its interior depression. Otherwise freshwater is scarce.

Some soil exists on the upper platform surface, but other areas are dissected, incredibly pinnacled, sharp limestone. Such pinnacled surfaces also exist on limestone in class 6, below.

Class 6: Mixed Volcanic and Limestone Islands

Especially in the Austral and Cook archipelagoes are low volcanic islands with substantial terracelike limestone masses resting on the volcanic slopes, well above sea level, or extending up from sea level. These are called *makatea* by the Polynesians. In extreme cases, such as Mangaia, this limestone is many meters thick and intricately dissected. On some islands of this type the central volcanic part is eroded down to a low hill, sloping down to the base of the surrounding limestone. At the base where the two formations come together is a marshy zone with taro patches. There is little soil on the limestone, but the silt from the volcanic slopes collects in the marshy area, providing a fertile soil. On most such islands the volcanic rock is deeply weathered, providing a soil layer which seems badly leached. The nutrients are, however, accumulated in the marshland at the base of the slopes. Most of these islands are in a fairly rainy zone.

Pre-Polynesian Environment

We have no reliable means of knowing what sort of environments the Polynesians found when they spread into the oceanic islands of the Pacific three to five thousand years ago. Even fossils are very scarce in Polynesia and give us little that is helpful in reconstructing the past. Selling's (1948) Hawaiian pollen studies indicate climatic fluctuations, and unpublished data on plant macrofossils from the Salt-Lake ash indicate forest at lower levels than at present on Oahu. We can speculate on the basis of present wind and rainfall patterns, and resulting vegetation patterns, but must allow for possible climatic changes even in the few thousand years since the beginning of Polynesian settlement.

It seems very likely that, except on the coral atolls in the driest zones, the islands were forested. Several forest types seem to have been characteristic of low, coral atolls. On these, in addition to mixed broad-leaved forests of a few very widely distributed strand tree species [especially *Messerschmidia argentea* (Boraginaceae), *Cordia subcordata* (Boraginaceae), *Hernandia sonora* (Hernandiaceae), *Pandanus tectorius* (Pandanaceae), *Guettarda speciosa* (Rubiaceae), *Pisonia grandis* (Nyctaginaceae), and in western Polynesia, *Neisosperma* (syn. *Ochrosia*) *oppositifolia* (Apocynaceae)], several single-species types occurred, an uncommon phenomenon in the tropics. Such were *Pandanus* forests, *Messerschmidia* forests, *Neisosperma* forests, and, especially, *Pisonia grandis* forests.

Evidence exists that *Pisonia grandis* forests may have occurred in low-island habitats from eastern Polynesia as far west as the western Indian Ocean. This type is of special interest because of an ecological interaction with sea birds to form atoll phosphate rock, the "guano," mining of which altered a number of Polynesian environments. Under *Pisonia* forests a thick layer of an acidic "raw humus" or mor accumulated. Sea birds, in great numbers, roosted and nested in these *Pisonia* trees. Their excrement, of pulverized fish bones (calcium phosphate), was washed by rainwater into the humus, became acidified, and dissolved. The resulting solution percolated down into the coral sand below. Neutralized, the phosphate then came out of the solution and cemented the limestone sand grains together into a layer of soft rock, or hard-pan. Further percolation of the acid solution gradually dissolved away the calcium carbonate sand grains and replaced them with calcium phosphate. The atoll phosphate rock thus formed is a characteristic brown substance, speckled with white, occurring in thin to thickish beds on many atolls.

Even on the driest atolls there may have been some *Pisonia* or *Messerschmidia* forest, probably dwarfed. Small areas of phosphate rock on Canton, in the

Phoenix group, suggest such *Pisonia* forests occurred there. Several pieces of atoll phosphate, picked up by Wayne Gagné on Laysan atoll, Leeward Hawaiian Chain, make it almost certain that a fairly dense *Pisonia grandis* forest must have existed there, with seabirds roosting and nesting in it.

On the higher, volcanic islands in the trade-wind belt we can say with some confidence that on the wet windward sides there were montane rain forests on the slopes and cloud forests higher up, similar to those still present on islands like Tahiti, Kauai, Oahu, Molokai, Maui, Hawaii, Kusaie, and Ponape. On the lower, drier, leeward slopes in the rain shadows, there were dry sclerophyllous forests. Examples of such still existed in the nineteenth century on the Hawaiian leeward slopes, and a few tattered remnants still do.

New and recent lava flows were bare, and early successional stages of vegetation on these probably were similar to those which exist at present. The very high elevation grasslands with open-to-sparse, shrubby, emergent individuals or clumps were probably similar to those at present, but more luxuriant than now because of the absence of large herbivores. The faunas found in the pre-Polynesian forests were undoubtedly similar to, but probably richer than, those still present. Likewise, plants now rare or extinct in these dryland forests may have been common then.

From what we know of the nature of the indigenous floras and faunas of Polynesian islands, the original Polynesian castaways and colonists found precious little that was edible in the terrestrial plant biota when they arrived. Whether certain widespread species were native is difficult to know with certainty, but it is generally believed that most of the obviously useful ones came with the Polynesians. The uses of endemic ones were not obvious and had to be learned. Birds, however, were plentiful, at least at first.

The marine situations and biotas were much richer in edible organisms, which were largely the same or similar to those farther west and could have been immediately exploited (see Abbott, this volume). Otherwise colonization would have been almost impossible.

In pre-Polynesian time, habitats suitable for immediate human occupation were mostly confined to the coastal strips and the deep stream or river valleys. Indeed, until the coming of Europeans, these lowland habitats were those principally occupied by humankind. Available native human foods in the pristine island environments were almost exclusively marine. The only exceptions were birds and a few small freshwater fish, eels, and shrimps, and a very few berries, possibly a few succulent leaves, and roots. The presence or absence of the scarcely edible kukui nut, *Aleurites moluccana* (Euphorbiaceae), before the Polynesians is a subject of argument (see below and Whistler, this volume).

In summary, the pre-Polynesian environment provided a potentially wide range of habitats, some of them climatically and physiographically suitable for humans. In terms of biological resources, there was scarcity except along the seacoast, where marine resources were abundant and largely familiar. Land suitable for aboriginal cultivation was confined to the coastal strips and bottoms of valleys, which were then doubtless very well vegetated with large trees. Noxious, predatory, or disease organisms were very few, except for sharks, poisonous fish, and a few stinging pelagic and reef-dwelling invertebrates. Even mosquitoes were probably absent. Away from the coast, starvation was about the only environmental threat or hazard, except for landslides and falling from cliffs. Even discomforts were few and mostly avoidable. Marine hazards were the same as everywhere else in the tropics.

Pre-European Environments

The physical environments in Polynesian islands—major rainfall patterns, geological and physiographic variations, regional climates—in all likelihood persisted with little change after humans had occupied the habitable islands in Polynesia. Changes in physical factors caused by aborigines would have been slight and local.

The coming of the Polynesians brought many other environmental changes, mostly beneficial to humans, at least for the short term. Direct changes by them were at first confined to clearing places along the coast at the mouths of rivers and streams to build their houses and plant gardens. Coconuts were planted, and changed the landscape locally about villages. Several other kinds of trees, such as breadfruit, *mape* or Tahitian chestnut (*Inocarpus fagifer*, Leguminosae), and probably the Tahiti apple or hog-plum (*Spondias dulcis*, Anacardiaceae) and the mountain apple (*Syzygium malaccense*, Myrtaceae) were also brought from the west, and produced minor changes, especially on the coastal strip and in valley bottoms. Only the mape and mountain apple tended to spread up the sides of the valleys, probably with the help of humans. Of these five common tree introductions only the coconut, mountain apple, and breadfruit were carried to Hawaii. A number of "root" crops-taro, giant taro, and several kinds of yams—also came with the Polynesians. The valley bottoms on the wet sides of the islands were altered by establishment of taro patches and other types of gardens. Ingenious irrigation systems changed the flow of some streams.

Whether or not the *kukui* (*Aleurites moluccana*) was brought by the Polynesians is not certain, as its nuts are common in beach drift. The theory that it is an introduction is favored and, indeed, suggested by the unlikelihood of its having climbed the steep mountain slopes up to its present habitat without human assistance. If it was brought by humans and carried up the hills by them, it spread to dominate a whole zone on many islands, forming pure stands and shading out almost all other plants, and made an important change. On some islands kukui forest occupies roughly the rainfall belt (between 1500 and 2250 mm of rainfall a year), with tongues of this forest running some distance down moist ravines to lower elevations. The landscape was modified conspicuously by the introduction of *Aleurites*, whether by the hand of humans or dispersed naturally.

Pandanus tectorius may have preceded man in Polynesia, as its fruits are a component of beach drift, and its seeds germinate readily and the trees grow well on back-beach sands and coastal flats. The edible varieties were selected and carried around by humankind, but never became an important food source in Polynesia, as they did in Micronesia. Just how much of the *Pandanus* used for plaiting mats and other items was from wild native trees and how much selection and planting took place may be determined by ethnobotanists. The species is amazingly variable, and forms an important component of coastal vegetation throughout Polynesia except in New Zealand and on Easter Island. It also provided a habitat for mosquito larvae when they arrived in the islands.

Bananas were brought by the Polynesians and carried by them into wet valleys, even up to elevations well above where any Polynesians lived. The *fe'i* banana (*Musa troglodytarum*, Musaceae), especially, became established in the mountain valleys, particularly in the Society Islands. An important food plant there, it never made its way successfully to Hawaii.

With increasing population the alteration in the environment became more and more pronounced. Lowlands and coral islands were in many island groups densely populated and, hence, modified extensively to accommodate human-kind's comfort and activities. The steeper and higher slopes and ridges were not much utilized or changed.

Fires, probably mostly set by man, made profound changes in the vegetation of lower slopes on many islands. It seems reasonable to think that the extensive areas of sword grass, *aiho* of the Tahitians (*Miscanthus floridulus*, Gramineae), were the result of repeated fires. They are on leeward slopes for the most part, and on some islands, as on Mangareva, are practically pure stands of 1- to 2-m tall coarse grass, very inflammable when dry, but with root systems that normally survive a fire. In the Hawaiian Islands, where *Miscanthus* is not known, pili grass (*Heteropogon contortus*, Gramineae) covered corresponding slopes. It is not known how far back in the history of human occupation of the islands these grasslands originated. They doubtless came about gradually. They are now almost completely confined to volcanic slopes.

On high wet islands, such as Tahiti, many wetter and more exposed slopes at relatively low elevation (100–600 m) have almost pure stands of *Gleichenia linearis* (Gleicheniaceae), a tangled, branching fern. How far back these fernlands date is not known, but they were probably present in pre-European time. Their origin is controversial, but ancient repeated fire may be responsible, as with the grasslands. Scattered in the blanket of ferns are shrubs and small trees of *Metrosideros* (Myrtaceae), *Wikstroemia* (Thymelaeaceae), *Melastoma* (Melastomataceae), *Decaspermum* (Myrtaceae), and occasional herbaceous species, such as *Lycopodium cernuum* (Lycopodiaceae). The soil in these areas is bright red, highly leached or lateritic, thoroughly decomposed volcanic material. One may speculate that this soil-vegetation complex was the result of deforestation by fires set by the Polynesians, but the possibility cannot be excluded that it is a response to extreme leaching of nutrients by the heavy rainfall at warm temperatures. Its occurrence is normally on very wet windward slopes. Similar *Gleichenia* stands in Hawaii occur on gently sloping, young and not yet completely vegetated lava or ash, and also on older, weathered, deforested substrata. *Gleichenia* is able to colonize bare, moist soil wherever exposed, and holds the soil well.

A number of exotic plants other than the food plants mentioned above are believed to have come with the Polynesians. These were either brought intentionally for medicinal and other purposes, or unintentionally as seeds or spores accidentally sticking to items carried in the canoes. It seems unlikely that many of these had a significant influence on the environment. Exceptions may be those such as *Aleurites moluccana* and *Hibiscus tiliaceus* (Malvaceae,) whose indigenous origin is controversial (see Whistler, this volume).

Of the animal species brought by the Polynesians, chickens and dogs probably did not become thoroughly naturalized and had only very local environmental influences, in the immediate vicinity of human settlements. Pigs did become naturalized, and at present have a very deleterious effect on vegetation. What the effect was in pre-European time is hard to assess, but the fact that the flora almost completely lacks defenses against large herbivores suggests that pigs may have influenced both the establishment and the survival and numbers of many plant species. Dogs may have affected the numbers and habits of the pigs. The Polynesian rat, *Rattus exulans*, a "camp-follower," doubtless came in the canoes, as it is found on almost all Pacific islands. It was a part of the environment and unquestionably affected it in various ways. It eats both plant and animal material, fruits, insects, birds, and eggs. Its effects in the natural ecosystems as well as the human ones, are hard to assess. It certainly is a less aggressive and perhaps less omnivorous animal than its post-European competitors, the brown and black rats. It does not seem to have been a major environmental factor, but was not negligible. Lizards—geckoes and skinks—also may have come with the Polynesians, or they may have arrived earlier. They undoubtedly helped control insect populations, as did the birds, which were certainly pre-Polynesian.

To sum up the changes after the arrival of the Polynesians—undoubtedly much of the lowland vegetation was changed or replaced in the islands that supported significant human populations. Tree gardens, dominated by coconuts and breadfruits, with several other trees in many areas, and with a strong lower, mostly herbaceous component, such as bananas, yams, pia (*Tacca leontopetaloides* Taccaceae), taro, plus a number of weeds, came to occupy large parts of the lowlands. A few weeds and ornamentals accompanied the houses and gardens. Artificial marshes, for taro culture, became an important part of the landscape, and furnished a new habitat for certain plants, and probably animals also. Bird populations may have been affected, both by habitat changes and by rats. Some birds were also caught by people, both for food and for decorative feathers. Fire made changes in landscape and vegetation.

The marine environment was certainly affected, but not drastically changed, by fishing, both with spears and with nets, and also by poisoning by use of certain plants. Waste and offal were disposed of in the sea, but pollution may have caused only very minor changes.

The changes brought about by human and human-caused activities, while in some respects profound, did not usually threaten the stability of the ecosystem as a whole. There seems to have existed, at least on some islands, a fairly stable dynamic equilibrium. Population increases unquestionably brought about wars and forced migrations, but perhaps not much overexploitation of the environment. Population estimates given by early visitors were in some islands very high, but, judging from these early accounts, there seems not to have been serious environmental degradation resulting from population pressure. Islands that could not support human populations over long periods were abandoned or never settled. Doubtless most small-island cultures evolved in such a manner as to come to terms with their environments. Religions may have played a major part in this, but much of the information on this may have been lost as the Christian missionaries tried to wipe out the competing indigenous religious cultures.

It must, of course, be kept in mind that most of the above discussion is more informed intelligent guessing and speculation than fact. Most of the early accounts of the islands under discussion were not written by trained observers but by casual recorders who wrote about what interested them, in the terms of the periods and cultures in which they lived. Ecological interpretations are now attempted, but on the basis of all too few facts.

Post-European Environments

The coming of Europeans, with relatively advanced technologies and weapons, and with traditions of conquest and convictions of cultural superiority, as well as fanatical religious missionary zeal, brought vast and rapid environmental changes. The European culture itself was based on exploitation and the idea that everything in nature and the environment had been put there not just for human benefit, but for the benefit and enrichment of Europeans.

Indicative of what was to come was the way the captains of ships who "discovered" these islands claimed them—inhabitants and all—for their European sovereigns. British, French, Germans, and Americans all built large or small empires of the multitude of tiny chiefdoms and kingdoms scattered over vast expanses of sea. Sometimes they went through motions of treaties and alliances with local rulers, but nothing stood in the way of imposing, by harsh or gentle means, their "superior" European cultures on the peoples and places that one of the earliest, and certainly most enlightened of them, James Cook, called the nearest to paradise that he was aware of on earth. Most ironic of all were the numerous attempts to improve this paradise. The Polynesian religions were supplanted by the several "superior" brands of Christianity. The people were taught to live in ill-adapted European houses instead of well-ventilated grass huts, to use clumsy European boats instead of their graceful, fast canoes, to wear imported cotton and woolen clothes instead of their grass skirts and bark-cloth garments, to prize imported European bread and preserved food rather than their locally grown vegetable foods and locally caught fish and shellfish, and to drink alcoholic beverages rather than their relatively harmless *kava*.

A great number of exotic plants were brought in to compete with the native floras; large four-footed herbivorous mammals were introduced to trample and devour the remarkable plants that had evolved in the islands. Unintentionally, of course, diseases, to which island people, birds, and plants were unadapted, were brought in to decimate native populations. These all had profound effects on the environments in the native and foreign settlements.

Large-scale commercial agriculture—plantations of coconuts and sugar cane—occupied vast acreages of the most favorable coastal flats and lowlands. These not only used up the best land, but necessitated the importation of various nationalities of laborers, with a number of alien cultures and their environmental effects. Possibly most serious of all environmentally was the importation, escape, and naturalization of goats, cattle, sheep, and other large herbivores. These opened up the stable, closed, native vegetation by browsing and trampling. This had two important environmental consequences: accelerated erosion, and the replacement of much of the unique native vegetation of endemic plant species by an exotic vegetation, relatively poor in species. The environment was drastically changed and impoverished, and much that was poorly or not at all known was lost. The remarkable results of millions of years of animal evolution, as well as plant evolution, disappeared or are disappearing before they can be studied and understood, or even discovered and described.

Lowland landscapes are utterly changed. Water supplies and water regimes are depleted, altered, and polluted. Marine resources, fish, and other marine animals and plants are depleted, and the sea water itself is in places so polluted that few organisms can live in it. Surface fresh water is in most places undrinkable and even ground water must be purified.

Conclusion

The above applies mostly to the relatively complex environments of the high islands. The coral atolls and islands, with far simpler terrestrial environments, have mostly been converted from luxuriant, if simple, forests to vast coconut plantations. Their productive taro pits have become weed-infested and abandoned. Some of their lagoons have become polluted and reefs have been ravaged by crown-of-thorns starfish infestations, possibly brought on by pollution. Channels have been blasted into lagoons, changing the natural equilibria. Phosphate mining has altered even the land surface of some coral islands, and has brought total change and devastation on elevated atolls.

What has all this done to the indigenous human populations? In most islands introduced disease has decimated them. Their religions, and consequently their social environments, have been destroyed and replaced. Their material cultures and, even more, their social cultures have been drastically changed, and in many islands destroyed. They have, in most islands, become dependent on outside help, imported foods, medicines, and other materials. The younger people have never even learned how to survive in their island environment without help, education, and political domination from outside or from immigrant leaders. Not only have they forgotten how to use their natural resources, native plants, animals, and medicines, but even these resources themselves have largely disappeared. Native species are replaced by pantropic weeds, a few of which, of course, are useful.

The connections between these environmental changes and ethnobotany seem obvious. Ethnobotanical knowledge has mostly been forgotten and the botanical materials are in many cases no longer available. And interest in it is vanishing. If ever contact with the outside world were broken off, the reestablishment of a viable subsistence culture would be a long and painful process. Many peoples, even the immigrant ones, might not survive, or might survive in a most unrewarding fashion.

The above is admittedly a most incomplete account of the Polynesian environment. To bring together all that is already known would require an enormous research effort, library and museum facilities, and knowledgeable personnel. To put together all that would be needed to give a complete and integrated account of the Polynesian environment would not only require assembly, organization, and integration of all that is known, but an immense research effort to discover and record what is yet to be known. The dispersed nature of the region, with its vast seas and myriad islands, would require the efforts of a great many people with specialized training and abilities, as well as others with the ability and interest to generalize and integrate this vast information. The transportation and living facilities necessary to cover such a diversity of far-flung islands are beyond imagination, let alone probability.

Anyone who visits an island, however, with active curiosity and open eyes, can discover and put on record important facts, heretofore lost sight of or unknown.

The saddest thing of all to me is that the many Polynesian cultures, by all accounts among the most interesting and attractive developed by human populations, which showed the remarkable capacity to adapt to an originally difficult environment, are mostly forgotten and have largely disappeared. This volume seems to be a step in the direction of saving what remains of one aspect of these cultures.

Literature Cited

Abbott, I. A. 1991. Polynesian uses of seaweed. In *Islands, Plants, and Polynesians*. Eds. P. A. Cox and S. A. Banack. Portland, Oregon: Timber Press, Dioscorides Press.

MacNeil, F. S. 1950. Planation of recent reef flats on Okinawa. Bul. Geol. Soc. Amer. 61:1307–1308.

Selling, O. H. U. 1948. Studies in Hawaiian pollen statistics. III. Bernice P. Bishop Mus. Special Publication 29:1–154.

Whistler, W. A. 1991. Polynesian plant introductions. In *Islands, Plants, and Polynesians*. Eds. P. A. Cox and S. A. Banack. Portland, Oregon: Timber Press, Dioscorides Press.

CHAPTER 2

Plants and Polynesian Voyaging

SANDRA ANNE BANACK

Department of Botany and Range Science
Brigham Young University
Provo, Utah 84602

The voyages of early Polynesians and the vessels in which they travelled have long been of interest to researchers (Bougainville 1772; London Missionary Society 1799; Wilkes 1845; Coppinger 1883; Haddon and Hornell 1936; Whitney 1955; Banks 1962; Neyret 1974; Finney 1977). With courage and confidence in their gods and their vessels, the ancestors of the Polynesians undertook migrational voyages across stretches of the Pacific Ocean. It is apparent that their tremendous knowledge of their physical environment enabled them to sail their canoes to distant islands, navigating by sun, stars, wind, waves, and sea life (Gladwin 1970; Lewis 1972; Finney 1977). In addition, their knowledge of the island floras enabled them to construct seaworthy vessels while relying totally on the natural resources at their disposal. It no doubt took much trial and error to determine the best use of resources for optimal canoe performance.

Unfortunately, not enough attention has been focused on this environmental expertise. Rapid modernization of Polynesian cultures has led to an astonishing reduction in the transfer of such ethnobotanical knowledge to succeeding generations. While recent attempts to preserve ethnobotanical data have made valuable contributions in this effort (Cox 1980a, b; Kirch 1980; Atchley and Cox 1985; Banack and Cox 1987), much remains to be done. Particularly needed is an analysis of the actual plant materials used in Polynesian sea going canoes.

An examination of the ethnobotany of Polynesian canoes involves three areas for consideration: first, the plants employed in the construction of the vessels; second, the ceremonial use of plants; and third, the use of plants during voyages.

S. Banack's present address: Museum of Vertebrate Zoology, University of California, Berkeley, California 94720

Plants Used in Construction

Upon first contact with Polynesia, Europeans marvelled at the magnificence of Polynesian canoes (Wilkes 1845). The quality of workmanship appeared to far exceed the stone and bone tools employed in their construction (Williams 1884; Stair 1897). In fact, after seeing Samoan sea going canoes, Bougainville (1772) asserted that the Samoans must have used steel tools. The choice of materials used to construct the canoes was limited to the available local resources. Thus the quality of canoes from different islands varied and corresponded to the quality of resources available to each island.

Islands with extensive forests and durable timber, such as Savaii Island in Samoa (Stair 1897) and Kabara Island in Fiji (Thompson 1940), were celebrated for their canoes. Savaii is mentioned in connection with many Samoan voyages. In fact, in the oral records of early Samoan voyages and settlements in Rarotonga and elsewhere, the name of Savaii has been given such prominence that it seems to have largely overshadowed the true starting place in Samoa. In many cases Savaii is spoken of as the fountainhead of such colonization rather than what it seems to have been in most cases, the last starting place and port of call, as well as the home of the vessel (Stair 1897). Kabara Island was traditionally known as the center of canoe building in Fiji, and in much of Tonga as well, because of its valuable hardwood forest interior. Ancestors of the Fijian and Tongan carpenter clans settled on Kabara largely because of its floristic resources.

Carpenters developed wood preferences for the various canoe parts following the material constraints involved in the production of a fine canoe. Some of these preferences were unique to a particular area while others tended to overlap in conjunction with local floras. This section examines the floristic choices made in the construction of the main structural parts of Polynesian canoes in relation to the material constraints behind those choices.

The Hull

The main hull of a sailing canoe required durable timber, usually of great length and girth. The immense time and effort involved in the canoe construction demanded a finished product that would withstand the stresses and weathering of ocean travel for many years, hence the emphasis on durability. The unpredictability and danger inherent in interisland travel necessitated not only durability but also a vessel of large dimensions so that fewer trips would be needed to carry the desired people and property.

In Hawaii, the *koa* timber, *Acacia koa* (Leguminosae), well known for its hardness and durability (Hillebrand 1888), was commonly employed for the hull (Malo 1903; Emory 1933b). Driftwood trunks of the Oregon pine or sequoia redwoods, however, were preferred for their greater size (Emory 1933b; Haddon and Hornell 1936; Buck 1964).

The Maoris from New Zealand valued *totara* timber, *Podocarpus totara* (Podocarpaceae), or *kauri*, *Agathis australis* (Araucariaceae), for canoe building (Barstow 1878). The use of *A. australis* was confined by its geographic distribution, being used exclusively in the northern part of New Zealand.

The Fijians were well noted for the fine quality and design of their sailing canoes (see Fig. 1). The *vesi* tree, *Intsia bijuga* (Leguminosae), was always used for the best canoes because of its fine hardwood properties (National Research Council 1979). *Intsia bijuga* is a strong, durable timber resistant to insect and water damage, and grows to large dimensions. Fijian and Tongan carpenter clans settled on the island of Kabara, Fiji, because it possessed substantial stands of large *Intsia bijuga* trees (Thompson 1940).

It is evident from these few examples that each island possessed specific timber species from which canoe hulls were made. Naturally, alternate species were employed if the first preference was unavailable (Barstow 1878; Emory 1969). These canoes, however, were viewed as inferior and only the best timber species were used for the canoes of chieftains.

Islands which possessed no suitable large timber trees either developed methods of planking canoes together from the best available wood, as on Easter Island and in the Ellice Islands (Best 1925; Metraux 1957), or the islanders used other materials. For example, in the Chatham Islands such materials as dry flowering stalks of flax, *Phormium tenax* (Agavaceae), lashed to a light wood framework with bull kelp and lianas, *Ripogonum scandens* (Liliaceae) were used (Best 1925). These canoes from the Chatham Islands naturally were not capable of making distant voyages but they do illustrate the ingenuity of the Polynesians in manipulating their plant resources.

Figure 1. Raising the sail on a Fijian *camakau* built on Kabara Island, Lau, Fiji, in 1985.

The Float

Polynesian outrigger canoes were equipped with a float that provided balance and stability. The float often rode above the waterline, only skimming the surface of the water, and was always built from the lightest wood available to enhance the speed of the canoe. In Hawaii, the buoyant *wiliwili* wood, *Erythrina sandwichensis* (Leguminosae), was preferred, with *hau, Hibiscus tiliaceus* (Malvaceae), being used as a substitute (Malo 1903; Emory 1933b; Judd 1933; Buck 1964). The carpenters from the Cook Islands used *hau, Hibiscus* sp. as a first choice and sometimes *puka* (Buck 1927). The carpenters from Kabara preferred *Macaranga graeffeana* var. *major* (Euphorbiaceae) for the float, but recognized *Artocarpus altilis* (Moraceae), *Barringtonia edulis* (Barringtoniaceae), and *Hernandia nymphaeifolia* (Hernandiaceae) as useful also (Banack and Cox 1987).

Other Canoe Wood Parts

There are numerous other parts of a canoe for which wood is used. Each part possesses inherent material constraints which must be taken into consideration. For instance, wooden bailers require a soft wood so as not to damage the interior of the hull during bailing (Banack and Cox 1987). On the other hand, the paddles, steering oars, masts, and poling sticks require strength and a certain amount of flexibility. Outrigger booms must be lightweight and, in the case of the curved Hawaiian boom, conform to shape configurations. Inserted midribs also must fit a shape criterion and wood was always chosen with these facts in mind (Banack and Cox 1987). The midribs fit snugly inside the hollowed hull and must be shaped to the contour of the hull. The Fijians chose *Messerschmidia argentea* (Boraginaceae) for those inserted ribs because the tree often grows with a curved trunk and was easily shaped to the needed contour.

Nonwood Accessories

Foliage, sap, and inner bark fiber were used in addition to timber on these canoes. The leaves from *Pandanus tectorius* (Pandanaceae) were commonly plaited and used for sails throughout Polynesia (Malo 1903; Best 1925; Buck 1927, 1964). The Maoris from New Zealand were known to make sails from *raupo, Typha angustifolia* (Typhaceae), laid flat edge to edge and sewn across with New Zealand flax or *harakeke, Phormium tenax* (Best 1925). In addition, the leaves of *P. tenax* and *kiekie, Freycinetia banksii* (Pandanaceae), were also commonly employed. Also used occasionally was *kuwawa, Eleocharis sphacelata* (Cyperaceae) (Best 1925). Sennit made from the mesocarp of the coconut fruit, *Cocos nucifera* (Palmae), was commonly used for lashing the various pieces together on canoes in all Polynesian areas.

The rope used for rigging sailing canoes varies more widely within Polynesia. Hawaiians were known for using *olona, Touchardia latifolia* (Urticaceae) (Bryan 1933; Emory 1969). *Hau, Hibiscus tiliaceus, mamake, Pipturus albidus* (Urticaceae), and the fibrous stalk of the banana, *Musa* sp. (Musaceae) were also used to make coarse ropes (Bryan 1933). The Kabarans from Fiji used *hau, Hibis-*

cus tiliaceus, for rigging ropes (Banack and Cox 1987). These were made by first removing the bark from the trunk, then separating the primary phloem from the outer layer of periderm. The phloem was then hung up to dry. Once dried, a long, thin length of rope was twisted from several overlapping fibers. Three of these lengths were then twisted together to form a rope resembling manufactured hemp.

Across Polynesia, specific ropes were also used as hauling lines to transport wood from an island's forest interiors to its beaches. Rope made from dried leaves of the *ti* tree, *Cordyline banksii* (Agavaceae) or *Cordyline australis,* was used for this purpose in New Zealand ('Indigena' 1914; Best 1925). In Kabara, *kadragi* vines, *Ventilago vitiensis* (Rhamnaceae) were used (Banack and Cox 1987). Additionally, *pirita, Ripogonum scandens,* was employed as a rope for positioning the felled tree in New Zealand (Best 1925).

Great care was taken to waterproof seams in a Polynesian canoe, although materials used for this purpose varied according to location. Carpenters from Samoa and the Society Islands used breadfruit, *Artocarpus altilis,* pitch between the joints (Wilkes 1845; Stair 1897; Best 1925). To make an accurate fit, the Samoans covered one of the edges with turmeric, *Curcuma longa* (Zingiberaceae), which easily showed where alterations were needed on the two edges being placed together (Stair 1897). Once an accurate fit was secured, a piece of tapa cloth was placed between the joint and covered with breadfruit pitch before the seam was lashed together with sennit.

For the canoe constructed in Kabara, Fiji, (Fig. 1) coconut husk was driven tightly into the seam between the washstrake and hull. (If water enters the seam during sailing, the coconut husk will swell, filling the aperture). The hull was then rolled on its side and Fijian glue made from the sap of *Canarium harveyi* (Burseraceae) was poured over the seam, sealing the crack from the outside. A layer of plastic retrieved from a used commercial flour sack was then laid over the glue, followed by a wooden batten held in place with sennit. The inside seam was covered with a leaflet from the coconut frond, which was in turn covered by a wooden batten. The Maoris used *hune,* down surrounding the seeds of *Typha angustifolia,* to assist in waterproofing seams. In some instances *Phormium* fiber, smeared with the sap from *Panax arboreum* (Araliaceae), was placed in the joints before lashing with sennit (Best 1925).

Other non wood accessories worth mentioning are the paints used by both the Hawaiians and the Maoris. Hawaiian paint called *pa'ele* was said to have the quality of lacquer and was mixed using the sap of a certain *Euphorbia* sp. (Euphorbiaceae), the sap of the inner bark of the root of the *kukui,* or candlenut tree, *Aleurites moluccana* (Euphorbiaceae), and the sap from the bud of the banana tree. This was mixed with charcoal made from the leaf of the pandanus (Malo 1903; Buck 1964). The paint was applied with a brush made from a piece of pandanus aerial root, one end of which was beaten to free the fibers from the soft inner fibrous material. A dressing of *A. moluccana* oil was applied over the paint for a finish.

Before the Maoris painted a wood surface it was first primed using the expressed sap of the *poporo* shrub, *Solanum aviculare* (Solanaceae). This dressing was said to have caused the paint to adhere and enhanced the color (Best 1925).

Red dye was made from a type of clay, although *hinau* dye was made from *Elaeocarpus dentatus* (Elaeocarpaceae). The bark of *E. dentatus* was pounded, placed in a wooden vessel with water, and boiled. A carved piece was set in this dye for two nights, then flung in a swamp for one night. The dye acted as a mordant to intensify the black stain produced by the swamp mud. The carved piece was then dried and smeared with *E. dentatus* oil or grease.

A second method of producing a black paint involved collecting the soot obtained by burning *mapara*, *Podocarpus dacrydioides* (Podocarpaceae), and mixing it with oil. The Maoris applied the paint using a brush made from the *Phormium* fiber tied to a stick.

Each Polynesian group seems to have developed specific plant preferences for the individual canoe parts. Some of these species were unique to an area while others had widespread distributions and were commonly used throughout the region. The important fact remains that the construction of oceangoing canoes was a precise science throughout Polynesia and arguably remains the supreme technological achievement of its cultures. It is apparent that each group adapted its canoe building techniques to the available resources.

Ceremonial Use of Plants

In addition to the use of plants in a purely functional manner, the building and sailing of a canoe included various ceremonial observances in which plants often played an integral part. Plants were used primarily in a ceremonial capacity to either compensate the carpenters or propitiate the gods.

Compensating Carpenters

Carpenters throughout Polynesia came from recognized social groups or clans. They consisted of an elite hereditary class with recognized prestige and distinction (Stair 1897; Thompson 1940). Only men from these specific groups were permitted to build the large oceangoing canoes, thus they possessed the power to exact stiff wages.

It was customary for the carpenters, their families, and their attendants to be fed daily meals while the construction was in progress (Stair 1897; Haddon and Hornell 1936; Thompson 1940). Included in the plants comprising a staple diet on most Polynesian islands are taro, *Colocasia esculenta* (Araceae), breadfruit, *Artocarpus altilis*, coconut, *Cocos nucifera*, and sweet potato, *Ipomoea batatas* (Convolvulaceae). In Fiji, carpenters traditionally did not own garden lands; thus daily sustenance was necessary for their support and permitted a distinct division of labor and specialization (Banack 1987). This daily food, though not ceremonial, was nevertheless part of the custom associated with canoe building. The amount of food involved rendered the construction of a large sailing canoe a formidable task for anyone but a chief, who could command the necessary resources. When a chief decided to build a canoe, extra supplies of taro were planted and satisfactory crops assured before the request was presented (Stair 1897). Gardens were often planted near the forest work area where the tree for the hull was located (Best

1925). In conjunction with this the tree would be felled in autumn when the crops were mature (Best 1925). Food was often cooked separately for the workers and eaten at a distance from the canoe area. In addition, the carpenters were required to eat any leftovers before the freshly prepared food was consumed (Best 1925). A report concerning a Ngapuhi war canoe ('Indigena' 1914) documents a *tapu* placed on both the log and the workers every morning after the morning meal, and taken off each evening. This *tapu* forbade the eating of food during the day. (*Tapu*, the Polynesian root of the English word "Taboo," refers to a system of religious prohibitions and consecrations in Polynesian culture.)

In addition to daily meals, food was ceremonially presented to the carpenters as feasts when various stages of the project were complete (Hocart 1929; Haddon and Hornell 1936; Banack and Cox 1987). On Kabara Island in Fiji, feast food included not only large quantities of the regular staples but also a special addition of pork and often chicken (Banack 1987). *Kava, Piper methysticum* (Piperaccac) was ceremonially drunk at these occasions (Titcomb 1948; Banack 1987) as is common throughout Polynesia (Cox and O'Rourke 1987) (see Lebot, this volume). In Hawaii, offerings of a pig, red *kumu* fish, coconuts, and *awa, Piper methysticum*, were presented to the gods before the tree was felled, and were subsequently eaten by the head builder, the prospective canoe owner, and the assistants (Buck 1964).

Gifts of native manufacture were also presented to the carpenters throughout the building of the canoe (Stair 1897; Hocart 1929). These gifts included whales' teeth, fine mats made from *Pandanus sp.* and *Freycinetia sp.*, tapa made from *Broussonetia papyrifera* (Moraceae) or *Artocarpus altilis*, fine axes, and probably other objects such as coconut oil (Stair 1897). Stair (1897) commented on the importance of presenting adequate gifts, lest the carpenters took offense and made exorbitant demands or just quit working altogether.

Gifts to the Gods

Just as it was important to maintain the favor of the carpenters, it was perhaps more important to possess the favor of the gods to ensure a swift and sturdy craft. The attitude of the Polynesians toward their ships was said to transcend the mental and emotional, and become spiritual (Buck 1938). Canoe building was consecrated to the gods and thus *kapu* or *tapu* (Handy 1933).

A well-known Maori legend (Best 1925) tells of a man, Rata, who forgot to gain approval from the gods before felling a tree for his canoe. The next day he returned to find the tree restored to its stump. The man felled the tree a second time only to find it standing again the next morning. Rata felled the tree a third time and then hid, watching. He observed the coming of the forest elves, who chanted a charm, whereupon the prostrate trunk was restored to its stump as before. Rata confronted the forest folk, who replied, "It is not your tree. You did not tell us that you wished to fell a tree." The forest elves then explained that they must consent to his cutting the throat of the ancestor Tane and proceeded to tell him to fell the tree and cover the stump with the *paretao* fern, *Asplenium falcatum* (Aspleniaceae). He did so, and was thus permitted to make his canoe. This legend illustrates the importance of the gods in the undertakings of the Polynesians.

In most parts of Polynesia the god of forests and canoe building was Kane (Tane). The Hawaiians held Ku (or Tu), known as the god of war in other parts of Polynesia, as the god of crafts. Buck (1964) concluded that the Hawaiians simply confused the functions of the two gods; however this is insignificant, as a god by any name would perform the functions attributed to it by its worshippers.

Ceremonial observances to the gods can be identified in all areas of canoe building, from choosing a tree for the hull to launching and sailing the canoe. This section is divided into three areas: (1) selecting and felling a tree; (2) building the canoe; (3) launching and sailing.

Selecting and Felling a Tree. The felling of a tree first required feast offerings to the gods and prayers to male and female deities (Malo 1903; Emory 1933a). In Hawaiian legends Lea was the wife of one of the forms of Ku, and was therefore the female deity of the craft, with a visible representation as a woodpecker. If this bird appeared on a felled hull and walked the entire length of the trunk without pausing, the wood was considered sound. If, on the other hand, the bird stopped and pecked at the bark, the tree was judged to have a hollow or flaw and was thus condemned (Buck 1964).

Buck (1964) further relates that a variation on this was the interpretation of a dream by a priest. After the prospective owner reported to the priest that a suitable tree had been located, the priest slept beside the shrine in the men's house. If a naked man or woman appeared in a dream, the tree was condemned as having some hidden flaw. If the priest dreamed that he saw a well-dressed man or woman, the tree was approved as sound.

Emory (1933a) reported the selection of the hull was made by the *kahuna kalai wa'a*, who slept in a house for a vision to guide him in his choice.

Immediately following the felling of the tree, the head builder mounted the fallen trunk and, facing the stump, called out to the gods. He then turned 180 degrees and donned a ceremonial white loin cloth. The head carpenter proceeded to strike the trunk with his adz until he reached the place for cutting off the branched end (Buck 1964). A piece of *ie'ie* vine, *Freycinetia scandens* (Pandanaceae), considered sacred and reserved for ceremonial purposes (Neal 1965), was tied around the point to be cut. The other craftsmen proceeded to sever the end which then removed the *tapu* invested in the tree, and allowed all to share in the work (Malo 1903; Buck 1964).

Best (1925) recorded the Maoris from New Zealand as having similar rituals concerning felling the hull. Early in the morning the person desiring a canoe fastened a leaf to the end of a stick in the semblance of an adz. After donning a special girdle the adept repeated a chant to the god Tane. He then hit the tree with the stick and leaf, repeated a second chant, and hit the tree with a real felling tool. The adept took the first chip and burned it out of hearing distance of the tree felling, and upon his return burned the subsequent wood chips in a fire near the tree, thus removing all *tapu*. An additional recitation placated Tane and prevented him from punishing the tree fellers, thus preventing the stone tools from breaking and preventing accidents by the workmen. The feast food was then cooked with a portion being set aside and chanted over by the adept, thus completing the lifting of the *tapu* from the food, the work, and the workmen, and supporting and imparting wisdom to the workmen.

An additional account (Best 1925) recorded "a singular ceremonial act performed when a tree was felled." This account described laying fronds of two ferns, *mauku, Asplenium bulbiferum,* and *paretao, Asplenium falcatum,* upon the stump. One informant claimed that a piece of fern was cast into the fire, while another informant stated that a piece of fern was fastened to the canoe hull when it was dubbed out. Both of these acts were performed as symbolic offerings to Tane.

Although descriptions of the use of plants in ceremonial observances are somewhat scanty and the significance of these rituals even less understood or recorded, it is apparent that offerings to the gods were commonplace and undoubtedly widespread throughout Polynesia. I now examine examples of ceremonial plant use related to the building of a canoe.

Building a Canoe. Once a tree was felled and roughly hollowed out in the forest, it was hauled to the beach front for construction and finishing. This process was traditionally marked on Kabara, Fiji, by two feasts (Banack 1987). The first of these feasts was held when the small roller branches, over which the canoe would be hauled, were laid on the limestone trail. The second feast was presented after the hull was lowered from the forest interior down the cliffs to the beach front, where canoe construction was continued.

A similar occasion was recorded concerning a Ngapuhi war canoe in which a feast was made in the bow of the canoe ('Indigena' 1914). A woman of high rank then climbed into the canoe and consumed the food before the hull was pulled on its journey seaward.

Best (1925) recorded that each Maori worker had one special garment which he wore whenever working on the canoe. The garment was made of flax, *Phormium tenax,* specially procured for the purpose and woven by *ruahine* or *tapu* women. This garment was left near the canoe when quitting for the day.

In Samoa, the work area was placed under *tapu* to ensure quiet for the workers and to compel villagers to detour around the work area, thus paying homage to the work (Stair 1897).

Launching and Sailing. The launching and sailing of a canoe was also performed with reverence and respect for the gods. Certain rituals were chanted over the new vessel, placing it under the care of the gods. The final completion of the canoe and subsequent maiden voyage was traditionally the anticipated high point of the canoe construction, and was prepared for well in advance with gifts and a great feast (Malo 1903; Best 1925; Banack 1987).

In Maori culture, as recorded by Best (1925), a priest entered the forest the day before the ceremony to seek a small shrub of *karangu, Coprosma* sp. (Rubiaceae), approximately three feet high. The priest laid his hands on the leaves and chanted to endow the plant with the power to foreshadow the vessel's success. The next morning the priest returned to the shrub and, after chanting, pulled it up by its roots; a good omen was indicated if the roots did not break. If some or all of the roots snapped off as the shrub was pulled up misfortune was predicted for the canoe and its owners. The operator would at once go and consult other priestly or shamanistic experts and obtain their assistance in order to avert the misfortune by means of invocations or charms. At a later stage of this ritual the *karangu* shrub was dipped in water and struck against the figurehead of the canoe. The name of the canoe was also repeated at a given point in the ceremony. This rite served to remove the *tapu* so non*tapu* persons could approach and use the canoe. After the launching, a large feast was held.

The Hawaiians sailed the canoe, then consecrated it with a ceremony and a feast consisting of pig, red fish, and coconuts before it was presented to the owners (Malo 1903).

The canoe built in 1985 on Kabara, Fiji (Banack 1987; Banack and Cox 1987), was ceremonially presented to its owners with *kava, Piper methysticum,* being served before the launching. As the vessel returned from its maiden voyage a *rovo* was held wherein a sailor jumped off the craft and chased an assembled group of children who held aloft banners of native and manufactured cloth, celebrating the return.

The Samoans were accustomed to taking on board the canoe a talisman during distant voyaging as a protection and a shield (Stair 1897). The legends of the Maori also claim that each vessel that came from Polynesia had on board some sort of talisman, regarded as a sacred object endowed with protective powers that brought good fortune to the vessel and its occupants (Best 1925). One tribe reported having a piece of seaweed stem they used as a talisman, which had been carefully dried after preparation in a steam oven and over which a priest had recited certain charms. This talisman was used to ward off evil and was carried in the bow on every voyage and deposited in a sacred place upon returning.

The Maoris were known to perform ceremonies before and after a distant journey (Best 1925). To make the ocean calm for sailing a priest first took off his clothes and wrapped himself in a seaweed apron. With seaweed in each hand he recited aloud a chant, cast the seaweed into the sea, then removed the apron and reclothed. During a war expedition, canoes were under *tapu* and no food could be cooked or eaten in them. Upon reaching land an adept priest produced two *kakaho*, or two flower stalks of *toetoe, Arundo conspicua* (Gramineae). One of these was thrown as a dart into the sea and the other was chewed or its end bitten off, thus freeing the members of the party from *tapu* and enabling them to partake of food.

Plants Used During Sea Voyages

The ceremonial use of plants during ocean voyages has already been discussed. This section concentrates on plants used or carried on voyages for (1) consumption during travel, (2) fishing, (3) repair of the canoe, and (4) propagation in new islands or cargo transfer to neighboring islands.

Plant Consumption During Ocean Travel

As mentioned in the previous section, the Maoris were at times under *tapu* and forbidden to eat anything during local interisland travel (Best 1925). When considering long voyages, such as would have occurred for migrational purposes, the question of food supplies presented special problems. It should be noted, however, that

> the unbroken sea stretches of most Pacific voyages are relatively short
> because every inhabited island, save only Hawaii, Easter Island and New

Zealand, can be reached from some other island without crossing much more than 300 miles of ocean (Lewis 1976, 26).

Thus the problems of food supplies were not insurmountable. Horvath and Finney's (1976) experiments concluded that paddling a Hawaiian double canoe would require 4000 to 4500 calories per day per paddler. They comment further that perhaps water is a more critical resource on such voyages:

> One of the major limiting factors to successful voyaging may be the availability of adequate water supplies to replenish the losses experienced by the paddlers (Horvath and Finney 1976, 53).

Banks reported that Tupaia, a Tahitian navigator, set about a twenty-day maximum duration for a crew at sea on an intentional voyage, without refurbishing supplies (Best 1925; Ferdon 1981). Although the sailors lived as sparingly as possible, need of proper provisions and a place to store them, as well as drinking water, set this limitation.

The traditions of Hawaii and New Zealand (Buck 1938) held that crews of expeditionary ships were trained beforehand to use self-restraint in the consumption of food and water. With such discipline, the supplies in a canoe could be rationed for three to four weeks, the time required to cross the widest ocean spaces between the island groups in Polynesia.

Buck (1938) stated that "the provisioning of the sea-going canoe offered no problem." While provisions were usually cooked, a fireplace was often provided on canoes, laid on a bed of sand and stones (Stair 1897; Emory 1933a; Buck 1938). In atoll areas of the Pacific, reserve provisions consisted of ripe pandanus fruit grated into a coarse flour, cooked, dried, and packed in cylindrical bundles with an outer wrapping of dried pandanus leaves (Buck 1938). Volcanic islands provided greater possibilities for voyage provision. Samoans were known for carrying preserved breadfruit cooked in large baskets (Buck 1938; Cox 1980a, b). The Maoris' main sustenance at sea was sweet potatoes, cooked and dried (Buck 1938). Dried shellfish were also carried, and were said to keep indefinitely without spoilage. Fowls were often carried live on board and fed with dried coconut meat until killed and eaten.

A good account of Hawaiian voyaging provisions was provided by Emory (1933a). He explained that a seven- to ten-day supply of fresh food was carried, including sweet potatoes, taro, bananas, green coconuts, and breadfruit. Fresh yams were known to keep for two months, so a larger supply of them would have been taken. In addition, a supply of lasting food was carried which consisted of mature coconuts, fermented breadfruit, dried taro, dried sweet potato, dried bananas, and pandanus. The pandanus food was a yellow dough the consistency of putty, made by scraping the starch from the base of the keys, mixing the starch with coconut milk, and baking it. In addition, Hawaiians kept fresh fish and shellfish alive in a bamboo aquarium on board. Dried fish formed a staple on long voyages. Live domestic animals were also carried on board and fed scraps of copra and fish. Carried provisions were supplemented with birds and fish caught at sea.

As mentioned earlier, fresh water was considered a limiting factor on ocean voyages. Water was traditionally carried in bamboo lengths, coconut bottles, and gourds where available (Stair 1897; Best 1925; Emory 1933a; Buck 1938).

Reverend John B. Stair (1897, 285) recorded the use of a herb to assuage thirst on long voyages.

> In answer to my query whether they did not often run short of water, they told me the early voyagers always took a supply of leaves of a certain herb or plant as a means of lessening thirst, and that these formed a valuable stand-by on a voyage. By chewing the leaves of this plant, they declared that to a certain extent they could drink sea water with some impunity.

The author could not obtain the name of the shrub as the custom had fallen into disuse and the Samoans themselves did not know. He was, however, confident that the custom did prevail in the past.

Plants Carried for Fishing

To supplement food supplies carried on voyages, the sailors caught fresh fish while at sea. Fishing equipment was traditionally made from local resources and would have included nets, lines, and hooks. In Tahiti, fishing lines were made from *roa*, *Pipturus argenteus*, but *Hibiscus tiliaceus*, *Ficus tinctoria* (Moraceae), and *Cocos nucifera* were also used (Ferdon 1981). Wooden fish hooks were constructed from small roots of ironwood, *Casuarina equisetifolia* (Casuarinaceae). These were made by twisting the living root into the desired shape, then allowing it to grow; when the soft outer layer was removed, the inner heartwood remained thick enough to serve as a hook (Ferdon 1981).

In the Cook Islands, hooks were made from a forked branch of ironwood with a point of bone attached. Nets were used in the Cook Islands to catch fish from canoes. The cord for making nets was prepared from the bast of trees such as *oronga*, *Pipturus argenteus*, *hau*, *Hibiscus tiliaceus*, *Cocos nucifera*, *papako*, and *Broussonetia papyrifera*, although *oronga* is noted as the best.

Malo (1903) recorded that the Hawaiians used nets 20- to 30-fathoms long and four- to eight-feet deep for deep-sea fishing. No mention was made as to the materials used in their construction. Samoans and Fijians both used *Hibiscus tiliaceus* to make fishing lines (Turner 1884; Stair 1897; Thomson 1908).

Plants Carried for Canoe Repair

Before a long voyage was attempted the canoe was always refurbished, with seams recaulked and boards relashed (Emory 1933a). On occasion a new canoe would be constructed specifically for the purpose of a journey. It was also common practice in the Caroline Islands, with the traditions of the Moriori, and logically on any voyage, to carry a large basket of cured coconut fiber for making rope, along with extra poles to splice booms, the mast, or outrigger supports that might be broken during the trip (McCoy 1976). To check leaking joints during sailing, caulking material was carried in the canoe (Indigena 1914).

Plants for Propagation

Canoes were used extensively for interisland trade throughout Polynesia and thus food crops and plant products were commonly carried (Thompson 1940; Ferdon 1981). It is apparent that some common food species were also of aboriginal introduction, no doubt carried on migrational voyages. The Maoris of New Zealand have passed down oral records concerning the arrival of some plant species to the land. Seeds of the *karaka* tree, *Corynocarpus laevigatus* (Corynocarpaceae), for instance, were said to have been brought from Rangi-tahua or the Sunday Islands to New Zealand on the ship *Aotea* (Best 1925). Likewise the vessel *Horouta* was said to have brought *kumara* or sweet potato, *Ipomoea batatas*, to New Zealand from Tahiti (Best 1925). Another legend claimed a local vessel, *Te Aratawhao*, left Whakatane to fetch seed tubers of the sweet potato from Polynesia (Best 1925). In addition, *Broussonetia papyrifera* or *aute*, a plant species used in the making of tapa cloth, was reported to have arrived in New Zealand on the *Uturereao* canoe (Best 1925).

It is evident that plants were intentionally carried on migrational voyages to distant lands with the voyagers and propagated in the new homes of the Polynesians. In addition, many plants were carried inadvertently with the early settlers (see Fosberg and Whistler, this volume).

Conclusion

It is apparent that the indigenous flora was integrally tied to traditional Polynesian canoes. Floristic resources were heavily used, not only for materials in construction, but also for ceremonial purposes, and for sustenance and practical uses on oceanic voyages. Plants were carefully and expertly chosen to fill the material requirements of canoe construction. A variety of plant species was used in different localities following common criteria of durability, growth form, density, and availability.

Certain plants were chosen for use in ceremonial observances. Common useful plants were used to compensate carpenters for their efforts and expertise. Other plants were set aside for use in ceremonial rituals to placate the gods and remove *tapu.*

During seaward voyages, plants provided food for consumption as well as containers for water. Local resources were used as materials for fishing implements and canoe repair items, and also carried on board a canoe during travel. In addition, seed crops were transported on migrational voyages to distant islands.

The Polynesians possessed an intimate knowledge of their plant environment and needed this knowledge for their survival. The ethnobotanical study of Polynesian canoes aptly shows the ability of the Polynesians to meet material, cultural, and social needs using their various local floras.

Literature Cited

Atchley, J., and P. A. Cox. 1985. Breadfruit fermentation in Micronesia. *Econ. Bot.* 39:326–335.

Banack, S. A. 1987. *Ethnobotany of Ocean-Going Canoes in Lau, Fiji; The Fijian "Camakau"—Construction Techniques; Tradition and Change: The Fijian "Camakau".* M.S. Thesis, Brigham Young Univ., Provo, Utah.

Banack, S. A., and P. A. Cox. 1987. Ethnobotany of ocean-going canoes in Lau, Fiji. *Econ. Bot.* 41:148–162.

Banks, J. 1962. *The Endeavour Journal, 1766–1771.* Vol. 1. Ed. J. C. Beaglehole. Sydney: Angus and Robertson.

Barstow, R. D. 1878. The Maori canoe. In The Maori canoe. E. Best, p. 40. New Zealand Dominion Mus. Bul. 7:1–312.

Best, E. 1925. The Maori canoe. *New Zealand Dominion Mus. Bul.* 7:1–312.

Bougainville, L. 1772. *A Voyage Around the World.* Trans. J. R. Forster. London: J. Nourse.

Bryan, E. H., Jr. 1933. Fiberwork. In *Ancient Hawaiian Civilization.* Eds. Handy et al. Honolulu: Kamehameha Schools. 125–129.

Buck, P. H. [Te Rangi Hiroa]. 1927. *The Material Culture of the Cook Islands (Aitutaki).* Memoirs Board of Maori Ethnological Research. Vol. 1. New Plymouth, New Zealand: T. Avery and Sons.

_____ . 1930. Samoan material culture. Bernice P. Bishop Mus. Bul. 75.

_____ . 1933. Polynesian migrations. In *Ancient Hawaiian Civilization.* Eds. Handy et al. Honolulu: Kamehameha Schools. 19–30.

_____ . 1938. *Vikings of the Sunrise.* New York: Stokes Company.

_____ . 1964. Arts and crafts of Hawaii. Section 6, Canoes. Bernice P. Bishop Mus. Special Publication 45.

Coppinger, R. W. 1883. *The Cruise of the "Alert".* London: D. B. Sonnenschein and Co.

Cox, P. A. 1980a. Masi and tanu 'eli: ancient Polynesian technologies for the preservation and concealment of food. Pac. Trop. Bot. Garden Bul. 10(4):81–93.

_____ . 1980b. Two Samoan technologies for breadfruit and banana preservation. *Econ. Bot.* 34(2):181–185.

Cox, P. A., and L. O'Rourke. 1987. Kava (*Piper methysticum* Forst.) *Econ. Bot.* 43:452–454.

Emory, K. P. 1933a. Navigation. In *Ancient Hawaiian Civilization.* Eds. Handy et. al. Honolulu: Kamehameha Schools. 237–245.

_____ . 1933b. Wooden utensils and implements. In *Ancient Hawaiian Civilization.* Eds. Handy et al. Honolulu: Kamehameha Schools. 229–236.

_____ . 1969. The island of Lanai. Bernice P. Bishop Mus. Bul. 12:1–129.

Ferdon, E. N. 1981. *Early Tahiti As the Explorers Saw It 1767–1797.* Tucson: Univ. of Arizona Press.

Finney, B. R. 1977. Voyaging canoes and the settlement of Polynesia. *Science* 196:1277–1285.

Fosberg, F. R. 1991. Polynesian plant environments. In *Islands, Plants, and Polynesians.* Eds. P. A. Cox and S. A. Banack. Portland, Oregon: Timber Press, Dioscorides Press.

Gladwin, T. 1970. *East is a Big Bird.* Cambridge, Massachusetts: Harvard Univ. Press.

Haddon, A. C., and J. Hornell. 1936. Canoes of Oceania. 1976. Bernice P. Bishop Mus. Special Publication 27:1–445.

Handy, E. S. C. 1933. Government and society. In *Ancient Hawaiian Civilization.* Eds. Handy et al. Honolulu: Kamehameha Schools. 31–42.

Hocart, A. M. 1929. Lau Islands, Fiji. Bernice P. Bishop Mus. Bul. 62:1–241.

Hillebrand, W., M.D. 1888. *Flora of the Hawaiian Islands.* London: Williams and Norgate.

Horvath, S. M., and B. R. Finney. 1976. Paddling experiments and the question of Polynesian voyaging. In *Pacific Navigation and Voyaging.* Ed. B. R. Finney. Wellington: The Polynesian Society. 47–54.

'Indigena'. 1914. A Ngapuhi war-canoe. In The Maori canoe. E. Best, pp. 68–69. New Zealand Dominion Mus. Bul. 7:1–312.

Judd, A. F. 1933. Trees and plants. In *Ancient Hawaiian Civilization*. Eds. Handy et al. Honolulu: Kamehameha Schools. 273–281.

Kirch, P. V. 1980. Polynesian prehistory: cultural adaptations in island ecosystems. *Amer. Sci.* 68:39–48.

Lebot, V. 1991. Kava (*Piper methysticum* Forst. F.): the Polynesian dispersal of an Oceanian plent. In *Islands Plants, and Polynesias*. Eds. P. A. Cox and S. A. Banack. Portland, Oregon: Timber Press, Dioscorides Press.

Lewis, D. 1972. *We, the Navigators*. Honolulu: Univ. of Hawaii Press.

———. 1976. A return voyage between Puluwat and Saipan using Micronesian navigational techniques. In *Pacific Navigation and Voyaging*. Ed. B. R. Finney. Wellington: The Polynesian Society. 15–28.

London Missionary Society. 1799. *A Missionary Voyage to the South Pacific Ocean (1796–1798) In the Ship Duff, Commanded by Captain James Wilson*. London: S. Gosnell for T. Chapman.

Malo, D. 1903. *Hawaiian Antiquities*. Trans. from Hawaiian by Dr. N. B. Emerson, 1898. Honolulu: Hawaiian Gazette Co.

McCoy, M. 1976. A renaissance in Carolinian-Marianas voyaging. In *Pacific Navigation and Voyaging*. Ed. B. R. Finney. Wellington: The Polynesian Society. 129–138.

Metraux, A. 1957. *Easter Island*. Trans. from French by M. Bullock. New York: Oxford Univ. Press.

National Research Council, Commission on International Relations. 1979. Tropical legumes: resources for the future. Washington, DC: National Academy of Science.

Neal, M. C. 1965. *In Gardens of Hawaii*. Bernice P. Bishop Mus. Special Publication 50:1–924.

Neyret, J. 1974. *Pirogues Océaniennes*. Vol. 1. Paris: Association des Amis des Musées de la Marine Palais de Chaillot.

Parkinson, S. 1764. *A Journal of a Voyage to the South Seas, in His Majesty's Ship the* Endeavour. London: Dilly and Phillips.

Stair, J. B. 1897. *Old Samoa*. Oxford: Horace Hart.

Thompson, L. 1940. Southern Lau, Fiji. Bernice P. Bishop Mus. Bul. 162:1–124.

Thomson, B. 1908. *The Fijians*. London: William Heinemann.

Titcomb, M. 1948. Kava in Hawaii. *J. Polynesian Society* 57:105–171.

Turner, G. 1884. *Samoa A Hundred Years Ago and Long Before*. London: Macmillan and Co.

Waterhouse, J. 1866. *The King and People of Fiji*. London: Wesleyan Conference Office.

Whistler, W. A. 1991. Polynesian plant introductions. In *Plants and Man in Polynesia*. Eds. P. A. Cox and S. A. Banack. Portland, Oregon: Timber Press, Dioscorides Press.

Whitney, H. P. 1955. *An Analysis of the Design of the Major Seagoing Craft of Oceania*. M.A. Thesis, Univ. of Pennsylvania.

Wilkes, C. 1845. *Narrative of the United States Exploring Expedition*. Vol. 3. Philadelphia: Lea and Blanchard.

Williams, T. 1884. *Fiji and the Fijians*. London: Kelly.

CHAPTER 3

Polynesian Plant Introductions

W. ARTHUR WHISTLER

National Tropical Botanical Garden
c/o Botany Department
University of Hawaii
Honolulu, Hawaii 96822

Categories of Polynesian Plants

Polynesia is usually thought of as a vast triangle with Hawaii at the northern angle, Easter Island at the eastern angle, and New Zealand at the southern angle. A single group of people, known as Polynesians, occupied the entire region at the onset of European contact. Prior to the arrival of the Europeans, Polynesia was almost totally isolated from the rest of the world by the wide expanse of the Pacific, except at the western border where interaction occurred between Fiji (whose inhabitants appear Melanesian but are culturally Polynesian) and Tonga, and, to a lesser extent, between Fiji and Samoa. The vast distances within Polynesia served to isolate the islands from each other, which impeded the flow of the Polynesians and their plants, and contributed to the numerous interesting problems to be found in the study of the dispersal of cultural plants in the Pacific.

Although the islands already had numerous native plant species prior to human occupation, the most useful plants in the ancient Polynesian culture were species brought in voyaging canoes. Based upon distribution and mode of dispersal, plants can be arranged into several categories and subcategories. Species native to an area (i.e., arriving by natural means unassisted by human transport) are termed "indigenous," the first of two major categories of useful plants discussed here. In Polynesia, which was colonized relatively recently (beginning in ca. 1300 B.C.), nearly all indigenous plants arrived long before the islands were discovered. Except for timber trees, very few useful plant species are indigenous; most are introduced plants, the second major category.

"Introduced plants" are species that arrived directly or indirectly in Polynesia by human agency, and this category can be further divided into two subcategories, Polynesian and modern introductions. "Polynesian introductions," also known as "aboriginal introductions," are plants which were transported from island to island by Polynesian voyagers before the beginning of European contact. "Modern introductions" or "Recent introductions" are plants brought to Polynesia after this time, mostly by the direct or indirect activities of Europeans. Unlike Polynesian introductions, which are mostly regional species originating in Polynesia and Melanesia, modern introductions have been brought, and are still being brought, to Polynesia from throughout the warm regions of the world.

A further categorization of introduced plants is based on whether the species were intentionally or unintentionally transported. "Intentional introductions" include plants purposefully transported between islands for food, clothing, shelter, and other needs. "Unintentional introductions," often called "weeds," arrived mostly as propagules adhering to clothing or contained in soil packed around intentionally introduced species. About forty plant species are unintentional Polynesian introductions, but only about five of these were dispersed as far east as Hawaii. This chapter will consider only the intentional Polynesian introductions.

Using the criterion of time of introduction to determine what is modern and what is aboriginal presents some difficulties, because the vast area of Polynesia and the different dates of European discovery make it impossible to accurately pinpoint the beginning of the European era. The European discovery of Polynesia dates to 1595 with the arrival of Mendaña in the Marquesas. Tonga was discovered by Schouten and LeMaire in 1616 and by Tasman in 1643, and Samoa by Roggeveen in 1722. However, the botanical impact of these early explorers was relatively insignificant. The real impact of Europeans began after the discovery of Tahiti by Wallis in 1767, and was highlighted by Captain James Cook's three extensive South Seas expeditions from 1769 to 1779. Cook visited most of the major archipelagos of Polynesia, and introduced plants such as pumpkin, melon, and corn.

If European influence is used to determine the beginning of the European era, then 1769 would be the preferred beginning date; that is, plants introduced to a Polynesian island or archipelago after this date would be considered modern introductions. However, plants introduced from Fiji to western Polynesia during the early years after European contact should be considered Polynesian introductions when they were transported by Polynesians sailing in native canoes unassisted by any Europeans. So perhaps the best definition of a Polynesian introduction would be a plant transported between islands by Polynesian voyagers before about 1850, without the assistance of Europeans. But even this definition will not settle the status of some species.

The Intentional Polynesian Plant Introductions

Using the definition above, 72 species can tentatively be classified as Polynesian intentional introductions. These are shown in Table 1, arranged in six groups based upon their range prior to European contact. For the arrangement, the collections from the Cook expeditions, noted in sources such as Drake de Castillo (1893), Merrill (1954a), Yuncker (1959), and St. John (1979), are very useful; of the 72 species, about 53 either were collected by the expeditions' naturalists or can be identified from the narratives in the journals (Beaglehole 1955–1967).

However, this information is only as reliable as the identifications. At least two of the species have until now been misidentified; *Benincasa hispida* (Cucurbitaceae), the wax gourd, has been confused in western Polynesia with *Lagenaria siceraria* (Cucurbitaceae), the bottle gourd, and *Veitchia joannis* (Palmae) in Tonga was misidentified as a variety of coconut by Beaglehole (1955–1967) and Merrill (1954b), despite its fruit being described as two inches long. There is also the problem of mislabelled specimens, which makes some of the information from the United States Exploring Expedition (U.S.E.E.) in Polynesia (1839–1840) unreliable. The botanical information of the U.S.E.E. was published by Pickering (1876).

Another problem is determining whether or not the 19 Polynesian introductions not collected or recorded during the Cook expeditions were actually present in Polynesia at that time. Two trees illustrate this problem: *Terminalia catappa* (Combretaceae) (tropical almond) and *Cananga odorata* (Annonaceae) (ylang-ylang). These were probably present in Samoa in pre-European times, but because that archipelago was not visited by the Cook expeditions, and the two trees were not collected in western Polynesia until 1839, their date of arrival and mode of introduction are uncertain.

It is also sometimes difficult to determine whether species are indigenous or introduced. The ti plant, *Cordyline fruticosa* (Agavaceae), for example, was probably a Polynesian introduction throughout Polynesia (including New Zealand), but is now widely naturalized in native forests. Several other species, such as *Thespesia populnea* (Malvaceae), *Pipturus argenteus* (Urticaceae), and *Cordia subcordata* (Boraginaceae), are probably native to some parts of Polynesia, but were aboriginal introductions to others.

The matter is also complicated by the introduction of species from Fiji to Tonga during the period just after European contact. Polynesians have always cherished their plants, and would introduce any useful or attractive plant when the opportunity arose. But the geographical isolation of the islands, and the inability of most species to survive long sea transport, limited the number of such species established in Polynesia prior to the arrival of Europeans. Two plants that may have been introduced by Polynesians shortly after European contact are Fijian sandalwood, *Santalum yasi* (Santalaceae) and *Intsia bijuga* (Leguminosae). The Fijian sandalwood was reported by Mariner (Martin 1981) to have been introduced to Tonga from Fiji before 1800. Mariner also noted that *Intsia bijuga*, which is indigenous to Fiji and Samoa, was brought from Fiji to Tonga at about that time. The introduction of plants from Fiji has continued; the Fijian endemic *Cryptocarya fusca* (Lauraceae) was introduced for its fragrant bark used in scenting coconut oil, and *Gardenia tannaensis* (Rubiaceae), a Vanuatu endemic, for its showy flowers.

Counting species may also be misleading, because some have several cultivars or varieties that were introduced at different times. Several distinct kinds of *Pandanus* (Pandanaceae) have been introduced to Polynesia, and present a particular problem since many of them do not reproduce sexually and are impossible to adequately classify. In Tonga, about a dozen types of screw pine are recognized and utilized for mat making, but only a few produce fruit. In Tokelau, about 20 different types are recognized (Whistler 1988), mostly with edible fruits, and although all are fertile, the seeds produce plants similar to the wild type rather

Table 1. Distribution of Intentional Polynesian Plant Introductions

Species	Islands					
	Tonga	Samoa	Cook	Society	Marq.	Hawaii
Western Polynesia to Hawaii (28 species)						
Aleurites moluccana	P	P	P	P	P	P
Alocasia macrorrhiza	P	P	P	P	P	P
Artocarpus altilis	P	P	P	P	P	P
Broussonetia papyrifera	P	P	P	P	P	P
*Calophyllum inophyllum**	N	N	N	N	N?	P
*Cocos nucifera**	N?	N?	N?	N?	P?	P
Colocasia esculenta	P	P	P	P	P	P
*Cordia subcordata**	N?	N?	N?	N?	N?	P
*Cordyline fruticosa**	P	P	P	P	P	P
Curcuma longa	P	P	P	P	P	P
Dioscorea alata	P	P	P	P	P	P
Dioscorea bulbifera	P	P	P	P	P	P
Dioscorea pentaphylla	P	P	P	P	P	P
Gardenia taitensis	P	P	P	P	P	P
Ipomoea batatas	P	P	P	P	P	P
Lagenaria siceraria	—	—	P	P	P	P
*Morinda citrifolia**	P?	P?	P?	P?	P?	P
Musa × paradisiaca	P	P	P	P	P	P
*Pandanus tectorius**	N/P	N/P	N?	N?	N?	N?
Piper methysticum	P	P	P	P	P	P
Saccharum officinarum	P	P	P	P	P	P
Schizostachyum glaucifolium	P	P	P	P	P	P
Solanum viride	P	P	P	P	P	P?
Syzygium malaccense	P	P	P	P	P	P
*Tacca leontopetaloides**	P	P	P	P	P	P
Tephrosia purpurea	P	P	P	P	P	P
*Thespesia populnea**	N?	N?	N?	N?	N?	P
Zingiber zerumbet	P	P	P	P	P	P
Western Polynesia to Southeastern Polynesia (12 species)						
Amorphophallus paeoniifolius	P	P	P	P	P	M
Benincasa hispida	P	P	P	P	P	—
Casuarina equisetifolia	P	P	P	P	P	M
Cucumis melo	P	P	P	P	P	—
Erianthus maximus	—	P?	P?	P?	P?	—
*Erythrina variegata**	P?	N?	P?	P?	P?	M
Hibiscus rosa-sinensis	P	P	P	P	P	M
Inocarpus fagifer	P	P	P	P	P	—
Musa troglodytarum	—	P	P	P	P	M
Pandanus spurius	P	P	P	P	M	—
Solanum repandum	P	P	P	P	P	M?
Spondias dulcis	P	P	P	P	M	—

P = Polynesian introduction; N = Native; M = Modern, or early European introduction, often brought in with its Polynesian name.

*These plants may be native over part of their Polynesian range.

† Totals exclude modern (M) introductions.

Table 1. Continued

Species	Islands					
	Tonga	Samoa	Cook	Society	Marq.	Hawaii
Western Polynesia to the Cook Islands (2 species)						
Bischofia javanica	P?	N?	P	—	—	—
Cyrtosperma chamissonis	P	P?	P	M	M	—
Western Polynesia Only (21 species)						
Atuna racemosa	P	P	—	—	—	—
Cananga odorata	P?	P	M	M	M	—
Citrus macroptera	P	P	—	—	—	—
Coix lacryma-jobi	P	P	M	M	M	—
Dioscorea esculenta	P	P	M	M	M	—
Dioscorea nummularia	M?	P?	M?	M?	M?	—
Erythrina fusca*	P	N	—	—	—	—
Euodia hortensis	P	P	—	—	—	—
Garcinia sessilis	P	P?	—	—	—	—
Gyrocarpus americanus*	P	N	—	—	—	—
Intsia bijuga*	P	N	—	—	—	—
Manilkara dissecta*	P	N?	—	—	—	—
Metrosideros collina*	P	N	N	N	N	N
Pandanus whitmeeanus	P	P	M	—	—	—
Parinari insularum	P	P	—	—	—	—
Pometia pinnata*	P?	N	M	M	M	—
Pritchardia pacifica*	N?	P	—	—	—	—
Pueraria lobata	P	P	—	—	—	—
Syzygium corynocarpum	P	P	—	—	—	—
Syzygium neurocalyx*	P	N?	—	—	—	—
Terminalia catappa*	P?	P?	M	M	M	M
Tonga Only (7 species)						
Aglaia saltatorum	P	—	—	—	—	—
Antiaris toxicaria	P	—	—	—	—	—
Citrus maxima	P	—	—	—	—	—
Diospyros major*	N?	M	—	—	—	—
Garcinia pseudoguttifera	P	—	—	—	—	—
Santalum yasi	P	—	—	—	—	—
Veitchia joannis	P	—	—	—	—	—
Introduced on Atolls (2 species)						
Ficus tinctoria*	N	N	N	N	N	—
Pipturus argenteus*	N	N	N	N	N	—
Totals †	72	69	64	45	43	41	28

than the desired cultivar. For the purposes of this paper, however, varieties and cultivars will not be considered.

According to one widely quoted theory, the original Polynesian migration from western to eastern Polynesia occurred about 300 A.D. as a colonization of the Marquesas from either Samoa or Tonga. Later, Hawaii, Easter Island, and the Society Islands are believed to have been settled by Marquesans. From the Society Islands, the Polynesian migrations moved to the Cook Islands, and on to New Zealand sometime before 1000 A.D.

It may be impossible to ever know just how and when most of the introduced plants made their way through the islands. The Polynesians criss crossed the area after the original western to eastern Polynesian migration, and in the process discovered virtually every island in Polynesia, and many in Micronesia and Melanesia as well (Polynesian outliers). Plants were probably carried on the initial voyage of discovery to eastern Polynesia, assuming it was intentional and not just a storm-blown accident, but most of the species introduced across Polynesia were probably carried during other, numerous, shorter, planned trips.

Of the 72 species, approximately 49 originated in the area from Indo-Malaysia to Africa. Some are undoubtedly native to Melanesia, but most were probably carried during the Polynesian migrations to Tonga and Samoa. Polynesians may have transported them the entire way to Tonga and Samoa, but many of the plants were undoubtedly picked up from the longer-established Melanesian cultures along the migration route during the centuries of Polynesian eastward expansion. Eleven of the 72 probably originated in Melanesia (excluding Fiji), and were similarly transported to Polynesia. Another nine are indigenous (mostly endemic) to Fiji, and were carried by Polynesians from there to Tonga or Samoa in the original migrations, or in later contacts during the more than 3000 years since western Polynesia was first settled. The remaining three (or perhaps only two) species were introduced from the opposite direction, from South America, and these are discussed in the section below.

The six plant groups in Table 1 are based on the aboriginal range of the introduced species. The first group, "Western Polynesia to Hawaii," includes 28 species successfully introduced to the farthest point of the Polynesian migrations, Hawaii. Much has already been written of these species (see St. John 1979, Merrill 1954b), so there is no need to discuss them any further here. (All 72 are described in more detail in Table 2.) One of the 28 may need more study; *Solanum viride* is recorded from Hawaii based on only two specimens, but these identifications may need review.

The second group, "Western Polynesia to Southeastern Polynesia," comprises 12 species. Among them are three common trees, *Spondias dulcis* (Anacardiaceae) (Otaheite apple), *Inocarpus fagifer* (Leguminosae) (Tahitian chestnut), and *Casuarina equisetifolia* (Casuarinaceae) (ironwood), which are propagated by seeds, and could easily have been transported to Hawaii had they been present in eastern Polynesia at an early enough time. The same is true for *Erianthus maximus* (Gramineae), a reed now uncommon and mostly restricted to wetlands.

Other common and important species, such as *Musa troglodytarum* (mountain plantain), which is a major food source in Tahiti, and *Hibiscus rosa-sinensis* (red hibiscus), were not successfully transported to Hawaii, but are propagated by stem or root cuttings and are less likely to have survived the long trip. Some species may have been in Tahiti and the Marquesas during the period of contact with Hawaii, and for some reason were not taken, but most of the 12 species probably came from western Polynesia after the original migration from western to eastern Polynesia, and after the end of contact with Hawaii. Two species, *Pandanus spurius* and *Spondias dulcis,* may have been in Tahiti in pre-European times, but were probably more recent introductions to the Marquesas. The Marquesas and Society islands both belong to French Polynesia, and their close colonial relations since 1842 have obscured the pre-European range of some of the introduced species.

The third group of plants in Table 1, "Western Polynesia to the Cook Islands," includes only two species, *Bischofia javanica* (Euphorbiaceae), a tree whose bark is used to dye tapa cloth, and *Cyrtosperma chamissonis* (Araceae), a giant aroid cultivated on atolls where few other food plants will grow; these apparently did not reach Tahiti until recent times. *Cyrtosperma* was probably aboriginally introduced to the atolls of western Polynesia (Tuvalu, Tokelau, Northern Cooks) from Micronesia, a route different than that taken by the other plants in Table 1. This Micronesian route is more likely than the usual one through the Melanesian islands because of the numerous Micronesian atolls suited to *Cyrtosperma* cultivation, and similarities between some Polynesian and Micronesian names.

The fourth group in Table 1, "Western Polynesia Only," includes 21 species that were never successfully established in eastern Polynesia, or were introduced but have subsequently disappeared without a trace. *Pritchardia pacifica* (Palmae), a fan palm indigenous to either Tonga or Fiji, was aboriginally introduced to Samoa and Tokelau. It is related to a native species, *Pritchardia vuylstekeana,* found on Makatea Island (north of Tahiti) and Miti'aro in the Cooks. *Metrosideros collina,* which is indigenous to most of the high islands of Polynesia, appears to have been an aboriginal introduction to Tonga where it is now extinct.

The fifth group, "Tonga Only," includes seven species probably introduced to Tonga from Fiji, with the possible exception of *Diospyros major* (Ebenaceae) which may be native to Tonga. These seven apparently were not introduced to Samoa, or if so, only in modern times. The most enigmatic of these is *Antiaris toxicaria* var. *macrophylla* (Moraceae), the upas tree. This variety, named from the Polynesian outlier of Tikopia in Melanesia where it still persists, was reported from Uvea in about 1852 and Tonga in the same year, but never again.

The sixth and last group, "Introduced on Atolls," includes two widely distributed Pacific species, *Ficus tinctoria* (Moraceae) and *Pipturus argenteus* (Urticaceae), which are indigenous to high islands of the region, but which appear to be aboriginal introductions to atolls. *Ficus* was introduced for its edible fruit, and *Pipturus* was esteemed for its bark fibers braided into nets and fishing line. Some botanists consider *Pipturus* to be native to Polynesian atolls, but that has not been my perception.

One category not mentioned here comprises Polynesian plants introduced to New Zealand. It is likely that many of the listed species were carried to New Zealand, but because of the temperate climate there, few survived. The only successful Polynesian introductions to New Zealand were sweet potato, bottle gourd, taro, paper mulberry, ti, and common yam, but only the sweet potato thrived.

Additional information on the 72 Polynesian introductions, such as usage and distribution, is recorded in Table 2. Another 12 species are listed in Table 3; these are plants that may have been aboriginal introductions in Polynesia, but probably were not. The spelling of the Polynesian names in both tables is in accordance with the most recent dictionaries of each of the island groups. The different Polynesian languages are consistent among themselves in spelling except for the letter *g*; in some islands it is spelled *g*, in others it is spelled *ng* but pronounced the same way. Also, the *w* of Hawaiian is often pronounced the same as the *v* in the rest of the Polynesian languages.

Polynesian Introductions From South America

Much has already been written about the origin of the yam in South America (see Yen 1974), but little about two other species apparently introduced from there to Polynesia. One is the bottle gourd, *Lagenaria siceraria*, which was one of, if not the only species grown in both Africa and South America in ancient times. Until now, most authorities, such as Purseglove (1968) and Heiser (1979), believed the bottle gourd was introduced to Polynesia from the Indo-Malaysian region. Eames and St. John (1943) suggested a farther eastward introduction to South America to account for the bottle gourd's pantropic distribution, but since the vine is known from archeological evidence to have been grown in South America thousands of years before the colonization of eastern Polynesia (Heiser 1979), this theory is invalid.

New information, however, suggests that the bottle gourd never reached western Polynesia. The attribution of the bottle gourd to western Polynesia has come from several sources; Anderson (Beaglehole 1955–1967) noted the presence of "gourds" in Tonga during the Cook expeditions there, and Rabone (1845) and Churchward (1959) identified the vine known as *fangu* as "calabash." In Samoa, Te Rangi Hiroa (Buck 1930) and Powell (1868) both noted the presence of small gourds (*fagu* used to contain coconut oil, the same use Churchward noted in Tonga. Bataillon's dictionary of Uvea (1932) also noted *fangu* as a small gourd for storing oil.

A recent collection of the Tongan *fangu* used as an oil container has been positively identified as *Benincasa hispida*, the wax gourd (see Whistler 1990b). Its small fruit is the size and shape of an orange. *Benincasa* was collected in Tahiti during the Cook expeditions. It is undoubtedly the same as that which Henry (1928) called *aroro* and described as a small spherical gourd, the size of a medium orange, used as a container for coconut oil. Merrill (1954b), however, incorrectly identified it as *Lagenaria siceraria*. Inquiries at various herbaria and ethnological museums have failed to turn up any evidence that the bottle gourd was cultivated in western Polynesia other than as a novelty in the last few decades. Also, the *Lagenaria* noted in Seemann (1865–1873) and Smith (1979–present) is a misidentified *Benincasa*, and there is no record of the bottle gourd from Fiji either. If it is true that the bottle gourd did not reach western Polynesia and Fiji, the most likely hypothesis is that it was introduced to eastern Polynesia from South America instead.

The third cultivated plant appearing to be a South American introduction, *Solanum repandum*, is distributed from the Marquesas to Fiji, but nowadays is rare or has disappeared over most of this range. The last record of its collection in Samoa is 1905, and in Tonga, 1926. The plant is now rare in Niue where it was last reported to have been collected in 1965 in a banana plantation (Sykes 1970). The only recent record of it from eastern Polynesia is from a banana plantation on Mangaia in the Cook Islands in 1985 (Whistler 1989, 1990a).

The closest relative to *Solanum repandum* is a South American species, *S. sessiliflorum*, according to Whalen et al. (1981), and the two are so similar that those authors suggested they may be conspecific. Their section of the genus is predominantly South American, which suggests the origin of *S. repandum* there. In Polynesia the plant is always associated with human activities, and is rarely, if ever, found in undisturbed habitats, which also suggests the plant is an introduction. It may have been introduced by the early Spanish explorers to the Marquesas in 1595, but its wide distribution in Polynesia suggests a much earlier, Polynesian introduction. Its Polynesian names, such as *koko'u* in the Marquesas, may be cognates of its South American name, *cocona* (Whalen et al. 1981, who spelled the Marquesan name as *kokoua*).

Another species mentioned as an aboriginal introduction, *Capsicum frutescens* (Solanaceae), was believed by Heyerdahl (1961) to have been present on Easter Island prior to the European era. Heyerdahl cited Gonsalez who noted the presence of the "chili pepper," but this identification is incorrect and is based on an error in translation from the original Spanish text (Langdon 1988). A species called *poroporo* present there prior to European contact was probably the native or weedy species, *Solanum americanum*, which is found throughout Polynesia and is called by cognates of *poro* throughout its Polynesian range. It was recorded there during the Cook expedition in 1774.

Cotton, *Gossypium hirsutum* var. *taitense* (Malvaceae), is another species sometimes cited as being an aboriginal introduction from South America. It may be a very early (i.e., Spanish) introduction, as Pickersgill and Bunting (1969) suggested, but because the plant had little use in Polynesia and was probably distributed all the way to Samoa (and Micronesia), this is unlikely. However, since the plant grows in native coastal vegetation (in Samoa at least), and was of little use, it is probably native to Polynesia. The cassava, *Manihot esculenta* (Euphorbiaceae), was suggested by Langdon (1988) to have been an aboriginal introduction to Easter Island, based on translations of manuscripts by early Spanish visitors. However, the first botanists to visit the island, the Forsters with the second Cook expedition, made no mention of its presence there.

Table 2. Intentional Polynesian Plant Introductions

The following 72 species are arranged alphabetically by family (dicots followed by monocots), then by genus and species.

Dicotyledoneae

ANACARDIACEAE

1. **Spondias dulcis** Parkinson
Fiji: *wi;* Tonga: *vi;* Samoa: *vi;* Cooks: *vi;* Societies: *vi;* Marquesas: *vi.*

The Otaheite apple is indigenous to Indo-Malaysia, but was aboriginally introduced to high islands eastward to the Society Islands. It is cultivated for its edible, mangolike fruit, one of the few fruits available to the early Polynesians.

ANNONACEAE

2. **Cananga odorata** (Lam.) Hook. f. & Thoms.
Fiji: *makosoi, mokosoi;* Tonga: *mohokoi;* Samoa: *moso'oi.*

The ylang-ylang is indigenous to southeast Asia, but was aboriginally introduced eastward to Fiji and Samoa, and perhaps Tonga. It was noted as a large timber tree in Samoa in 1839 (Pickering 1876), but was not recorded from Tonga until ca. 1845 (in Rabone's vocabulary list) and thus may be an early European introduction there. The tree, esteemed for its showy, fragrant flowers used for fashioning leis and scenting coconut oil, spread in recent times throughout Polynesia where it is usually called by cognates of its Fijian and western Polynesian names.

BORAGINACEAE

3. **Cordia subcordata** Lam.
Fiji: *nawanawa;* Tonga: *puataukanave;* Samoa: *tauanave;* Cooks: *tou;* Societies: *tou;* Marquesas: *tou;* Hawaii: *kou.*

Cordia is distributed from tropical Asia to Polynesia, but was an aboriginal introduction in the eastern part of its range (Hawaii at least). Its status as a native species is debatable in many islands because the tree is not a common component of littoral forests, and is often associated with disturbed vegetation. The beautiful wood is esteemed for making boats, houses, and handicrafts, and the seeds are eaten in times of famine.

CASUARINACEAE

4. **Casuarina equisetifolia** L.
Fiji: *nokonoko;* Tonga: *toa;* Samoa: *toa;* Cooks: *toa;* Societies: *'aito* (originally *toa*); Marquesas: *toa.*

The ironwood or she oak is distributed from southeast Asia to the Marquesas, and although common now in native littoral and inland habitats, it is probably a Polynesian introduction throughout the area. The extremely hard wood was used for making spears, clubs, tapa beaters, and other artifacts.

CHRYSOBALANACEAE

5. **Atuna racemosa** Raf.
Fiji: *makita;* Tonga: *pipi fai lolo;* Samoa: *ifiifi.*

This tree is indigenous from the Philippines to Fiji, but was aboriginally introduced to Tonga, Uvea, Futuna, and Samoa. In the latter three it is called by the same name, *ifiifi.* It is grown for its large, fragrant seed used to scent coconut oil.

6. **Parinari insularum** A. Gray
Fiji: *sea;* Tonga: *hea;* Samoa: *sea.*

This tree is indigenous to Fiji, but was aboriginally introduced to Tonga, Samoa, Uvea, and Futuna where it is rare and restricted to cultivated areas. Its fragrant fruit was used to scent coconut oil and hung around the neck in aromatic leis. In Tonga, and perhaps on the other islands, a varnish from the fruit was formerly used to paint tapa cloth.

COMBRETACEAE

7. **Terminalia catappa** L.
Fiji: *tavola*; Tonga: *telie*; Samoa: *talie*.

The tropical almond is indigenous to tropical Asia, but was probably aboriginally introduced as far east as Tonga and perhaps Samoa; in the latter archipelago it occurs in native forests. Although not collected in Tonga during the Cook expeditions, it was first reported from there in 1840 and from Samoa in 1839 (Pickering 1876). It is naturalized in some places in Tonga, but is predominantly found in villages. The tree is esteemed for its wood, and for the almondlike kernel which is eaten by children, or by others in times of famine.

CONVOLVULACEAE

8. **Ipomoea batatas** L.
Fiji: *kumala*; Tonga: *kumala*; Samoa: *'umala*; Cooks: *kumara*; Societies: *'umara*; Marquesas: *'uma'a, kuma'a*; Hawaii: *'uala*; New Zealand: *kumara*.

The sweet potato is indigenous to South America, but was aboriginally introduced into the Pacific islands, possibly by Marquesans, centuries before European contact. It is widely cultivated as a major food crop on high islands, not only in the tropical Pacific islands, but also in temperate areas such as New Zealand. Its Polynesian names, all cognates of *kumara*, are believed to have been derived from a similar Indian name from Peru (Yen 1974). Some authorities believe that the sweet potato was not present in western Polynesia prior to European contact, but it was recorded in Tonga in 1777 where it was noted as "a kind of sweet potatoe of a yellow colour" (Ellis 1782).

CUCURBITACEAE

9. **Benincasa hispida** (Thunb.) Cogn.
Fiji: *vago*; Tonga: *fangu (fagu)*; Samoa: *fagu*; Cooks: *'ue roro?*; Societies: *hue 'aroro*; Marquesas: *hue puo?*

The wax gourd is indigenous to southeast Asia, but was aboriginally introduced as far east as the Societies or Marquesas. Although collected in Polynesia (Tahiti) in 1773, it was often misidentified by later authors as *Lagenaria siceraria*, the bottle gourd. Its globose, orange-sized fruits was used as a calabash for scented coconut oil. Burkill (1935), Heiser (1979), and Purseglove (1968) did not record its use as a calabash, and this, along with its smaller, differently shaped fruit, may indicate that the Polynesian plants comprise a separate variety (Whistler 1990b).

10. **Cucumis melo** L.
Fiji: *timo?*; Tonga: *'atiu*; Samoa: *'atiu*; Societies: *'atiu*; Marquesas: *katiu, 'atiu*.

The melon is indigenous to Africa and India, but was aboriginally introduced as far east as the Marquesas. The Polynesian form is now rare, but was noted by Brown (1935) as naturalized in Marquesan valleys in 1921. The most recent records of it in Polynesia are a collection from Samoa (1959) and one from the Marquesas (1977). The small fruits were probably mostly a famine food, but Brown described them as esteemed by the Marquesans for making fragrant leis. The name *'atiu* was first reported from Samoa by Powell (1868) as a vine with a fruit the size of an apricot, which is presumably this species. The only record of this plant from Tonga is its inclusion in early vocabulary lists such as Rabone (1845). Since it is listed as *atiu* [*'asiu*] rather than *katiu* as would be expected, it is likely that this species was introduced to Tonga from Samoa where no *k* was present. It may still exist on Rotuma where it is well known to the inhabitants (Whistler, unpublished data).

11. **Lagenaria siceraria** (Molina) Standl.
Cooks: *'ue;* Societies: *hue;* Marquesas: *hue;* Hawaii: *hue;* New Zealand: *hue.*

The bottle gourd is indigenous to the Old World tropics, possibly originating in Africa, but was widely distributed throughout the world in pre-European times. It has usually been considered to have been introduced eastward during the Polynesian migrations, but recent information suggests that it was instead introduced into eastern Polynesia via South America, perhaps at the same time as the sweet potato (Whistler 1990). There are no early records of it from western Polynesia or Fiji, and reports to the contrary have arisen from a mistaken identification of *Benincasa hispida.* Bottle gourds were employed as calabashes for storing water, food, fishing gear, and so forth, and in Hawaii the fruit pulp was eaten.

EBENACEAE

12. **Diospyros major** (Forst. f.) Bakh.
Fiji: *maba;* Tonga: *mapa.*

This species of persimmon is indigenous to Fiji, but was possibly aboriginally introduced to Tonga, Uvea, and Futuna where it is cultivated in villages. It appears to be a modern introduction to Samoa where it is rare or absent now; in Tonga, it is sometimes found in native forests, which may indicate a native status. The fragrant fruits are suspended around the neck in leis, or used to scent coconut oil; less commonly they are eaten, but mostly by children.

EUPHORBIACEAE

13. **Aleurites moluccana** (L.) Willd.
Fiji: *lauci, sikeci;* Tonga: *tuitui;* Samoa: *lama;* Cooks: *tuitui;* Societies: *tutu'i, ti'a'iri;* Marquesas: *'ama;* Hawaii: *kukui.*

The candlenut tree is indigenous to Indo-Malaysia, but was aboriginally introduced throughout Polynesia. It is naturalized in Hawaiian forests, but in much of Polynesia it is mostly cultivated in villages and plantations, or is found in secondary forests as a relict of former cultivation. The oily nuts were burned on skewers for illumination, and the soot produced from them is the source of the black color of tapa cloth, particularly in Samoa and Tonga.

14. **Bischofia javanica** Bl.
Fiji: *koka;* Tonga: *koka;* Samoa: *'o'a;* Cooks: *koka.*

This tree is indigenous to Indo-Malaysia, but was probably aboriginally introduced eastward as far as Rarotonga. Its absence from the rest of eastern Polynesia suggests a comparatively recent Polynesian introduction from western Polynesia. It is casually cultivated for its bark, which is used to produce the characteristic brown color of Tongan and Samoan tapa cloth, and is seminaturalized in secondary forests, even appearing to be native in primary forests (e. g., in Samoa).

GUTTIFERAE

15. **Calophyllum inophyllum** L.
Fiji: *dilo;* Tonga: *feta'u;* Samoa: *fetau;* Cooks: *tamanu;* Societies: *tamanu;* Marquesas: *temanu;* Hawaii: *kamani.*

This stately tree is indigenous from Africa to eastern Polynesia, but was aboriginally introduced to Hawaii, and perhaps to some of the other islands of eastern Polynesia. Its fine-grained wood is highly esteemed by Polynesians for making houses, boats, bowls, slit-gongs, and handicrafts. The crushed leaves are often used to treat eye ailments, and the oil extracted from the seed is used in massage. The eastern Polynesian names are cognates of the western Polynesian names for an inland species of *Calophyllum.*

16. **Garcinia pseudoguttifera** Seem.
Fiji: *(none?);* Tonga: *mo'onia.*

This tree is indigenous to Fiji and Vanuatu, but was probably aboriginally introduced to Tonga where it is rare and restricted to cultivation. It may have been introduced from Fiji after the beginning of the European era since the first record of it in Tonga is Rabone's vocabulary list (1845). Its fragrant fruits are used in scenting coconut oil and making aromatic leis.

17. Garcinia sessilis (Forst. f.) Seem.
Fiji: *'elala?* (Lau Islands); Tonga: *heilala;* Samoa: *seilala.*

This small tree is indigenous to the Santa Cruz Islands and Fiji, but was aboriginally introduced to Tonga where it is commonly cultivated for its fragrant flowers esteemed for making flower leis and scenting coconut oil. It also appears to be a Polynesian introduction to Samoa, where its name was first recorded in early dictionaries, such as that of Violette (1879), but it is rare or absent there now.

GYROCARPACEAE

18. Gyrocarpus americanus Jacq.
Fiji: *wiriwiri;* Tonga: *pukovili;* Samoa: *vili, vilivili.*

This tree is pantropic in distribution, and in Polynesia is reported from the Marquesas, Societies, Samoa, and Tonga. In the latter archipelago, however, it is restricted to cultivation in villages. It may have been introduced to Tonga in the nineteenth century since the first record of it is Rabone's vocabulary list (1845). It is grown primarily for its medicinal bark used to treat stomach disorders. Children play with the winged fruit which spins while falling.

LEGUMINOSAE

19. Erythrina fusca Lour.
Fiji: *drala kaka;* Tonga: *ngatae (gatae) fisi;* Samoa: *gatae.*

This coral tree is pantropic in distribution, but in Polynesia is restricted to Samoa and Tonga. Although it appears to be native to coastal swamp forests of Samoa, it is probably an aboriginal introduction to Tonga since its Tongan name is *ngatae fisi,* literally "Fijian coral tree," and it is restricted mostly to cultivated or disturbed places. It was first collected in Tonga in ca. 1889, but is on Rabone's vocabulary list (1845) as *ngataefekefisi,* a name variant not used today. Although not a particularly useful tree, it is probably cultivated for its showy red flowers.

20. Erythrina variegata L.
Fiji: *drala dina;* Tonga: *ngatae (gatae);* Samoa: *gatae;* Cooks: *'atae;* Societies: *'atae;* Marquesas: *natae.*

The coral tree is distributed from the Indian Ocean to the Marquesas, but appears to be aboriginally introduced over some of this range; in Tonga and elsewhere, it is restricted mostly to villages and plantations, but in Samoa it appears to be native to coastal forests. The soft wood is sometimes used in boat building and light construction, but the tree is probably best known as an ornamental because of its spectacular red, seasonal flowers.

21. Inocarpus fagifer (Parkinson) Fosberg
Fiji: *ivi;* Tonga: *ifi;* Samoa: *ifi;* Cooks: *i'i;* Societies: *ihi, mape;* Marquesas: *ihi.*

The Tahitian chestnut is indigenous to Indo-Malaysia, but was aboriginally introduced to high islands eastward to the Marquesas. It is casually cultivated, but is often naturalized in coastal forests and along streams. The tree is valued for its large seed which is eaten roasted or boiled.

22. Intsia bijuga (Colebr.) Kuntze
Fiji: *vesi;* Tonga: *fehi;* Samoa: *ifilele.*

This large tree is indigenous from east Africa to Samoa, and although native to coastal and lowland forests of Samoa, it was apparently aboriginally introduced from Fiji to Tonga at about the time of European contact. Mariner (Martin 1981) noted that the tree was found in Fiji and not Tonga (ca. 1806), and that it was esteemed for making large canoes. Nowadays it is rare in cultivation in Tonga, but its wood is prized for the carving of bowls and other artifacts.

23. Pueraria lobata (Willd.) Ohwi
Fiji: *yaka;* Tonga: *aka;* Samoa: *a'a.*

This kudzu vine is probably indigenous to southeast Asia, but was aboriginally introduced as far east as western Polynesia. Although nowadays only a weed of disturbed places, it was formerly cultivated, or perhaps only harvested from the wild for its root, which although inferior in taste, was cooked and eaten, especially in times of famine.

24. Tephrosia purpurea (L.) Pers. Fiji: *tuvakei;* Tonga: *kavahuhu;* Samoa: *'avasa;* Cooks: *mata'ora;* Societies: *hora;* Marquesas: *kohuhu;* Hawaii: *'auhuhu, 'auhola, hola.*

This shrub is distributed from East Africa to Hawaii, but was probably an aboriginal introduction throughout Polynesia. Although no longer cultivated, it persists on rocky coasts and sometimes in rocky, inland habitats. The plant, which contains a fish poison called "tephrosin", was mashed and poured into lagoons to stun fish.

MALVACEAE

25. Hibiscus rosa-sinensis L.
Fiji: *senitoa;* Tonga: *kaute;* Samoa: *'aute;* Cooks: *kaute;* Societies: *'aute;* Marquesas: *'oute, koute.*

The red hibiscus is indigenous to somewhere in the Old World tropics, possibly Africa, but was aboriginally carried as far east as the Marquesas for its showy red flowers. It is possible that more than one distinct variety was present in the islands before European contact, the normal cultivar, and another with short, double petals which is recognized on some islands as being the original variety.

26. Thespesia populnea (L.) Sol. ex Correa
Fiji: *mulomulo;* Tonga: *milo;* Samoa: *milo;* Cooks: C miro; Societies: *miro, 'amae;* Marquesas: *mi'o;* Hawaii: *milo.*

Milo, or Pacific rosewood, is pantropic in distribution, but was probably an aboriginal introduction to the eastern part of its range, to Hawaii anyway. The tree is occasional in littoral forests of high islands, but is often found in disturbed habitats. Its hard, durable wood is highly esteemed for carving canoe parts, calabashes, bowls, and handicrafts.

MELIACEAE

27. Aglaia saltatorum A. C. Sm.
Fiji: *lagakali;* Tonga: *langakali (lagakali).*

This tree is indigenous to Fiji, but was aboriginally introduced to Tonga, Futuna, and perhaps Uvea, and probably more recently to Niue. It is cultivated in villages for its tiny, fragrant flowers used in fashioning leis and for scenting coconut oil. Another related species, *Aglaia samoensis,* native to Samoa and called *laga'ali,* is used similarly.

MORACEAE

28. Antiaris toxicaria Lesch. var. *macrophylla* (R. Br.) Corner
Fiji: *mavu ni Tonga?*

This variety of the upas tree is distributed from the Philippines and Australia to Tonga, but was an aboriginal introduction into the eastern part of its range, including Tikopia (a Polynesian outlier), Fiji, Tonga, and Uvea. It was collected only once on Uvea and Tonga (both in ca. 1852), and not since 1875 in Fiji (Smith 1979). Its Fijian name was reported to be *mavu ni Tonga,* literally "fig from Tonga," which suggests a puzzling introduction from Tonga to Fiji instead of the reverse; equally puzzling is its apparent introduction from Tikopia (where it is called *mami*) to Tonga, and its subsequent disappearance in the latter archipelago. The latex of var. *toxicaria* is a deadly poison, but the Polynesian variety is not as toxic. Burkill (1935) reported the tree was used to make bark cloth in Fiji, but there is no indication that the latex was used there for poison arrows as it was elsewhere.

29. **Artocarpus altilis** (Parkinson) Fosberg

Fiji: *uto;* Tonga: *mei;* Samoa: *'ulu;* Cooks: *kuru;* Societies: *maiore, 'uru;* Marquesas: *mei;* Hawaii: *'ulu.*

The breadfruit tree is indigenous to southeast Asia, but was aboriginally introduced eastward to Hawaii. Many different varieties are cultivated on the high islands and atolls of Polynesia, particularly in the Marquesas (see Ragone, this volume). Most of these lack seeds, and trees found in forests are mostly relics of former cultivation. Although cultivated primarily for its large, seasonal, edible fruit, its wood is also highly esteemed for making canoes and houses. Another breadfruit species, *A. mariannensis,* was introduced from Micronesia to Tuvalu and Tokelau, but there is no indication that this occurred before European contact. Most of the Polynesian names for breadfruit are cognates of *kuru,* which itself is a cognate of the Malayan name for the tree, *kulur* (Burkill 1935).

30. **Broussonetia papyrifera** (L.) Vent.

Fiji: *malo, masi;* Tonga: *hiapo;* Samoa: *u'a;* Cooks: *aute;* Societies: *aute;* Marquesas: *ute;* Hawaii: *wauke;* New Zealand: *aute.*

The paper mulberry tree is indigenous to China and Japan, but was aboriginally introduced throughout the high archipelagos of Polynesia. The tree does not set seed in Polynesia, but is propagated vegetatively. It has been widely cultivated for its bark, which is stripped from the stems, pounded, and prepared into tapa cloth.

31. **Ficus tinctoria** Forst. f.

Fiji: *nunu?;* Tonga: *masi'ata;* Samoa: *mati;* Cooks: *mati;* Societies: *mati;* Marquesas: *'ata.*

This species of fig is indigenous from India to the Marquesas, and grows in coastal and lowland forests throughout its Polynesian range. The plant was probably aboriginally introduced to some atolls (it was reported from Tokelau in 1839) where it is mostly found in cultivation for its edible fruits. On the high islands of Tahiti and the Cook Islands, the fruits were also formerly used to prepare a red dye.

MYRTACEAE

32. **Metrosideros collina** (J. R. & G. Forst.) A. Gray

Fiji: *vuga;* Tonga: *vunga (vuga);* Cooks: *rata;* Societies: *puarata;* Marquesas: *heua;* Hawaii: *'ohi'a lehua.*

This tree is distributed from Vanuatu to the Marquesas, and possibly to Hawaii where it is, however, often considered a different species. It is apparently an aboriginal introduction to Tonga where it was collected only three times (between 1826 and 1855), but there is no indication that it ever grew in native habitats there. A tree called *vunga* matching its description was cultivated on Tongatapu until the last one reportedly died within the last twenty years. I collected the buried root of this individual on Tongatapu, and this was tentatively classified as *Metrosideros* sp. (Patel, pers. com.). This identification is also supported by its Fijian and Tongan names being the same.

33. **Syzygium corynocarpum** (A. Gray) C. Muell.

Fiji: *seasea;* Tonga: *hehea;* Samoa: *seasea.*

This small tree is indigenous to Fiji, but was aboriginally introduced to Samoa, Tonga, Futuna, and Uvea where it is restricted to cultivation in villages and plantations. The fruit is edible, although eating it is mostly an activity of children; more commonly, it is suspended from the neck in fragrant leis.

34. **Syzygium malaccense** (L.) Merr. & Perry

Fiji: *kavika;* Tonga: *fekika kai;* Samoa: *nonu fi'afi'a;* Cooks: *ka'ika;* Societies: *'ahi'a;* Marquesas: *kehika;* Hawaii: *'ohi'a 'ai.*

The Malay apple is indigenous to Indo-Malaysia, but was aboriginally introduced across the Pacific and throughout Polynesia. It is cultivated for its edible fruit, one of the few fruits available to the early Polynesians. The bark and leaves have also widely been used in native medicines. The tree is mostly found in plantations and around houses, but sometimes appears in native forests where it is most likely a relict of former cultivation.

35. Syzygium neurocalyx (A. Gray) Christoph.
Fiji: *leba;* Tonga: *koli;* Samoa: *'oli, fena.*

This small tree is indigenous to Fiji, and perhaps to Samoa where it has been found growing in native forests, but was probably aboriginally introduced to Tonga, Futuna, and Uvea. It is cultivated for its fragrant fruits used in leis. Its presence in Tonga was first noted in Rabone's vocabulary list (1845).

PIPERACEAE

36. Piper methysticum Forst. f.
Fiji: *yagona;* Tonga: *kava;* Samoa: *'ava;* Cooks: *kava;* Societies: *'ava;* Marquesas: *kava, 'ava;* Hawaii: *'awa ('ava).*

Kava is indigenous to Melanesia, but was aboriginally introduced as far east as Hawaii (see Lebot, this volume). It was commonly cultivated in plantations, and although no longer grown over much of its range, relict populations can still occasionally be found in mature forests. Only male plants are known, but *kava* has been shown to be a sterile cultivar of an indigenous Vanuatu species, *P. wichmannii* C. DC. The root contains a mild narcotic which is drunk ceremonially (as in Samoa) or socially (as in Tonga and Fiji).

RUBIACEAE

37. Gardenia taitensis DC.
Fiji: *tiare, bua?;* Tonga: *siale;* Samoa: *pua;* Cooks: *tiare;* Societies: *tiare;* Marquesas: *tia'e, tiare.*

The Tahitian gardenia is indigenous to Vanuatu and possibly Fiji, but was probably an aboriginal introduction throughout Polynesia. The showy, fragrant flowers are worn in leis or individually in the hair, and are esteemed for scenting coconut oil, but are much more popular in eastern than in western Polynesia.

38. Morinda citrifolia L.
Fiji: *kura;* Tonga: *nonu;* Samoa: *nonu;* Cooks: *nono;* Societies: *nono;* Marquesas: *noni;* Hawaii: *noni.*

The Indian mulberry is distributed from India to Hawaii, but was probably aboriginally introduced over the eastern part of its range, as it was in Hawaii. It is casually cultivated in villages and plantations, often as a weed of disturbed places, but is also naturalized in coastal forests. The bark and roots were used to make red and yellow dyes, and the fruit is a famine food. Various parts of the plant are also widely employed in native Polynesian medicines.

RUTACEAE

39. Citrus macroptera Montr.
Fiji: *moli kurukuru;* Tonga: *moli 'uku;* Samoa: *moli 'u'u.*

This orange is indigenous to southeast Asia and perhaps as far east as Melanesia, but was aboriginally introduced to Fiji and western Polynesia. Its fruit is nearly inedible, but the juice was used as a shampoo. Although rarely cultivated nowadays, it persists in forests and old plantations.

40. Citrus maxima (Burm.) Merr.
Fiji: *moli kana;* Tonga: *moli Tonga.*

The pummelo, or shaddock, is indigenous to southeast Asia and Indo-Malaysia, but was aboriginally introduced as far east as Fiji and Tonga. It was first collected from Tonga in 1773, but apparently did not reach the rest of Polynesia before the beginning of European contact. The tree is cultivated for its edible fruit, and is also seminaturalized in forests in Tonga and Fiji.

41. Euodia hortensis J. R. & G. Forst.
Fiji: *uci;* Tonga: *uhi;* Samoa: *usi.*

This shrub is probably indigenous to New Guinea or western Melanesia, but was aboriginally introduced as far east as Niue. The plant is cultivated in villages for its strongly aromatic leaves employed mostly to scent coconut oil used in massage, and often medicinally as a repellent of evil spirits.

SANTALACEAE

42. Santalum yasi Seem.
Fiji: *yasi;* Tonga: *ahi.*

This sandalwood tree is indigenous to Vanuatu and Fiji, but was aboriginally introduced to Tonga, possibly at the beginning of European contact. It was not recorded in Tonga by the Cook expeditions, but Mariner (Martin 1981) recorded it there in 1806. Mariner noted a Tongan chief who tried to bring a large shipment of the wood by canoe from Fiji to Tonga (ca. 1800) because the tree had been grown in Tonga with little success (i.e., it produced little or no scent). The scraped wood is used to scent coconut oil. Labillardière (1800) also noted the same lack of successful cultivation during his visit to Tonga in 1793.

SAPINDACEAE

43. Manilkara dissecta (L. f.) Dub.
Fiji: *bau?;* Tonga: *ngesi;* Samoa: *pau.*

This tree is distributed from New Caledonia to western Polynesia, and although appearing to be native in coastal forests of Samoa, it is probably an aboriginal introduction to Tonga where it is rare and restricted to cultivation in villages. It was first collected in Tonga in 1840, and is probably cultivated for its wood and for its bark used to produce a dye.

44. Pometia pinnata J. R. & G. Forst.
Fiji: *dawa;* Tonga: *tava;* Samoa: *tava.*

Tava is distributed from Ceylon to western Polynesia, and although native to lowland and foothill forests of Samoa, it appears to be an aboriginal introduction to Tonga where it is a common tree in villages and plantations. It is esteemed in Tonga for its edible litchilike fruit, but in Samoa it is known primarily as a major timber tree. In recent times it has been introduced to eastern Polynesia where it is occasionally in cultivation, sometimes even commercially, as it is in the Cook Islands.

SOLANACEAE

45. Solanum repandum Forst. f.
Fiji: *boro sou sou;* Tonga: *to'uloku;* Samoa: *taulo'u;* Cooks: *morerei;* Societies: *pua;* Marquesas: *hoko'u, koko'u.*

This species of *Solanum* is distributed from Fiji to the Marquesas; there is also a recent (ca. 1850) record of it from Hawaii, but this may be the result of a modern introduction. Since it is found only in villages and disturbed habitats, and was cultivated for its edible fruit, it is almost certainly an aboriginal introduction to the region, but recently the plant has become extremely rare or extinct over most of its range. The fruits were usually cooked with other food. See the earlier discussion of the origin of this species under "Polynesian Introduction From South America".

46. Solanum viride Forst. f. ex Spreng.
Fiji: *boro dina;* Tonga: *polo tonga;* Samoa: *polo'ite;* Cooks: *poro'iti;* Societies: *porohiti;* Marquesas: *porohito?*

Several different varieties of this shrub exist, some described as separate species, but they all probably belong to *S. viride* which ranges from Hawaii (Wagner et al. 1990) to at least Fiji, depending upon how the species will finally be delineated. Its fruits are edible, but nowadays are more commonly fashioned into leis, particularly in the Cook Islands where a large-fruited variety is commonly grown around houses. *Solanum viride* is naturalized (but uncommon) on some Polynesian islands, and apparently extinct on others. The Polynesian and Fijian names are all cognates of *poro*, which generally refers to native and aboriginally introduced species of *Solanum*.

URTICACEAE

47. **Pipturus argenteus** (Forst. f.) Wedd.
Fiji: *roga?*; Tonga: *'olonga* (*'ologa*); Samoa: *soga, fausoga*; Cooks: *'oronga* (*'oroga*); Societies: *ro'a*; Marquesas: *hoka*.

This tree is distributed from Vanuatu to the Marquesas, and is probably indigenous over its whole range as a tree of disturbed habitats and secondary forests. It appears to be an aboriginal introduction on atolls, however, and was collected on several of them in the Tuamotus and Tokelau in 1839 (Pickering 1876). The bark contains strong fibers that were braided into fishing line and nets.

Monocotyledoneae

AGAVACEAE

48. **Cordyline fruticosa** (L.) Chev.
Fiji: *ti, masawe*; Tonga: *si*; Samoa: *ti*; Cooks: *ti*; Societies: *ti*; Marquesas: *ti*; Hawaii: *ki*.

The *ti* plant is distributed from tropical Asia to Hawaii, but is probably an aboriginal introduction throughout Polynesia. It is entirely naturalized in forests and other habitats, but a number of cultivated varieties, some with red leaves, are recognized. Ti is sacred in much of Polynesia, and was also very important for providing clothing and food wrappers from its leaves and food from its root. It is also valued as an ornamental shrub around houses.

ARACEAE

49. **Alocasia macrorrhiza** (L.) G. Don
Fiji: *via, viadranu*; Tonga: *kape*; Samoa: *ta'amu*; Cooks: *kape*; Societies: *'ape*; Marquesas: *kape, 'ape*; Hawaii: *'ape*.

The giant taro is probably indigenous to tropical Asia, but was aboriginally introduced as far east as Hawaii. The plant, which does not require wet soil as taro usually does, is cultivated for its large aroid rhizome, but is usually considered inferior in taste to taro.

50. **Amorphophallus paeoniifolius** (Dennst.) Nicolson
Fiji: *daiga*; Tonga: *teve*; Samoa: *teve*; Cooks: *teve*; Societies: *teve*; Marquesas: *teve*.

This aroid is indigenous to tropical Asia, but was aboriginally introduced as far east as the Marquesas. Although probably once grown as a supplemental food crop, it no longer is, but is seminaturalized in disturbed habitats. The rhizome is poisonous and much preparation is needed to make it edible, hence it was probably never much more than a famine food.

51. **Colocasia esculenta** (L.) Schott
Fiji: *dalo*; Tonga: *talo*; Samoa: *talo*; Cooks: *taro*; Societies: *taro*; Marquesas: *ta'o*; Hawaii: *kalo*; New Zealand: *taro*.

Taro is native to southeast Asia, but was aboriginally introduced as far east as Hawaii. The plant rarely flowers in Polynesia, and is thus mostly restricted to cultivated areas, usually in running water where it thrives. Numerous varieties were recognized in each island group, with perhaps the greatest number in Hawaii. Taro is the most esteemed of the four aroids grown by Polynesians, but its growth requirements preclude its cultivation on most atolls. In addition to its edible tuber, the leaves, which must be thoroughly cooked, are eaten like spinach throughout its Polynesian range.

52. **Cyrtosperma chamissonis** (Schott) Merr.
Fiji: *via kana*; Tonga: *via*; Samoa: *pula'a*; Cooks: *puraka*.

This giant aroid is probably indigenous to New Guinea or elsewhere in Melanesia, but was aboriginally introduced to Micronesia and Polynesia as far east, perhaps, as the Cook Islands. It is less esteemed as a root crop than taro or kape, but unlike these two, thrives on atolls in standing brackish water, in pits excavated in the sandy soil. Its aboriginal range is thought to include Tuvalu, Tokelau, and the northern Cooks, and its introduction east of there is thought to be modern. It was first noted from Tonga in Rabone's vocabulary list (1845). The apparent later introduction into French Polynesia is supported by the common names there, which are unrelated to the Polynesian cognates of *puraka, pulaka,* and *pula'a.* Its aboriginal introduction to Polynesia from the atolls of Micronesia rather than through the high island route of Melanesia is suggested by its Trukese name *pura* (Barrau 1961), probably a cognate of the Polynesian names.

DIOSCOREACEAE

53. Dioscorea alata L.
Fiji: *uvi;* Tonga: *'ufi;* Samoa: *ufi;* Cooks: *u'i;* Societies: *uhi, ufi;* Marquesas: *puauhi;* Hawaii: *uhi.*

The common yam is widespread in cultivation from tropical Africa to Hawaii, and was aboriginally introduced throughout Polynesia where numerous varieties are recognized. It is cultivated for its large edible tubers, and is the most common yam species in the region. All the Polynesian names are cognates of the Malayan name for the plant, *ubi* (Burkill 1935).

54. Dioscorea bulbifera L.
Fiji: *kaile;* Tonga: *hoi;* Samoa: *soi;* Cooks: *'oi;* Societies: *hoi;* Marquesas: *hoi;* Hawaii: *hoi.*

The bitter yam is distributed from tropical Africa to Hawaii, but was an aboriginal introduction throughout Polynesia. The tuber is edible, but because it is acrid and poisonous, much effort is required in its preparation. Consequently, it was mostly a famine food and rarely if ever cultivated, but is now naturalized in disturbed and undisturbed habitats.

55. Dioscorea esculenta (Lour.) Burk.
Fiji: *kawai;* Tonga: *'ufilei;* Samoa: *ufilei.*

The lesser yam is probably indigenous to tropical Asia, but was aboriginally introduced as far east as western Polynesia, and more recently to eastern Polynesia. It is cultivated for its small, edible tubers, but is not grown as frequently as the common yam, *D. alata.* A yam matching this description was noted in Tahiti in 1839 (Pickering 1876), but this may have been something else.

56. Dioscorea nummularia Lam.
Fiji: *tivoli;* Tonga: *palai;* Samoa: *palai;* Cooks: *u'i parai;* Societies: *parai, pirita?;* Marquesas: *pauhi.*

This spiny yam is probably indigenous to southeast Asia, but was aboriginally introduced eastward to Fiji and perhaps Polynesia. Pickering (1876) described a spiny yam in Fiji in 1840 that fits the description of this species, but none of the yams noted by Pickering elsewhere in the islands were described as being spiny. The first mention of the yam's name (*palai*) in Tonga is from Whitcombe (1930). In Samoa, Te Rangi Hiroa (Buck 1930) noted the *palai* in a story about a folktale heroine named Sina who married a Fijian king, and *palai* is in an early Samoan dictionary (Pratt 1862), although it was the only one of the five Samoan yams omitted in Powell's list of plant names (1868). It was first noted in Tahiti (as *parai*) in Davies' dictionary (1851), but was not mentioned by Henry (1928) whose book was based on notes made by her grandfather before 1848. Barrau (1961) noted the species as aboriginally introduced to Tahiti, but the first collection of the plant there was by Nadeaud (1873) in ca. 1857; Nadeaud called the plant *pirita,* which is the western Polynesian name for *D. pentaphylla. Dioscorea nummularia* may have been introduced to much of Polynesia in the nineteenth century, possibly by missionaries.

57. Dioscorea pentaphylla L.

Fiji: *kaile tokatolu;* Tonga: *lena;* Samoa: *pilita, lena?;* Cooks: *pirita, makatirau, ma'ararau;* Societies: *patara;* Marquesas: *utau;* Hawaii: *pi'a.*

The five-leaved yam is probably indigenous to tropical Asia, but was aboriginally introduced as far east as Hawaii. It is sometimes cultivated for its edible tuber, but is more of a famine food that grows seminaturalized in disturbed areas.

GRAMINEAE

58. Coix lacryma-jobi L.

Fiji: *sila;* Tonga: *hana;* Samoa: *sanasana.*

Job's tears is native to tropical Asia, but apparently was an aboriginal introduction to western Polynesia where it was first collected in Tonga in 1773, and is a modern introduction to eastern Polynesia. It was probably casually cultivated for its hard, white to black seeds employed as beads, but is now a weed of taro patches and other wet places.

59. Erianthus maximus Brongn.

Fiji: *vico;* Samoa: *fiso;* Cooks: *to kaka'o;* Societies: *to 'a'eho;* Marquesas: *to kakaho?*

This large cane is distributed from Indo-Malaysia to the Societies or Marquesas, but is probably an aboriginal introduction throughout its Polynesian range. It appears, however, to be a hybrid, or perhaps a hybrid swarm, and may have arisen independently in the different archipelagos by hybridization between sugar cane and the native reed, *Miscanthus floridulus.* It was formerly cultivated for its stems used for making fences, house walls, rafter sticks, and darts; its pith may have been utilized as a low-grade source of sugar, and its leaves can be used for house thatch. It is no longer cultivated, but occasionally persists in wet places.

60. Saccharum officinarum L.

Fiji: *dovu;* Tonga: *to;* Samoa: *tolo;* Cooks: *to;* Societies: *to;* Marquesas: *to;* Hawaii: *ko.*

The sugar cane is indigenous to the Old World tropics, but was an aboriginal introduction throughout Polynesia where it was cultivated for its sugar-laden stems and its leaves were used for house thatch. Numerous varieties were recognized, differing mostly in sugar content, stalk color, and length of internodes.

61. Schizostachyum glaucifolium (Rupr.) Munro

Fiji: *bitu;* Tonga: *kofe;* Samoa: *'ofe;* Cooks: *ko'e;* Societies: *'ohe, 'ofe;* Marquesas: *kohe;* Hawaii: *'ohe.*

The Polynesian bamboo is native to Fiji, but was an aboriginal introduction to most of the high archipelagos of Polynesia, where clumps growing in montane forests are probably relicts of former cultivation. It was grown for its stems used to make water containers, nose flutes, and house parts; the sharp, freshly split edges of the stem were used as knives. The common bamboo, *Bambusa vulgaris,* was an early European introduction to Polynesia, and because of its superior qualities, soon superceded *Schizostachyum* in common usage.

MUSACEAE

62. Musa × paradisiaca L.

Fiji: *vudi;* Tonga: *fusi;* Samoa: *fa'i;* Cooks: *meika;* Societies: *mei'a;* Marquesas: *meika, mei'a;* Hawaii: *mai'a.*

Bananas and plantains are usually classified as subsp. *sapientum* and *paradisiaca* respectively, but the taxonomy of this group is very confusing due to the presence of hybridization and polyploidy. However, they are probably indigenous to, or originated somewhere in, southeast Asia or Indo-Malaysia, but were aboriginally introduced as far east as Hawaii. Numerous varieties, both aboriginal and recently introduced ones, are recognized.

63. Musa troglodytarum L.

Fiji: *soaga;* Samoa: *soa'a;* Cooks: *'uatu, fehi;* Societies: *fe'i;* Marquesas: *huetu;* Hawaii: *polapola.*

The mountain plantain is probably indigenous to New Caledonia and perhaps as far east as Fiji, but was aboriginally introduced eastward to the Marquesas, and was an early European introduction to Hawaii (possibly from Borabora, judging by its Hawaiian name, *polapola*). It is a minor food plant in western Polynesia, where it is known for certain only from Samoa and Uvea; in Tahiti it is an important food crop.

PALMAE

64. **Cocos nucifera** L.

Fiji: *niu;* Tonga: *niu;* Samoa: *niu;* Cooks: *nu, niu;* Societies: *ha'ari;* Marquesas: *niu;* Hawaii: *niu.*

The coconut is indigenous to somewhere in the Old World tropics, but was aboriginally introduced to eastern Polynesia (Hawaii anyway) and even into tropical America (Purseglove 1972). It is the most useful plant in Polynesia where it provides food, drinking water, an alcoholic beverage (toddy), oil, charcoal, utensils, cordage, thatch, weaving materials, timber, and firewood. It appears to be native or naturalized in littoral forests on atolls, but probably does not persist in undisturbed littoral forests on high islands. Nowadays, it is cultivated in large plantations, but this is a Western practice instituted for commercial purposes. The Polynesian names are cognates of its Malayan name, *nyiur* (Burkill 1935). Its South American distribution was limited at the beginning of the European era, which would support the hypothesis that it was an aboriginal introduction there. This possible introduction could have been accomplished by American Indians, but Polynesians are the more likely candidates because of their tradition of eastward exploration in large, voyaging canoes.

65. **Pritchardia pacifica** Seem. & H. Wendl.

Fiji: *viu;* Tonga: *piu;* Samoa: *piu, niu piu.*

This fan palm is indigenous to Tonga and/or Fiji, and was aboriginally introduced to most of western Polynesia, including Tokelau where it was noted in 1839 (Pickering 1876). It has probably been grown mostly as an ornamental, but its small fruits are edible, and in Tonga the leaves were used to make fans.

66. **Veitchia joannis** H. Wendl.

Fiji: *niu sawa;* Tonga: *niu kula.*

This palm is indigenous to Fiji, but was aboriginally introduced to Tonga where it was noted in 1773 by Anderson, one of Captain Cook's officers. However, Beaglehole (1955–1967), Merrill (1954b), and Whitcombe (1930) all misidentified it as a variety of coconut, despite Anderson's description of the fruits as being two inches long. It is grown for its leaves used as thatch (as it is in Fiji), its small fruits which are edible, and its value as an ornamental palm.

PANDANACEAE

67. **Pandanus spurius** Miq.

Tonga: *tutu'ila;* Samoa: *fala;* Cooks: *rau'ara, pae'ore;* Societies: *papa, pae'ore.*

This sterile type of screw pine is a cultivar known as "putat," but has often been called *Pandanus tectorius* var. *laevis.* It is probably indigenous to Indo-Malaysia or Melanesia, but was aboriginally introduced as far east as Tahiti, and probably more recently to the Marquesas where it goes by the Tahitian name. The name of the plant in Tonga and Uvea, *tutu'ila,* suggests an introduction to those islands from Tutuila (Samoa). The thornless leaves are used for weaving mats.

68. **Pandanus tectorius** Parkinson

Fiji: *balawa, vadra;* Tonga: *fafa;* Samoa: *lau'ie;* Cooks: *'ara;* Societies: *fara;* Marquesas: *fa'a, ha'a;* Hawaii: *hala.*

The screw pine is probably indigenous throughout Polynesia and Melanesia, but several cultivars, some of which do not produce fruit and are restricted to cultivation, were aboriginal introductions. The taxonomy is very confusing, however, and literally hundreds of species have been named. Most of these, however, represent just morphological variation within a species. The Polynesians themselves, particularly those living on atolls, recognize numerous kinds, but the offspring produced from seed of most of these revert to a wild type and hence are cultivars that can be propagated only vegetatively. Many of the varieties are carried from island to island, particularly among atolls where the tree assumes great importance for survival. The fruits provide a major source of food for atoll dwellers since both the seeds and succulent bases of the phalanges are utilized as food; the leaves are important for weaving and thatching on both high islands and atolls; and the trunk and prop roots are used for timber on atolls.

69. Pandanus whitmeeanus Martelli

Fiji: *voivoi;* Tonga: *paongo (paogo);* Samoa: *paogo;* Cooks: *'ara 'amoa.*

This screw pine species ranges from Vanuatu to the Cook Islands, and is probably indigenous to the New Hebrides, an aboriginal introduction to western Polynesia, and judging by its name *'ara'amoa* (Samoan screw pine), a modern introduction to the Cook Islands. Its name *paongo,* recorded by Mariner (Martin 1981) in Tonga in about 1806, suggests an aboriginal rather than a recent introduction. It is cultivated for its leaves valued for weaving mats and baskets, and for the fruits which are strung into colorful leis, and it is sometimes naturalized in native habitats.

TACCACEAE

70. Tacca leontopetaloides (L.) Kuntze

Fiji: *yabia;* Tonga: *mahoa'a;* Samoa: *masoa;* Cooks: *pia;* Societies: *pia;* Marquesas: *pia;* Hawaii: *pia.*

The Polynesian arrowroot is distributed from India eastward to Hawaii, but was probably an aboriginal introduction to Polynesia. It is naturalized in littoral areas, and was probably mostly harvested rather than cultivated. The starch extracted from the tuber is bitter and poisonous, and must be washed thoroughly before being baked and eaten. It is also used as an additive to other foods, and as a glue in making tapa cloth.

ZINGIBERACEAE

71. Curcuma longa L.

Fiji: *cago;* Tonga: *ango (ago);* Samoa: *ago;* Cooks: *renga (rega);* Societies: *re'a;* Marquesas: *'eka, 'ena;* Hawaii: *'olena.*

The turmeric probably originated somewhere in southeast Asia, but does not occur today in the wild state. It was aboriginally introduced throughout Polynesia where it was cultivated for the yellow powder extracted from its rhizome; this was used as a dye for tapa and mats, and as body paint in ceremonial and medicinal practices.

72. Zingiber zerumbet (L.) J. E. Smith

Fiji: *drove;* Tonga: *angoango (agoago, ango (ago) kula;* Samoa: *'avapui;* Cooks: *kopi'enua;* Societies: *re'amoruru;* Marquesas: *'eka pu'i, 'ena pu'i;* Hawaii: *'awapuhi ('avapuhi)*

The wild ginger is probably indigenous to southeast Asia, but was aboriginally introduced as far east as Hawaii. It is naturalized in forests, but in these situations is mostly a relict of former disturbance or cultivation. The fragrant fluid that accumulates in the flowering bracts was esteemed by Polynesians for washing their hair, and the rhizomes were sometimes employed in scenting tapa cloth, and perhaps also as a condiment.

Table 3. Other Possible Intentional Polynesian Introductions

The following 12 species are arranged alphabetically by family, then by genus and species.

APOCYNACEAE

1. **Cerbera manghas** L.
Fiji: *rewa, vasa;* Tonga (the Niuas): *leva;* Samoa: *leva;* Marquesas: *'eva.*

Cerbera manghas is distributed from Indo-Malaysia to the Marquesas, but is not known from the islands between Samoa and the Marquesas. In Tonga, the other species of this genus is the common one, and *C. manghas* is restricted to the Niuas. It is an uncommon littoral forest tree in Samoa, but in the Marquesas, where the flowers are somewhat larger, it is an inland tree. It is difficult to believe that this large-fruited tree could have this disjunct distribution without human intervention, but it is equally difficult to believe that it was aboriginally carried by ancient voyagers from Samoa to the Marquesas and nowhere else. It has minor use as an ornamental, and the fruits were reportedly eaten in the Marquesas as a means of suicide.

2. **Cerbera odolla** Gaertn.
Tonga: *toto;* Cooks: *reva,* Societies: *reva.*

Cerbera odolla is distributed from Indomalaysia to the Gambier Islands east of Tahiti. It is uncommon in littoral forests in Tonga, but in Samoa, Rarotonga, and the Society Islands where it is uncommon to rare, it is mostly an inland forest species, possibly being a relict of cultivation. This species has often been confused with *Cerbera manghas,* but differs in having a yellow rather than a red eye, and a slightly different corolla shape.

BARRINGTONIACEAE

3. **Barringtonia asiatica** (L.) Kurz
Fiji: *vutu;* Tonga: *futu;* Samoa: *futu;* Cooks: *'utu;* Societies: *hutu, hotu;* Marquesas: *hutu.*

The fish-poison tree ranges from the Indian Ocean to the Marquesas. It is probably native over its whole range and occurs on, and often dominates, rocky coasts, but may have been introduced to atolls, which lack optimal conditions. There are, however, apparently no early records of it on Polynesian atolls, and its occurrence there now (e.g., in Tokelau) is probably a result of a modern introduction. The fruits and sometimes the bark are grated and used as a fish poison.

BURSERACEAE

4. **Canarium harveyi** Seem.
Tonga: *'ai;* Samoa: *mafoa?*

This tree is found in Fiji, Tonga, Niue, and Samoa, but in the latter archipelago appears to be a modern introduction first collected in 1929 and now naturalized in lowland forests. It was first collected in Tonga from a cliff-edge forest on Vava'u in 1855, and is cultivated there for its edible, almondlike kernel.

CUCURBITACEAE

5. **Luffa cylindrica** (L.) M. Roem.
Fiji: *vusovuso;* Tonga: *mafa'i;* Cooks: *po'ue.*

The wild loofah is probably indigenous to tropical Asia, and is indigenous or aboriginally introduced as far east as the Marquesas. Nowadays, it is mostly weedy in disturbed habitats. There is little evidence of any aboriginal use, but its fibrous pulp (dried fibrous vascular bundles) may have been used as a sponge.

EUPHORBIACEAE

6. **Acalypha grandis** Benth.
Fiji: *kalabuci;* Tonga: *kalakala 'a pusi.*

Acalypha grandis is distributed from the Philippines to Samoa, and although it is sometimes found in seemingly native coastal habitats, it may be a European introduction over some of its range, including western Polynesia. It was first collected in Fiji in 1840, but not in Tonga until 1852, and from Samoa in ca. 1862. Also, its native names in both Fiji (particularly in the Lau Islands where it is reported to be most common) and Tonga (rare there and perhaps now restricted to Niuafo'ou), which literally mean "cat's tail," would have to date to European times, since cats were absent from the area prior to European contact. It may have been introduced and cultivated as an ornamental.

HERNANDIACEAE

7. Hernandia moerenhoutiana Guillemin
Fiji: *pipi;* Tonga: *pipi tui;* Samoa: *pipi.*

This large tree is distributed from the Solomon Islands to the Societies, and is probably native over this entire range growing in coastal to montane forests. In Tonga, where it was first noted on Rabone's vocabulary list (1845), it is cultivated for its fruits and flowers, which are strung into necklaces, but the tree is sometimes found in native forest.

LEGUMINOSAE

8. Abrus precatorius L.
Fiji: *lele damu;* Tonga: *matamoho;* Samoa: *matamoso;* Cook Islands: *pitipiti'o, mata koviriviri, uiui;* Tahiti: *pitipiti'o;* Marquesas: *poponiu.*

The rosary pea is distributed from Africa to the Societies where it is uncommon in coastal forests. It is probably native over its entire range, although Brown (1935) believed it to be introduced to the area by Catholic missionaries; however, it was present in Tahiti before Cook's arrival. It was first collected in Samoa and Tonga in 1839 and 1840 respectively (Pickering 1876). The seeds are used as beads, but are poisonous if swallowed.

9. Lablab purpureus (L.) Sweet
(No common names.)

The hyacinth bean is distributed from Africa to the Pacific islands, but its only early record in Polynesia is a specimen reportedly collected in Tahiti during one of Cook's expeditions. The listed collector is Cook, but since Captain Cook is not known to have collected any specimens, it was presumably one of his crew or officers. It is strange, however, that none of his botanists recorded it, an omission which suggests its possible collection from somewhere other than Tahiti. Its first record from Samoa is in 1893, and from Tonga in 1872. Its seeds are edible when cooked, but Seemann (1865–1873) noted that the Fijians were unaware of this. In recent times it has been reintroduced to the islands as a fodder crop.

LOGANIACEAE

10. Fagraea berteroana A. Gray ex Benth.
Fiji: *bua;* Tonga: *pua tonga;* Samoa: *pualulu;* Cooks: *pua;* Societies: *pua;* Marquesas: *pua.*

Fagraea berteroana is distributed from New Guinea to the Marquesas, and is probably native over this entire range. Because of its large, showy, fragrant flowers, it is sometimes cultivated in villages in various parts of Polynesia, especially in Tonga. However, because of its occurrence in native forests, there is no need to postulate its introduction from other archipelagos. Its flowers are used for decoration and to scent coconut oil.

MALVACEAE

11. Hibiscus tiliaceus L.
Fiji: *vau;* Tonga: *fau;* Samoa: *fau;* Cooks: *'au;* Societies: *purau;* Marquesas: *fau, hau;* Hawaii: *hau.*

The beach hibiscus is pantropic in distribution, and is common on disturbed coasts, edges of mangroves and estuaries, and inland in disturbed places. Because of its seawater-dispersed seeds, it is probably native over most of its range, but because of its great utility, the tree may have been introduced to much of Polynesia (especially Hawaii). In Hawaii, the new flora (Wagner et al. 1990) considers it to be native. The soft wood is used for light construction, boat parts, and other artifacts, and its bark is used for cordage and weaving.

MORACEAE

12. **Artocarpus mariannensis** Trécul
Tokelau: *'ulu lalo, 'ulu 'elihe.*

   This species of breadfruit is native to the limestone forests of Guam and elsewhere in Micronesia, but was aboriginally introduced over much of Micronesia. In Polynesia, it is reported only from Tuvalu and Tokelau, apparently introduced from the former to the latter, judging by its Tokelauan name (*'elihe,* meaning Ellice Islands, the former name of Tuvalu). It may have been an aboriginal introduction to Polynesia, but this may never be known. See *A. altilis* in Table 2.

Literature Cited

Baker, S. 1897. *An English and Tonga Vocabulary; Also a Tongan and English Vocabulary, with a List of Idiomatic Phrases; and a Tongan Grammar.* Auckland: Wilsons and Horton.

Barrau, J. 1961. Subsistence agriculture in Polynesia and Micronesia. Bernice P. Bishop Mus. Bul. 223:1–94.

Bataillon, P. 1932. *Langue d'Uvea.* Paris: Librairie Orientaliste Paul Geuthner.

Beaglehole, J. C., ed. 1955–1967. *The Journals of Captain James Cook on his Voyages of Discovery.* 3 vols. Cambridge: Hakluyt Society.

Brown, F. B. H. 1935. Flora of southeastern Polynesia. Bernice P. Bishop Mus. Bul. 130:1–386.

Buck, P. H. [Te Rangi Hiroa]. 1930. Samoan material culture. Bernice P. Bishop Mus. Bul. 75:1–724.

Burkill, M. A. 1935. *A Dictionary of the Economic Products of the Malay Peninsula.* 2 vols. London: Crown Agents.

Churchward, C. M. 1959. *Tongan Dictionary.* Nuku'alofa: Government of Tonga.

Davies, J. 1851. *A Tahitian and English Dictionary.* Tahiti: London Missionary Society Press.

Drake de Castillo, E. 1893. *Flore de la Polynésie Français.* Paris: G. Masson.

Eames, A. J., and H. St. John. 1943. The botanical identity of the Hawaiian *ipu nui* or large gourd. *Amer. J. Bot.* 30(3):255–259.

Ellis, W. 1782. *An Authentic Narrative of a Voyage Performed by Captain Cook.* London: G. Robinson.

Heiser, C. B., Jr. 1979. *The Gourd Book.* Norman: Univ. of Oklahoma Press.

Henry, T. 1928. Ancient Tahiti. Bernice P. Bishop Mus. Bul. 48:1–651.

Heyerdahl, T. 1961. Prehistoric voyages as agencies for Melanesian and South American plant and animal dispersal. In *Plants and the Migrations of Pacific Peoples.* Ed. J. Barrau. Honolulu: Bishop Mus. Press. 23–35.

Labillardière, M. 1800. Voyage in Search of La Perouse . . . during the Years 1791, 1792, 1793, and 1794. Trans. from French. 1971 ed. Amsterdam: N. Israel.

Langdon, R. 1988. Manioc, a long concealed key to the enigma of Easter Island. Geogr. J. 154(3):324–336.

Lebot, V. 1991. Kava (*Piper methysticum* Forst. f.): the Polynesian dispersal of an Oceanian plant. In *Islands, Plants, and Polynesians.* Eds. P. A. Cox and S. A. Banack. Portland, Oregon: Timber Press, Dioscorides Press.

Martin, J. 1981. *Tonga Islands: William Mariner's Account.* 4th ed. Tonga: Vava'u Press.

Merrill, E. D. 1954a. Bibliographic notes on G. Forster's "De plantis esculentis insularum oceani australis" (1786). *Pac. Sci.* 8(1):35–40.

_____ . 1954b. The botany of Cook's voyages. Chron. Bot. 14:164–383.

Nadeaud, J. 1873. *Enumération des Plantes Indigénes de l'île de Tahiti.* Paris: F. Savy.

Pickering, C. 1876. *The Geographical Distribution of Animals and Plants in Their Wild State.* Salem, Massachusetts: Naturalists' Agency.

Pickersgill, B., and A. H. Bunting. 1969. Cultivated plants and the Kon Tiki theory. *Nature* 222:225–227.

Powell, T. 1868. On various Samoan plants and their vernacular names. *J. Bot.* 6:278–285, 342–347, 355–370.

Pratt, G. 1862. *A Grammar and Dictionary of the Samoan Language with English and Samoan Vocabulary.* Malua, Western Samoa: Malua Press.

Purseglove, J. W. 1968. *Tropical Crops: Dicotyledons.* 2 vols. London: Longmans.

_____ . 1972. *Tropical Crops: Monocotyledons.* 2 vols. London: Longman Group.

Rabone, S. 1845. *A Vocabulary of the Tongan Language, Arranged in Alphabetical Order.* Neiafu: Wesleyan Mission Press.

Ragone, D. 1991. Ethnobotany of breadfruit in Polynesia. In *Islands, Plants and Polynesians.* Eds. P. A. Cox and S. A. Banack. Portland, Oregon: Timber Press, Dioscorides Press.

Seemann, B. 1865–1873. *Flora Vitiensis: A Description of Plants of the Viti or Fiji Islands with an Account of their History, Uses, and Properties.* London: L. Reeve and Co.

Smith, A. C. 1979–1991. Flora Vitiensis Nova; A New Flora of Fiji. 5 vols. Lawai, Hawaii: Pac. Trop. Bot. Garden.

St. John, H. 1979. The first collection of Hawaiian plants by David Nelson in 1779: Hawaiian plant studies 55. *Pac. Sci.* 32(3):315–324.

Sykes, W. R. 1970. *Contributions to the Flora of Niue.* Christchurch: New Zealand D. S. I. R.

Violette, L. 1879. *Dictionnaire Samoa-Français-Anglais.* Paris: Maisonneuve et Cie.

Wagner, W. L., D. Herbst, and S. H. Sohmer. 1990. *Manual of the Flowering Plants of Hawaii.* Honolulu: Univ. of Hawaii Press and Bishop Mus. Press.

Whalen, M. D., D. E. Costich, and C. B. Heiser. 1981. Taxonomy of *Solanum* section *Lasiocarpa. Gentes Herbarium* 12(2):41–129.

Whistler, W. A. 1988. Ethnobotany of Tokelau: the plants, their Tokelau names, and their uses. *Econ. Bot.* 42(2):155–176.

_____ . 1990a. Ethnobotany of the Cook Islands: the plants, their Maori names, and their uses. *Allertonia* 5(4):347–424.

_____ . 1990b. The other Polynesian gourd. *Pac. Sci.* 44(2):115–122.

Whitcombe, J. D. 1930. Notes on Tongan ethnology. Bernice P. Bishop Mus. Occ. Paper 9(9):1–20.

Yen, D. E. 1974. The sweet potato and Oceania. Bernice P. Bishop Mus. Bul. 236:1–389.

Yuncker, T. G. 1959. Plants of Tonga. Bernice P. Bishop Mus. Bul. 220:1–283.

Polynesian Cultigens and Cultivars: The Questions of Origin

D. E. YEN

Department of Prehistory
Research School of Pacific Studies
Australian National University

Besides the Bread fruit the earth almost spontaneously produces Cocoa nuts, Bananas of 13 sorts the best I have ever eat, Plantains but indiffer(e)nt, a fruit not unlike an apple which when ripe is very pleasant, Sweet potatoes, Yamms, Cocos, another kind of Arum known in the East Indies by the name of Arum (illegible word), a fruit known by the name of (Eug mallacc) and reckond most delicious, Sugar cane which the inhabitants eat raw, a root of the Salop kind calld by the inhabitants *Pea*, the root also of a plant calld *Ethee* and a fruit in a pod like a large Hull of a Kidney bean, which when roasted eats much like Chestnuts and is calld *Ahee*, besides a fruit of a tree which they call *wharra* in appearance like a pineapple, the fruit of a tree calld by them *Nono*, the roots and perhaps leaves of a fern and the roots of a plant calld *Theve* which 4 are eat only by the poorer sort of people in times of scarcity. For tame animals they have Hogs, fowls and doggs, which latter we learn'd to eat from them . . . ; this indeed must be said in their favour that they live intirely on vegetables, . . . (Banks' journal entry for August 1769, qtd. in Beaglehole 1962, 1:342–343).

As the first Pacific expedition of Captain Cook left the Society Islands, Sir Joseph Banks interrupted his day-to-day journal to consolidate his observations during the four-month-long sojourn of the *Endeavour*. The passage quoted is a summary of the domesticated food resources of the islanders ("these happy people may almost be said to be exempt from the curse of our forefather [i.e., work]"), but read in context, it becomes a part of a portrayal of the Tahitian subsistence system of the time in its structural components. Accentuated is the role of arboriculture within the terrestrial resources and the subsidiary role of animals in the diet. However, in the full account of "Manners and customs of the S. Sea Islands" (Beaglehole 1962:

1:333–386), Banks added the importance of inshore and deep-sea fishing, with his descriptive accounts of marine species, fishing gear, and consumption. He also supplemented the list of cultigens with three fiber plants (*Broussonetia* as *Morus papyrifera,* breadfruit as *Sitodium altile,* and *Ficus prolixa* (Beaglehole 1762: I, 353). Through accounts of the manufacture and dyeing of cloth and the construction of canoes and houses, he pointed to the essential utility of the natural flora in the provision of raw materials. The practice of pit storage of breadfruit as food (Banks wrote *mahai* for *mahi*), a sign of agricultural intensification that can leave archaeological remains, was described by Banks. However, pond-field irrigation of *Colocasia* taro for Tahiti was first described by the senior Forster (Hoare 1982, 341) during the second Cook voyage.

Indeed, in this compressed analysis of the subsistence system of the Society Islands of the eighteenth century, there was conveyed an image, perhaps idealized, of an environment suited to the adaptation of the originally introduced economic plants. This environment provided the supplementary and not necessarily minor products elaborating an economy that was not exclusively agricultural, but had a strong component of (what we have to uncomfortably call) hunting and gathering. Thus, if we view Polynesian subsistence—and indeed Oceanic subsistence generally—in diffusional terms, the reassortment or segregation of the domestic species as representative of the parent systems was dependent on the character of the environments into which those species were introduced.

The deterministic, or perhaps opportunistic, imperatives of environment on the exotic genetic materials that this view espouses should be placed into some general prehistorical perspective. This portrayal of the pioneering, exploratory stage of early settlement can have far-reaching and virtually permanent consequences for subsequent development of systems (Yen, in press). The developmental stages were more culturally determined, whether for social production or in response to population rise, and were most often indicated by water control technology or concentration of field boundary features as the most obvious lines of evidence for intensification by archaeologists (Kirch 1984). The result of these processes is what we perceive as the endpoint, the ethnographic record of system as the result of indigenous development of which Banks has given an example. "An endpoint" may, however, be a more accurate rendition, for we cannot predicate the course of development without the advent of the European explorers.

Thus, we have the possibility of one cause of emigration in the fourth or fifth century A.D. from the Marquesas to the Hawaiian Islands that is perhaps attributable as drought or famine (Kirch 1985, 1). If this were the case, it is obvious that the intensive characteristics of Marquesan agriculture, such as irrigation of taro and the pit preservation of breadfruit, *ma*, (Handy 1923, 181–191), either had not been developed before the effects of environmental stress made the islands incapable of supporting the extent of human population, or the measures adopted at this early stage in the archipelago's prehistory were inadequate for a significant increase in population. However, if it is held that the Societies, rather than the Marquesas, were the immediate homeland of the Hawaiians (Malo 1951, 6; Suggs 1960, 149) and if the same conjectural cause (e.g., food shortage [Oliver 1974]) can be applied, then we cannot view Banks' Tahitian island subsistence system as the stable state that "endpoint" implies, but perhaps more realistically as a relatively stable episode that Cook's voyagers happened upon. In other words, the subsistence system could underwrite the social conditions of the time—the population, the institutions, the disputes, political or familial. It neither reflected a static state for the past, nor for an unrealized indigenous future.

I chose to begin this chapter with the enumerative passage from Banks' Tahitian account, obviously without any illusion of historical precedence in the Polynesian or Oceanic agricultural record. Not only does it represent a species base (i.e., the genetic materials in the formation of an "ideal" Polynesian system), but it further exemplifies, together with Sydney Parkinson's more formal and extended list (1784, 37–50) from the same voyage, an early application of a Linnean-like binomial system of plant classification to Pacific cultigens. It acts as a bridge between the often confusing plant descriptions of the earlier voyagers and the later and increasingly accurate records. However, fully developed catalogues had to await the work of Barrau (1958 for Melanesia; 1961 for Micronesia and Polynesia).

Banks' and Parkinson's accounts of the wide range of food and industrial species were to have a considerable influence on the future issues of prehistoric migration of plants and humans in the ultimate settlement of Polynesia. Furthermore, their inferences of variability at the intergeneric and intraspecific levels, exemplified through the confusion of the "Arum" and the subspecific discriminations of banana respectively, offer a further developmental consequence in terms of transfer and genetic variability conferring the potential for artificial selection by cultivators. It is because of this last topic that I have tried to introduce the social imperatives, however sketchily, as a part of the total environment under which subsistence intensification and change, as well as selection by cultivators (perhaps another manifestation of intensification), may be enacted. This is not new. Conklin (1961) stated it most clearly. Patrick Kirch's recent influential work (1984) on the development of Polynesian chiefdoms, with its strong emphasis on production systems, demonstrates its application for prehistory.

To continue then, we turn to an expansion of the early stage of Polynesian agricultural colonization, on the wider canvas of the Pacific plant records that extend back before the time of Cook by over two centuries.

The Southeast Asian Theory for Pacific Agricultural Origins

The widely accepted exposition of the theory for the origins of Pacific agriculture has been that of Buck (1938), who traced the "trail of plants and animals" from the Indo-Malaysian region. He espoused a southern route through New Guinea rather than the northern, Micronesian pathway through which he traced the advent of the Polynesians to Samoa and Hawaii. He also allowed for return contact of the Marquesans to Peru to accommodate the prehistoric acquisition of the sweet potato. Ethnological implications aside, the beginnings of this theory may be traced to the records of the voyages of Cook.

Banks (Beaglehole 1962, II, 203–217) in his account of the agriculture of Batavia of 1770, was impressed by its produce, as he was earlier for Tahiti. He noted yams, sugar cane, sweet potato, *Gnetum gnemon* (Gnetaceae), and bread-fruit "incomparably inferior to the South Sea ones," in a profusion of cultivated crops. These included dryland and pond-field rice, millet (without further identification), many kinds of vegetables European, Asiatic, and American, and a list of 37 trees that included coconut and *Eugenia* (Myrtaceae) as well as *Canarium commune* (*C. indicum*), the most westerly recording of this species (Leenhouts 1959), *Terminalia Catappa* [*sic*] and *Musa* bananas among, again, a surprising range of exotic as well as local domesticates.

The doctoral thesis of George Forster (1786) on the edible plants of the Pacific islands drew heavily on Banks for his frequent allusions to Indonesian homologues (including the sweet potato), because the second voyage of Cook when he accompanied his father, Johann Reinhold Forster, did not visit the East Indies. Banks (Beaglehole 1962), in turn, made frequent reference to George Rumphius who, in a residence in eastern Indonesia from 1653 until his death in 1702, was the earliest natural scientist to work in the Pacific. Rumphius' major work, which appeared in six volumes between 1741 and 1750 and was inter-preted in Linnean terms by Elmer Merrill (1917), must have been a major resource for Cook's botanists on their return. All the botanists on Cook's three voyages had knowledge of some American plants, exemplified in Banks' reference to "Cocos," the West Indian name for *Xanthosoma* sp. (Araceae), but here applied to *Colocasia* taro. And indeed, many of the earlier Spanish voyagers used their familiarity with American plants as referents to the unfamiliar plants that they saw in the vast new ocean.

Pigafetta, in his narrative of Magellan's voyage, wrote one sentence on the resources of Guam in 1521 that enumerated "coches/batates/oyseaux/figures longues/une palmae/cane doucle/poissons bolans avec autre chose." This was translated by Skelton (1969) as coconuts, yams, birds, figs a span long (i.e., bananas), sugar cane, flying fish, and other things. Recognizable instantly are some of the main plant resources of Polynesia at the time of European discovery, but the earlier rendition of "batates" by Safford (1905) was as sweet potato, reflect-ing a West Indian name for the plant. This was one of the precipitants of a long-standing controversy.

An earlier English version (Burney 1803) of the Pigafetta sentence seemed to have had added rice gratuitously to the list of plants, stimulating another, more recent argument on the significance of this for prehistory (Craib and Farrell 1981; cf. Pollock 1983). The possible presence of a grain crop in the root crop-dominant Pacific islands gains some credence from a further record, that of Legaspi's main expedition of 1564–65 (Sharp 1960, 37) describing the first contact with Mejit in the eastern Marshall Islands, and identifying "patatas," translated as potatoes, and "a grain like millet." It is perhaps possible to posit indigenous transfer of sweet potato, but what about the grain? This illustrates the confused nature of the early plant records.

The chronicles of the voyages of Mendaña in 1568 and 1595, the latter with Quiros as pilot, and of Quiros as captain in 1606 to the central and eastern Solomon Islands and to the northern New Hebrides produced records of agricul-ture analyzed by Yen (1973b). It seems, from Cook's journal of the first voyage (Beaglehole 1955), that he either had a copy of Quiros' 1606 journal with him, or he had made extensive notes from it, because he often checked the position of the *Endeavour* with that of the *San Pedro* for navigational purposes. Banks (Beaglehole, 1962) mentions Quiros also in the same terms, but gives no hint of attempting comparisons of Tahitian and Espiritu Santo plants.

The tree species of Banks' Tahitian listings have been convincingly described and identified from the Spanish journals as *Artocarpus, Eugenia, Inocarpus, Spondias, Cocos, Pandanus,* and the perennial sugar cane and bananas. The crop plants, however, were identified with deductive difficulty—"three or four kinds of roots . . . which form their bread . . . one of them has a sweet taste, the other two prick a little when eaten" (Markham 1904, for Santa Cruz in 1595). Some forms of the aroids *Colocasia, Alocasia,* or *Amorphophallus* (the Polynesian *taro, kape,* and *teve*) as well as *Dioscorea bulbifera* are candidates for the irritant tubers, but the one with the sweetness could be, contentiously, the sweet potato.

This has been only a sampling of the historical plant evidence that has contributed to the southeast Asian theory of origin for Pacific and Polynesian agriculture, for if we transpose the species names of recent determination for those given in 1769 in Tahiti, there is considerable correspondence with the equivalent interpretations by Merrill (1917) of the Indonesian domesticated flora of Rumphius. The recently determined Melanesian plants from the early Spanish voyages form a common bridge to Polynesia, and a more fragmentary one to Micronesia, where more direct Asian connections through rice may yet be shown.

If we look further into the Spanish documents, it may be seen that they record more than the cultigens, the genetic units of the indigenous Melanesian island agricultural systems. The observation of irrigation on Guadalcanal in 1568 (Amherst and Thomson 1901, 306) is an indication of intensive cultivation technology shared with Indonesia, and with Tahiti and Hawaii, in the early records. Furthermore, the pit preservation of breadfruit was first noted for Polynesia by the Spanish during the 1595 Mendaña voyage on Tahuata in the Marquesas (Markham 1904, 28), in the Marshall Islands in the 1568 voyage of Mendaña (Amherst and Thomson 1901, 68, 440–441), and with a more equivocal, but convincing to this writer, description by Quiros for Espiritu Santo of northern Vanuatu (Markham 1904). This intensive technique of provision for emergency, as well as creating a preferred food, is not shared outside of Oceania, and is probably a unique innovation. Thus, in the broadest terms, we have a model of possible diffusion of plants, animals, and irrigation technology to Polynesia, out of southeast Asia through Melanesia. The storage technique is something else; here is an example of an indigenous development that was to diffuse in the narrower ambit of eastern Melanesia and tropical Polynesia.

The Mendaña-Quiros documents are interesting in another respect. The identification of *Canarium harveyi, Barringtonia procera, Pometia pinnata,* and *Burckella obovata* (Sapotaceae), among others, as cultigens (Yen 1974a) demonstrated the continuing process of Oceanic domestication that itself was to extend to the ultimate ends of Polynesia (Yen 1985), being enacted on indigenous species by the agricultural colonizers as supplemental to the plants they carried and adapted.

The connection of Pacific agriculture to mainland Asia was made comparatively recently by Haudricourt and Hedin (1943) on the basis of homologous sets of root crops cultivated in the two regions. That these represented an earlier stratum of domestication than *Oryza* (Graminae) is one of the influential yet controversial points in Sauer's hypothesis (1952) of mainland southeast Asia as the "cradle of earliest agriculture." Reading these sources now, it is apparent that there was room left for the possibility of newer, indigenous domesticates within the diffusion patterns of agriculture on its journey to Polynesia.

Cultigens and Diffusion

At the symposium on Oceanic Cultural History at Sigatoka in 1969 I delivered a paper in which I expressed doubt that the diffusion out of southeast Asia was sufficient explanation for Pacific agricultural origins (Yen 1971). This was founded on the then recent and accepted view that among the endemic domesticates of New Guinea were two cultigens, sugar cane and the Australimusa banana—and I added *Cordyline fruticosa*—that were to reach into most of Polynesia in prehistoric times. A further influence was probably the subtle inferences in Jacques Barrau's extension (1965) of the Vavilovian center of Indo-Malaysia of the crop plants of the Pacific to western Melanesia. Thus, for those who have gained the impression that my thesis is that Pacific island and therefore Polynesian agriculture is solely derived from New Guinea, I make the following statement that was further elaborated at the Pacific Science Congress in 1971 (Yen 1973c): The actual model was that the Austronesian people, carrying domesticated plants out of southeast Asia, encountered other sets of cultures, especially in the New Guinea region, where agriculture based on locally domesticated plants was already being practiced. It was a complex adaptation, for here the Austronesian migrants met a range of species, some strange to them, some familiar (since some domesticates could have been in common, at least at the generic level—remembering that the New Guinea flora has strong affinities with the Malaysian).

I must admit that the plant evidence was suggestive rather than persuasive, for most of the other plants assigned to New Guinea origin were noncoastal or highland in their distribution. Species like the nut *Pandanus,* the vegetable *Rungia klossii* (Acanthaceae), and *Setaria palmifolia* (Graminae) were of highland distribution, and, anyway, had no island dispersal. *Saccharum edule* (Graminae) was one exception; this adaptable species found its way to the New Hebrides and Fiji in a disjunctive distribution. All these species had earlier been noted for Melanesia by Barrau (1958) without comment on origin. One plant however, *Piper methysticum,* which provides the source of the drink *kava,* had a distribution from southwest New Guinea, again to Vanuatu and Fiji, but, in this case, with extension to most of the high islands of tropical Polynesia and Hawaii, but in Micronesia, only on Ponape (see Lebot, this volume).

Irrigation technology, which in the Pacific applied most widely to *Colocasia* taro, is of considerable import for issues of plant diffusion. Here I took the view that this technology could be an independent invention, just as Peruvian prehistoric systems are taken to be independent of Old World developments. This is plausible, especially if we view irrigation as a part of the developmental process of water control technology. There is evidence for extensive drainage systems at some 6000 years B.P. in the New Guinea highlands (Golson et al. 1967). There was (and still is) considerable difficulty with this notion, for the Austronesian voyagers were unlikely to have reached the highlands. Except for Serpenti's ethnographic study (1965) of drainage or island bed cultivation on Frederik Hendrik Island, there is little evidence for intensive water control technology on the lowlands of New Guinea, and certainly nothing to convey the time depth of such agriculture. Thus, a diffusion bridge to the highlands does not exist, on present knowledge. The comparatively advanced drainage technology in Golson's site makes the transfer of taro across this coastal and lower montane region a difficult feat to conceptualize, even with the temporal allowance of the pushing backwards of the dates for the breaking up of proto-Oceanic language in the western Pacific (Pawley and Green 1973, 52) to "no later than 3000 B.C."

For the other Pacificwide technology, the pit preservation of breadfruit, there was the archaeological evidence from Samoa of Roger Green and his colleagues of fireless pits at time levels reaching the first century A.D. (Green and Davidson 1969). The source of this technique for eastern Polynesia therefore seems clear enough, but whether Samoa was a recipient early in its prehistoric sequence from eastern Melanesia (without archaeological attestation for earliness), or whether it was within the area of invention (and therefore a sign for cultural exchange with proximal Melanesia) is a question that remains open.

I used a concept that the results of agriculture as a part of cultural contact would be more evident away from the immediate area of contact; that the reactive synergy of that contact would have a segregative consequence as it was transported to islands of varying ecologies and isolation. Using then a border concept that must have been a shifting of the concept of Burrows (1938) for Polynesia, I attempted to portray the variability of systems in their components. The wide region of the Melanesian-Polynesian border, encompassing the Solomon Islands, New Caledonia and the New Hebrides to Fiji, and the nearby Polynesian archipelagos, contained agriculturally all the species and their combinations that were to arrive in Polynesia, and all the techniques as well. The region also portrayed the negative in this respect—those plants and therefore their associated technologies and utilizations that did not become a part of Polynesian subsistence. Some of the latter, and their variable distributions, even within the border region, have already been mentioned.

St. John (1953) interpreted the agricultural diffusion out of Asia as the gradual loss of domesticated species eastward. It can be seen that my 1971 definition may be viewed as an augmentation and modification that adheres largely to the original concept, which superficially recalls the founder effect in gross (generic) terms. However, the randomness of the process is rather denied in exposition of some of the principal features that indicate directive selection and the application of high-level change to environments that blunts the effect of natural selection. But here we cannot lose sight of variability in respect to the region's systems as their transition character is summarized: It incorporates the easternmost distribution of *Metroxylon* (Palmae) sago cultivation with differentiation of species in a shift from *M. sagu* of New Guinea to *M. salomonense* (which also occurs in New Guinea) in the Solomons and the New Hebrides, and the emergence of the endemic species *M. vitiense* in western Polynesia (Barrau 1959) and

M. upoluense in Rotuma. This exemplifies diffusion and local speciation, as well as the conversion of a plant predominantly used for food to a plant used predominantly for other purposes (i.e., house thatch). This can be seen in the use of *M. upoluense* for thatch, but never for food, in Samoa.

Selection in Malaysian genera of trees resulted in endemic domesticate species of fruit and nut food resources. But I will modify this claim later. Breadfruit selection did not operate against seed production, but the occasional seedless forms found on Santa Cruz seemed to have been multiplied at the east of the "border" region in the Samoa-Tonga archipelagos (see Ragone, this volume).

Forms of *Alocasia macrorrhiza* and *Dioscorea bulbifera* were selected for edibility, minimizing the "poisonous" principles contained in the wild types. The first named became important in western Polynesian subsistence; the latter seemed restricted to New Caledonia and the Solomons (Santa Ana and San Cristobal), although the dispersal of the species as far as the Marquesas, the Societies and Hawaii, if by human agency, would suggest a more general series of domesticated forms, and a loss, perhaps through vegetative mutation, or recombination through seed reproduction—and reduction in selection pressure. These are examples of genetic manipulation through selection or domestication.

Of the horticultural and utilization measures that may be seen as innovative for the region, we can merely list the conversion of *Cordyline fruticosa* to the status of a food plant for which no evidence has been found for New Guinea or SE Asia, the cultivation of *Broussonetia* for *tapa* manufacture as a pruned shrub, and the preservation of breadfruit by drying as well as the pit preservation method.

The drinking of *kava* as ritual recorded ethnographically by Serpenti (1965, 49–50) for Frederik Hendrik Island, seems typical of indigenous life in the Marind area of southeastern New Guinea, and apparently extended, in the past, to Vanuatu and Fiji. Lebot (this volume) posits a Vanuatuan domestication and origin of *kava* preparation. We have no way of knowing whether Cook's account (Beaglehole 1961, 236) of preparation of *kava* and reference to Lemaire's 1616 encounter with it on Futuna implied secular drinking or even, perhaps, the manifestation of an earlier breakdown of a social institution. Whatever the case, the "border" region is the easternmost extension of the betel nut chewing habit, the cultivation of the *Areca catechu* (Palmae) fruits and the *Piper* leaf accompaniment, that marks the diffusion through the intervening area from southeast Asia that indeed shows an ancient and rare surviving connection with India.

Finally, there was the incidence of irrigation in the border region, and the tentative hypothesis of a possible independent technological invention. The irrigation systems of New Caledonia (as well as dryland terracing) described by Barrau (1956) were viewed as the most elaborated of Oceanic agricultural environment control, while those in Vanuatu (Guiart 1958) were more simple hydrological measures taking advantage of stream valleys rather than sculpturing the hilly landscape. These necessitated canal structures for long-distance water carriage.

On the Polynesian edge of the region I recorded for Futuna (Yen 1971) what seemed to be the apogee of the valley system of irrigation that was to be mimicked in the Society and Marquesas islands, but brought into full florescence in the great valleys of the Hawaiian chain. The Futunan example, in comparison with the closest islands, for water control provided contrasts of a much narrower geographic and cultural range that emphasized the importance of the environmental factor in agricultural development. Alofi, an offshore island of Futuna without streams, was naturally devoid of irrigation; in 1969, the cultivators of the main island used Alofi for the cultivation of large stands of *Broussonetia*. Uvea, to Futuna's northeast, has cultural ties with that island. *Dioscorea alata*, the greater yam, is important to both islands' subsistence, but the other dominant, taro, is grown on the extensive swamps of dissecting valleys. Here the patterns of raised islands with the provision of organic mulch bear resemblance to drainage systems of New Guinea, and to those in some of the Cook Islands.

Agricultural technology in the Pacific has a major role in changing the environment within the natural limits such as has been portrayed in the preceding example. Where applicable, its initiation opened the way to the intensification alternative to the often limited agricultural expansion as a response to population increase or the demand for social production (Sahlins 1972). Furthermore, it had a biological implication, for the selection on genetic plant stocks became much more dependent on the directed substrate of managed soil and plant association, and less on what we may term, in shorthand, natural selection.

The Modified Model and the "Tests"

Since the 1970s there have been a number of studies that can be grouped as prehistorical and that are able to contribute to the issue before us as independent and often inadvertent "tests." Of considerable interest has been the field of linguistic reconstruction of proto-languages (e.g., Blust 1976), in which lexical items indicate archaeological significance in terms of an earlier Austronesian tradition for rice agriculture; also Pawley and Green (1973, 37) for western Austronesian languages. When it comes to when these languages were spoken, we seem to have considerable and confusing cross-referencing between archaeologists and linguists; as Irwin (1988) says in another context, "they have each known too well what is in one another's pocket!" Be that as it may, we now turn to the "tests . . ."

The Southeast Asian Source

The absence of rice in the Oceanic roster of crop plants from southeast Asia is one of the most difficult questions for Pacific archaeology. Bellwood (1979) held the view that the cereal was brought into western Oceania by the early Austronesians, but it failed because of the plant's sensitivity to "temperature, length of daylight, cloud cover and light intensity." In elaborating this thesis, Bellwood (1985, 233) referred to the physiological experiments of Oka and Chang (1960), among others, comparing photoperiodism among cultivated varieties and forms of two wild species thought to be possibly the progenitors of *Oryza sativa*. The reasoning is that "early *indica*" varieties of rice must have been sensitive to the short day equatorial conditions to which they were introduced, and as such mirrored the photosensitivity of wild types (which do vary in their reactions), while the modern varieties are virtually insensitive, and thus latitudinally more adaptable. There is some evidence that the cultivated rice of central Thailand at 3600 B.C. to A.D. 1200 was variable and displayed primitive characteristics (Yen 1982a). If this is typical of southeast Asian rice of the time, and if the Austronesian transferrers were in the west New Guinea region, then (Tryon 1985, 153, quoting Bellwood) the possibility of this negative selection of the grain crop in favor of the taro-yam root crop complex exists.

In another linguistic analysis in the same volume, Pawley and Green (1985, 177) suggest, "though unattested," a date earlier than 2000 B.C. for the Austronesian penetration of western Melanesia. This suggests over a millennium of potential selection in these early forms of *indica* rice, which we might assume displayed the heterozygosity that Oka and Chang (1961) found in hybrid swarms between wild and cultivated *Oryza* species. In this scenario, it seems unlikely that the early agricultural transferrers, with knowledge of rice cultivation, would have failed to select non-photoperiodic forms.

Perhaps it is mischievous to admit that I do not believe my own amendments to Bellwood's negative hypothesis for rice adaptation in early Austronesian Oceania either. What they serve to illustrate is that reasoning on biological grounds, seldom absolute, may be directed to either of differing views. There is a need for a greater emphasis on agricultural archaeology in Indonesia, west and east—not merely the incidental recovery of rice remains and more historical perspective on the *javanica* race, the adaptation to the vast region of rice-growing of the southeast Asian archipelagos, but also exploration of the antiquity of irrigated rice cultivation techniques and field systems. This is especially the case since it seems to be a consensus (Bellwood 1985, 208) that the plant originated as a wetland plant, so that the earlier (not earliest perhaps) stage in adaptation should leave archaeological imprints.

New Guinea Agricultural Archaeology and Taro

The ethnobotanical indications of indigenous domestication in New Guinea would have remained just indications were it not for Golson (e.g. 1977b; Golson and Hughes 1980) at Kuk in the Wahgi Valley of the Papua New Guinea highlands, following up his earlier work already mentioned. For here was a 9000-year sequence of agricultural drainage with a developmental sequence of simple to complex technology of drainage water control that took the changes virtually to the ethnographic present. Geomorphic features, studied over a wider-ranging set of researches into palynology (Powell 1982), had implications for an earlier and continuing form of dryland agriculture involving forest clearance that precipitated the infilling of the drains at various levels. As early as most firmly dated primary agriculture in the world, this progressive system is interpreted as being adapted to *Colocasia* taro well prior to the dominance of sweet potato, but obviously adapted for it also in the latter part of the sequence. Thus, as evidence for adaptive technology, its implication for taro cultivation makes it too early by some millennia for Austronesian transfer. That the species could therefore be a local domesticate is explored in the next section.

In New Guinea, the incidence of wild *C. esculenta* is common. Although we have tended to think of *C. esculenta* as garden escapes, this is not the view of indigenous cultivators. While in many areas these are simply wild taro, in others, like a group of agricultural villages encountered in the Brownie River area, Papua New Guinea, some wild types are deemed edible and cultivatable, but not preferred (Yen, field notes 1979). The wild taro is more variable in phenotype at such low altitudes than those occurring, for example, at Kuk, some 1550 m above sea level. This is the basis for the suggestion by Yen (1980) that earlier agriculture than that uncovered for Kuk might be found at lower altitudes.

The Origin of Pacific Taro

Yen and Wheeler (1968) addressed the problem of taro origin through a cytological study of southeast Asian and Pacificwide clonal varieties. Determining that all Pacific taro had a chromosome complement of $2n = 28$ or 42, they discussed a sequence of introduction of first 28-chromosome forms that reached out to New Guinea, the Melanesian islands, and Polynesia, and the 42-form only to the coastal areas of the Philippines, Timor, New Caledonia, and New Zealand. For the latter two locations, there were grounds for suspecting post-European contact introduction.

In 1981, I was made aware of wild taro in Australia that was foraged by the northern tropical peoples as a food resource with cultural affinities. My co-workers and I found these taro to have the same chromosome complement as the New Guinea and Pacific samples of the earlier study, $2n = 28$. By then we were well aware of the sundering of the Sahul continent, New Guinea, from Australia, at 12,000 to 8000 years ago by rising sea levels and the influence on perceived plant distributions of modern times (Golson 1971). Were the Australian and New Guinea wild and cultivated forms related—at least cytologically? This was the original question which led again into an Asian and Pacificwide cytological survey of cultivars and wild representatives of the species where we could find them. We applied karyotype analysis to chromosome morphology in addition to the numerical approach to give a finer-grained analysis that might give us a greater range of variability on which to base transfer patterns for the plant. The results of this project (Coates et al. 1988) I attempt to summarize here, using Figures 1, 2, and 3 as the basis for discussion.

We can use the $2n = 28/42$ differentiation in accounting for taro distribution in the Pacific, but there appear to be two separate lines of evolution under cultivation, according to the karyotyping. In the Pacific, two 42-forms appear to be derived from types with normal metacentricism in the 3 indicator pairs of chromosomes. The other line is incomplete and hypothetically derived from an earlier evolved Asiatic (Indian?) form of homologic 28 *acrocentric* indicator pairs. We have reasonable evidence to suggest that the Australian and New Zealand representatives are recent arrivals. The "Pacific line" cannot, however, be interpreted as an "endemic" line without qualification, since the putative progenitor type I is also found in the Asian material. However, the possibility does exist for a New Guinea or Sahul domestication, so that now, with residue analysis on artifacts and in soil becoming more sophisticated and of wider application, Golson, at the Kuk site, may yet come up with a testament of the inference of early taro through direct evidence of starch grains. Already my colleagues, Loy and others (n.d.), have come up with an identification of aroid starch and raphides on Pleistocene tools from Buka in the northern Solomons of New Guinea that could yet be shown to be from *Colocasia*.

There is a further biological approach to the taro material assayed cytologically; P. Matthews (per. com.) at the Australian National University is applying methods from molecular genetics to investigating variability in ribosomal DNA. From this work to date, two points seem to be clear. The cytotype II–3 (Fig. 3) seems to be Asian in origin. His collection of Australian populations that were phenotypically uniform and thus looked to be clonal populations gave evidence for genetic variability that suggests sexual reproduction in addition to the observable vegetative mode. This has relevance to a later discussion.

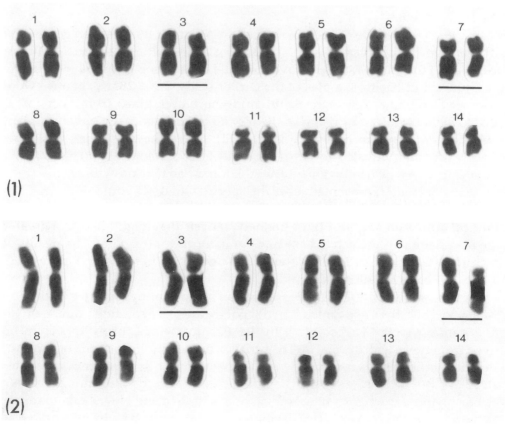

Figure 1. Karyotyping of the two diploid forms ($2n = 28$) of *Colocasia esculenta*. Marker chromosome sets are underlined. In (1) top, the three marker sets (pairs) are uniformly metacentric, while in (2) bottom, set 7 shows one of the pair as acrocentric. (From Coates, Yen and Gaffey 1988)

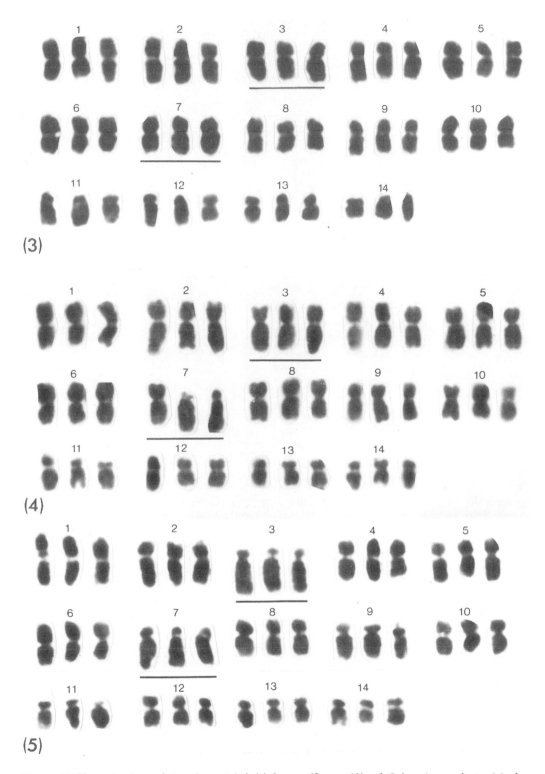

Figure 2. Karyotyping of the three triploid forms ($2n = 42$) of *Colocasia esculenta*. Marker chromosome sets are underlined. In (3) top, the marker sets are uniformly metacentric while in (4) middle, set 7 shows two of the three chromosomes acrocentric. (5) bottom shows that sets 3, 7 and 9 are uniform for acrocentricism. (From Coates, Yen and Gaffey 1988)

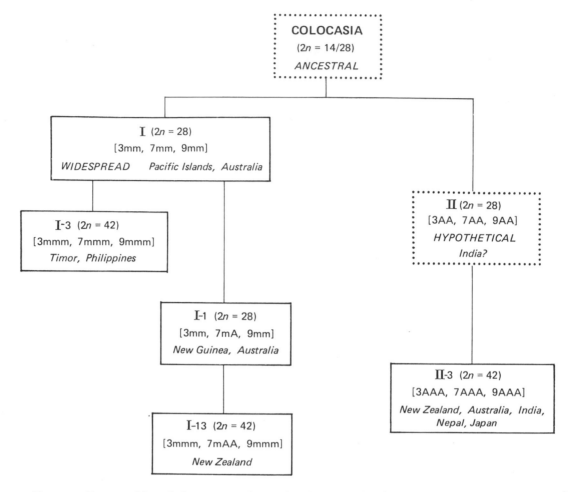

Figure 3. Proposed by phylogenetic relationship between the five cytotypes based on karyotype and ploidy level; whether the marker chromosomes 3, 7 and 9 are metacentric (m) or acrocentric (A) and the number of copies of each type are indicated for the different cytotypes. From a figure by W. Mumford in Coates, Yen and Gaffey 1988.

Taro Irrigation

Spriggs (1982) has made a study of taro irrigation in Melanesia which shows ethnographically the variability in technique—simple flooding (New Guinea highlands), furrow conduction (Aneityum in Vanuatu), raised island beds (eastern coastal New Guinea), and pond-fields (Mussau and some of the Solomon Islands).

Spriggs' subscription to a southeast Asian origin and diffusion into the Pacific is based on two points: that irrigation was practiced in New Guinea, and that island southeast Asian pond-field morphology and techniques are physically similar. The first contention is difficult, for now the Mussau pond-fields (the sole representation of true irrigation in New Guinea) appear to be nonexistent from direct field observation (H. McEldowney, per. com.). The furrow irrigation seems to be a unique Vanuatu, indeed Aneityum, innovation, as perhaps is the positively spectacular transfer of water source from one valley to the other described by Spriggs (1981).

I still feel from my own fieldwork that island beds, whether in swamp drainages of the Baliem Valley, the Wahgi Valley, Fiji, Rarotonga, or Uvea—or the Melanesian islands—are a drainage system with the facultative capacity for irrigation in dry seasons. One such system was actually in operation in Utupua, eastern Solomons, in its irrigation mode in 1978, but the normal purpose of the "islands" was to lower the water table relative to the planting surface. In his newer writing on irrigation, Spriggs (n.d.) seems to allow that, with the omission of Mussau, the techniques that remain could well be endogenously developmental. I do not find the linguistic correlate of irrigators as Austronesian speakers convincing, unless it can be shown that most Austronesians under the same ecological conditions practice irrigation, or that there are direct linguistic connections in the lexicon of water control.

The physical morphology of the pond-field terracing of New Caledonia, Bali, and the Ifugao and Bontoc in Luzon have in common varying extents of sculpturing of the landscape, hill, gully, and valley, and the long water conduits necessary to supply the fields. They are a long way from the valley systems of Kolombangara, Futuna, the Cook Islands, eastern tropical Polynesia, and Hawaii—in this Oceanic group, the morphological resemblance applies. It seems to me that it is the "social morphology" that may differentiate within the systems. They are just as likely to be expressions of independently developed systems whose social dictates towards intensification reveal more about their physical shape. Perhaps it is the basic hydrological theory that they all share, that water runs down rather than up—unless that is the level for diffusion. Certainly diffusion from the border area of Polynesia to its northern extremity, to dominate much of Hawaiian agriculture, seems a fair proposition for prehistoric Polynesia. I am not up with the recent contract reports in Hawaii, now the major source for Hawaiian archaeology, I believe. Are all irrigation systems like those in the upper valley of Makaha (Yen et al. 1972), with later dates than the beginning of the valley sequence, and certainly the Hawaiian cultural sequence (Kirch 1985)? If so, perhaps this is a case for diffusion of plant and idea rather than technique?

The Other Root Crops

A recent revision of the small number of *Dioscorea* yams in Australia (Telford 1986) has shown that two Melanesian species are naturalized, *D. pentaphylla* and *D. alata*. These are regarded to be adventive. *Dioscorea bulbifera* is present over the whole tropical north; there are two forms, one of whose tubers retain poisonous principles and thus need special preparation by the Aborigine hunter-gatherers. In addition, there are two endemic species important in Aboriginal subsistence. *Dioscorea hastifolia* is restricted to Western Australia to a maximum latitude of over 30 degrees S, while *D. transversa* is tropical in distribution but extends on the east coast again to some 30 degrees. We can say no more, in view of the fact that our knowledge of New Guinea wild forms has not likewise advanced. We are left with the prospect of a parallel possibility to the New Guinea-Australian situation in taro, with the distinction that in this case we have potentially divergent speciation in Australia.

Recent explorations of the plant resources of the northern coast of Papua New Guinea (Allen et al. 1984) have revealed wild *Cyrtosperma* of considerable variability. These are encountered alongside stream courses, sometimes at quite considerable distances from the sea (e.g., on small tributaries of the Yuat River). *Cyrtosperma* is not found cultivated in the area; the closest that we found it grown for food was on coastal New Ireland. This genus is, of course, the dominant crop plant grown in atoll agriculture under pit cultivation regimes exploiting the freshwater lens called the Ghyben-Herzberg effect (e.g., Small 1972, 27). Sometimes assigned to a southeast Asian origin, its absence in wild form in the southern Philippines and the fact that it is not noted by Rhumpius for eastern Indonesia (Merrill 1917) nor as a vegetable by Ochse with Bakhuizen van den Brink (1931) means that an origin in New Guinea for the Oceanic forms may be a serious possibility.

I arrive reluctantly at the sweet potato, but happily to say that the controversy over American origin has not been resurrected. Not even studies recently initiated on Australian wild species used by the Aborigine tribes of the arid central desert include any modification. Only the secondary distribution to Melanesia from the early Polynesian introduction (Yen 1974b) that the equivocal Mendaña record could indicate has had some materialization with Golson's claim (1977a) for a possible arrival of the plant in the New Guinea highlands at 1200 years B.P. on palynological and soil depositional evidence. This has been taken up by Gorecki (1986), who proposes a three-stage introduction, at 1200 and 300 years ago, and in the 1930s, the time of the opening of the highlands.

The Cultivated Trees of Melanesia

In the 1977–78 extension of the Bishop Museum's southeastern Solomons prehistory project (Yen 1982b), the ethnobotanical concentration was on the trees described by the Spanish explorers, specifically on the intraspecific variability of *Canarium.* Now securely identified as *C. harveyi,* its wider distribution as a cultigen beyond the Santa Cruz archipelago was confirmed with the addition of Tikopia to its range—its presence on Anuta was recorded in the 1970–71 phase of the project (Yen 1973a). Locally, the study narrowed to Utupua and Vanikoro, two islands to the south of the main Santa Cruz. There was little doubt that the greatest variability was found on Vanikoro, variation that exceeded Leenhouts' subspecific divisions (1959) for *C. harveyi;* this has been attested by comparisons of the Santa Cruz project collection of some 30 trees. In fact, with hitherto undescribed forms like one with entirely red foliage, if we subscribed to a splitting philosophy in taxonomy, we might have further subdivision! We can, however, suggest that the westerly distribution to San Cristobal and Shortland Islands and the easterly to Samoa and Fiji of the subspecific forms of Leenhouts (1955) may simply reflect an earlier sampling or founder effect in human transfer of the species to the western edge of Polynesia and into the central Solomons where the dominant cultivated nut species is *C. indicum*. It should be added here that the fruit domesticate *Pometia pinnata* also reached into Polynesia, being recorded for Uvea (Kirch 1978), Tonga (Thaman 1975), and Niue (Yuncker 1943), so that among the array of Santa Cruz trees, two species reflect a transfer in the past.

We were to find that *Canarium,* together with *Cocos,* left the best archaeological remains of all cultivated species of domesticates. The Tikopia excavations of Kirch (Kirch and Yen 1982) indicated the introduction of *Canarium* at the beginning of the Christian era, with cultural evidence for connections with Vanikoro. *C. harveyi* was also found in the 1977 excavations on Santa Cruz Island of McCoy and Cleghorn (1988) but the plant remains and their place in the cultural sequence are unreported.

Ethnobotany in the Lapita Homeland Project

This project, the initiative of the Australian National University (Allen et al. 1984), centered on the Bismarck archipelago of northern Papua New Guinea, but incorporation of the northern coast and hinterland of the main island for ethnobotany has yielded the following results:

1. This region is a further center of Oceanic arboriculture, where the same species of *Artocarpus, Pometia,* and *Burckella* are domesticated cultigens. *Barringtonia* is present but recognized everywhere as an introduction from the Solomons, while, as earlier noted, *Canarium* is dominated by *C. indicum*.

2. *Canarium* domesticates in the region (Figure 4) are also represented, in association with *C. indicum*, by the giant-fruited *C. decumanum* on Manus Island and northern coastal West Irian, extending to the Papua New Guinea border area, and *C. lamii* (provisionally named by Leenhouts, per. com. but with recognition of some reproductive and vegetative characters inconsistent with the type of that species), grown on the northern coast of Papua New Guinea from the Markham Valley to beyond the Sepik, and inland in the Torricelli range (Yen, field notes 1988). It should be noted that the wild forms of the two species are a part of the vegetation of the low-altitude rain forests of New Guinea, as is *C. indicum,* on soils of generally volcanic or mixed origin (with elements of raised limestone). *Canarium decumanum* seems to be restricted to the forests of the "Bird's head" area of West Irian, and I was unable to find *C. lamii* there at all. While all species have been found as village cultigens in the areas indicated, including *C. indicum,* the domestication process has adapted them all for coastal village planting on soil media like riverine alluvium, enriched beach sand, and cobbly limestone—a process to some degree paralleled by *Pometia pinnata.* This phenomenon had earlier been noted for these two genera in the eastern Solomons. In the recent fieldwork, however, we noted that *C. lamii* had been adapted to higher levels than the observed natural distribution, at some 530 m altitude at Lumi in the Torricellis.

The distribution of these *Canarium* species is shown in Figure 5. The disjunctive distribution is at least suggestive of a New Guinea origin, and further evokes the dictum of Leenhouts (1959, 328) in his revision of the genus, that on a geological time scale "in more recent times the main centre of speciation developed in New Guinea, and from there, some groups spread into Polynesia."

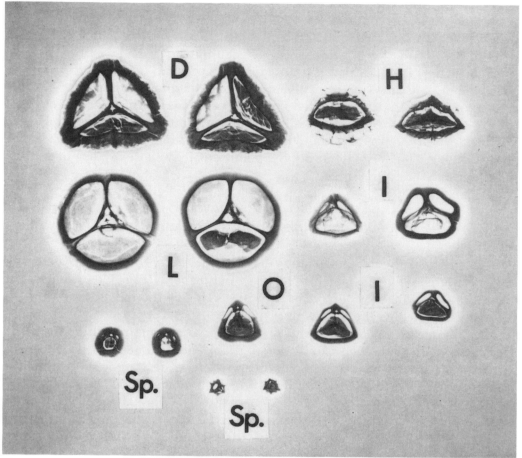

Figure 4. A cross-sectional view of the endocarps of domesticated Pacific species of the genus *Canarium*. D = *C. decumanum* (basal measurement or width 5cm.); H = *C. harveyi*; L = *C. lamii*; I (four nut sample) = *C. indicum*; O = *C. ovatum*, from Luzon, Philippines. The two groups of two marked Sp. are Western Pacific species of wild *Canarium*. (Xeroradiograph by W. R. Ambrose; photograph by D. Markovic)

In archaeological recoveries, the species recovered is predominantly *C. indicum*. Figure 6 shows the results of work in progress from the Lapita project. Of course, we cannot say whether the early Holocene dated specimens from Paul Gorecki's Sepik excavation represent domestication, but the absence of species with large seed cases may indicate a later direction of species selection, or at least the basis on which later selection might have been made. Notable is the incidence of *C. harveyi*-like specimens from New Britain, that might indicate the transfer east of mixed genotypes that allowed for progressive selection and domestication in the Santa Cruz group.

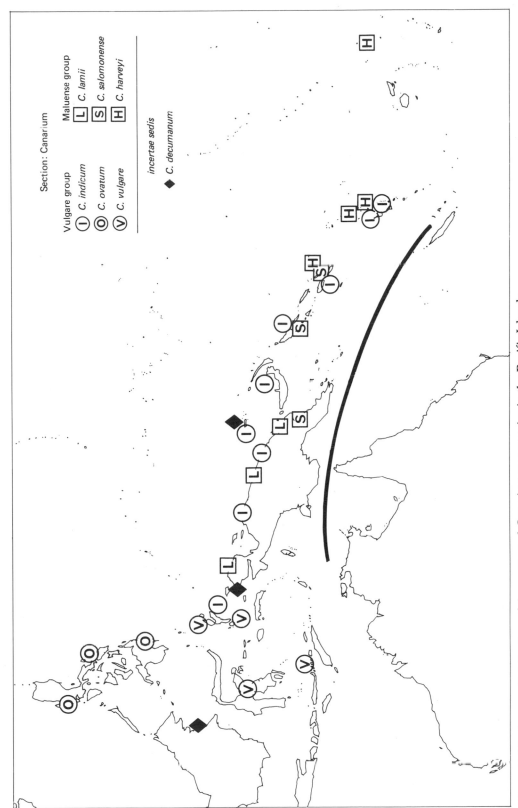

Figure 5. The known distribution of domesticated *Canarium* tree species in the Pacific Islands. See Figure 4 for species coding. (Map by W. Mumford)

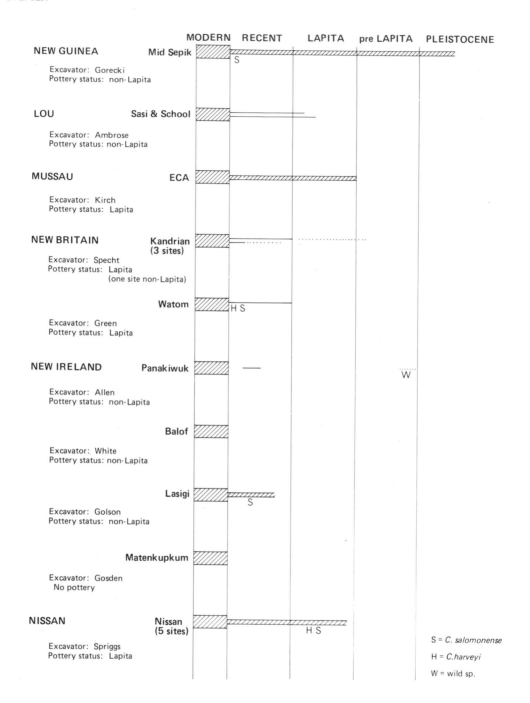

Figure 6. A preliminary diagram of archaeological remains of *Canarium* from archaeological sites in the Western Pacific that *suggest* a New Guinea mainland domestication, and the later movement into the islands to the north in Lapita times. S and H signify less certain identifications of material remains of low incidence in the sites, while W suggests that the early flora of at least New Ireland contained wild *Canarium*. (Diagram by W. Mumford)

Western Pacific Breadfruit and Issues of Domestication

Without going into all the possibilities of domestication of these tree species, only some of which reached the periphery of Polynesia, it may be appropriate here to address breadfruit in New Guinea. Barrau (1957) summarized the taxonomic differentiations of the Pacific *Artocarpus* and indicated an immediate southeast Asian origin.

Foresters of Papua New Guinea recognize *A. altilis* as a constant part of the low-altitude forests. The indigenous cultivators in the region recognize the polymorphic nature of the species in two ways: the variability of leaf forms and, in a more utilitarian sense, the seedy and fleshy fruit forms. Under cultivation, the types are similarly described, but "fleshy" does not mean the parthenocarpic forms of Polynesia, but fruits with less-fibrous flesh and fewer seeds. The seeded forms are valued for their edible seeds, often a feature of the products on offer in local markets today. As with *Canarium*, the cultivation extends to shoreline as well as 600-m montane village environs; the distribution on coral atolls is, of course, well known. Parthenocarpic forms are not known in nature, nor indeed is the vegetative reproductive habit, which would hardly be adaptive in the close competition of the tropical rain forest. Both these features are characteristic of Polynesian varieties, but even in Tahiti Wilder (1928) recorded a one seeded variety that had been retained through the spatial and temporal screen of Polynesian selection.

Whether New Guinea had a larger role in the origin of Oceanic breadfruit than was earlier supposed is unknown, but the selective role of the Polynesians and Micronesians in achieving the seedless character (Barrau 1959, 119) is conclusive (see Ragone, this volume). In the Melanesian islands, true seedlessness seems to be unknown. In the Admiralties, McEldowney (per. com.) describes forms with aborted but distinct flattish seeds; Ruth Spriggs (per. com.) says all Bougainville varieties in her experience are seeded, but that seedless forms occur in the neighboring Mortlock Islands. In Santa Cruz, as we have noted, seedless forms are known. These could represent the early parthenocarpy on which selection was exercised and then transferred on the eastward journeys of the Lapita people, but since this island is so close to the Polynesian outliers in the Reef group, as well as Tikopia and Anuta, an adventive, westward introduction by Polynesians late in prehistory may be as likely. That the Mortlock group is also a Polynesian outlier is support for the latter accounting. There are thus two implications for Oceanic breadfruit:

1. If the seedless character was established in western Polynesia, there was a westward as well as eastward movement of such forms of *Artocarpus*.

2. The apparent cline of increasing seedlessness (and vegetative reproductive capacity) was not necessarily a random genetic process, but one guided by indigenous agricultural selection. The most obvious explanation for such artificial selection pressure was the preference for seed-free fruit in the manufacture of the pit-fermented *ma*, so important in old Polynesia and Micronesia.

Plant Remains From Mussau

Kirch (1988b) has reported on one of the most informative sets of seed remains to be found in the western Pacific. As well as the archaeologically often-found fragments of coconut shell, there are 19 tree species represented, including *Canarium* sp. (*?indicum*), *Inocarpus, Aleurites, Spondias, Pometia pinnata,* and *Burckella obovata.* Among these are species discussed earlier. The significance is that these plants are associated with the classic Lapita ceramicware dated to 1600–500 B.C. It also indicates, if we take *Canarium indicum* as the marker for arboriculture, that the domesticated status of that species was well in place in western Melanesia for the Lapita people to adapt the tree species recovered from the site in its early phases. This should not be taken to mean that the Lapitan colonizers adopted a purely Melanesian agriculture; it is the arboricultural component on which Kirch's data focusses. Thus *Canarium, Pometia, Burckella,* and debatably *Artocarpus* may have been carried with the taro-yam complex to the eastern Solomons—the next great area for classic Lapita from where the complete set of tree species was to be dissembled, with disjunct and discontinued distribution of some at the Polynesian edge. Others, like *Cocos, Artocarpus, Spondias, Syzygium,* and *Inocarpus* were to go on, and to be further adaptively segregated through the effect of distance and isolation in their penetration of the farther reaches of Polynesia.

The Speed of the Lapita "Train"

The question of when these arboricultural, agricultural, and animal domesticates left such areas as Mussau remains unanswered, unless we refer to the one controversy that has exercised the participants in the Lapita Homeland Project. If it is the fast train hypothesis (see Kirch 1988b), then it is early in the 1600–500 B.C. period that is probably meant. While it might be more "comfortable" to adopt the hypothesis of slow travel for the prior adaptation of Melanesian crops into a travelling subsistence with elements of southeast Asian crops, the number of trains making the journey on a temporally (and perhaps spatially) staggered schedule might fit the prehistoric situation as well. However, there is one very new factor: the revision of the theory for a New Guinea origin of sugar, *Saccharum officinarum.*

It has been held for some time that sugar cane evolved in New Guinea (Brandes 1958)—as has been the assumption at the beginning of this paper. Daniels and Daniels (unpublished ms.) are presenting a revision of the situation. Briefly, the early hypothesis was that *S. officinarum* arose from *S. robustum,* that in turn evolved in New Guinea from a complex set of hybridizations of *S. spontaneum, Miscanthus sinensis,* and *Erianthus arundinaceus.* The phylogenetic situation remains unquestioned, but Daniels and Daniels investigated the wild distribution of the three parent species of *S. robustum. Saccharum spontaneum* is distributed in the wild in South China from where it was transported to Micronesia and Melanesia; *M. sinensis* has a natural distribution from East Asia through Indo-China to Malaysia and Sulawesi; *E. arundinaceus* does occur wild in southern New Guinea but has a distribution in Indonesia, the Philippines, Okinawa, and South

China through southeast Asia to India. The thesis is that these three species were actually brought to New Guinea by humans—and, Daniels and Daniels say, by Austronesians because of the plants' usefulness for building, pig-fencing, arrow manufacture, and so forth. The Austronesian identity attributed to Bellwood (1985) is based on proto-Austronesian word reconstructions (Blust 1976) and on the mainland Austro-Thai of Benedict (1975) while the date of 6000 years ago refers to the early Austronesian expansion from the Asian mainland to Taiwan.

If, however, this expansion occurred as the Lapita-bearing people reached western Melanesia or New Guinea at 3500 B.C. or 2000 B.C. as the earlier quoted linguists assert, then there was some one or two millennia in which the complex evolutionary process produced *S. officinarum* from parents which, if modern representatives reflect the species of earlier times, had chromosome complements of differing numbers. This is not an insurmountable barrier necessarily, but requires time to evolve sugar cane. Bellwood, however, says that the proto-Austronesians carried sugar cane, not its progenitors, so Daniels and Daniels suggest that the Asiatic sugar *S. sinense* had to be the species in that case, since clearly *S. officinarum* was a relatively late adventive to Asia. Thus there are two alternatives offered: in New Guinea, either the Asiatic sugar was replaced by locally domesticated sugar, which was lower in fiber and had a less tough rind or *S. officinarum* was then developed there from the high chromosome-numbered *S. sinense*.

If I may be granted the luxury of mixing metaphors, this is a red herring in the train issue, for it is obvious that with either model for evolution of sugar cane in New Guinea, any Lapita train, fast or slow, could pick up its product, depending on the rate of evolution of the species—fast or slow! The testing of the new hypotheses for the origins of sugar in their biological implications has not begun; the issue of nonAustronesian carriers of useful, industrial plants that were to produce a food source is one that may go against present wisdom. The case, however, is a demonstration of some of the pitfalls of the interdisciplinary studies to which most of us are committed. There is the whole question of the influence of the Laurasian collision of Sunda and Sahul in geological history and the indications of floral exchange that occurred. An alternatively parsimonious theory is that wild *S. robustum* evolved in southeast Asia, and was dispersed to New Guinea to provide the substrate for human selection—and the emergence of domesticated sugar cane.

The Nature of Prehistoric Plant Transfers

I would now like to address the Polynesian plant transfers directly. So many times anthropologists and archaeologists have likened Polynesia to a laboratory, and used biological phenomena as analogies for cultural variability, that perhaps it is opportune to inspect the cultigens as biological entities, and attempt to construct the consequences on them of the shift from the polyglot "homeland" to the far-flung highly variable island world that is Polynesia.

The people who were to pioneer Polynesia are generally agreed to have been represented ancestrally in the immediate Melanesian border area by a reasonably uniform culture bearing the Lapita-styled pottery whose complexity of design was to dissipate to an aceramic condition. But the culture certainly did not dissipate; it effloresced into divergent and complex social forms (Kirch 1984; Kirch and Green 1987). Kirch (1988a), who has long recognized the role of subsistence in the formative Polynesian ranked societies, finds resonance in the theory of circumscription of land resources, and the coercive social control that gave rise to the statelike structure that he sees some Polynesian cultures approaching at European contact. In 1971 I said something like this with reference to Hawaii and agriculture, but I could not consummate the argument with the eloquence and background of evidence as Kirch (1985) has done. This seems an irrecoverable digression, but I see this factor as the penultimate selection pressure on agriculture—and on the plants themselves. I well remember minor arguments on whether it was agriculture or horticulture that Pacific islanders practiced. A late reply might be that horticulture was transformed into agriculture through social dictates that converted single plant selection into group selection, the individual animal into the herd, the plant into the crop.

But back to the beginning. The breaching of the border region by canoe to unpopulated islands of vastly varying soil and climate meant the carriage of small stocks (Ferdon, 1988, is the latest of a long line of writers to make this observation) of the quite amazing numbers of cultigens. Plants are strong evidence for this diffusion being a process rather than an event, involving many craft over time, different tracks, different destinations. This, however, set up the prerequisites for the enactment of the founder principle that the dictionary entry of King (1968) states so succinctly:

> [T]he principle that, when a newly isolated population is established, its gene pool soon diverges from that of the parent population because of sampling errors. These differences are further enhanced because the different evolutionary pressures in the different areas occupied by the parent and daughter populations will be operating on different gene pools.

The first requisite for a colonizing population—and I stress that I am speaking about plants—is that the species must possess a breeding system that assures reproduction of adapted genotypes in abundance (Brown and Marshall 1981; Brown and Burdon 1987). Asexual or vegetative reproduction is one of these systems, and the Polynesian cultigens—yams, taro genera, banana, sweet potato, *ti* (*Cordyline*) as well as the breadfruit tree—all have that character as the normal means of propagation by Polynesian cultivators. Survival of crop plants after landfall would be comparatively easy on high tropical islands with water resources, varied soil media, and the ethnobotanical knowledge of the migrants.

On the more marginal soils, like the atolls and raised limestone platforms, with little water other than rainfall, it would be more difficult, but many of these conditions would have been known from the border region of immediate provenience. It was on islands like Easter Island and especially New Zealand, outside of normal latitudinal adaptational ranges for the species, that horticultural skills would need to have been directed toward initial survival. But whether tropical or temperate or high or low island, sufficient variability of small stocks for first, natural selection, and later, artificial selection was the first requisite, or the arrival of migrants with additional planting material was required. Whatever the case, the surviving gene pool would be small, and the effect should be observable in the modern populations.

As efficient colonizers through their vegetative reproductive systems, the Polynesian tuber plants are facultatively sexual reproducers, producing seed that allows for gene recombination and, thus, the formation of varieties through the agronomic selection of seedlings as well as vegetative mutants. It is by this means that the large number of varieties recorded or observed among Polynesian botanical and agricultural studies is putatively accounted for, although somatic mutation may have played a minor role. It is, indeed, the horticultural penchant of Oceanic peoples as a whole, that is expressed in plant propagation as selection. This can be exemplified through the examples of Barrau (1956, 74) for New Caledonia and Handy (1940, 17) for Hawaii, of varietal descriptions of *Colocasia* taro that are also discriminated on their adaptation to dryland or irrigated wetland, as well as other utilitarian characteristics such as suitability for leaf consumption, *poi*-making and the like.

By and large, the number of varieties within a given society of agriculturists can sometimes give a false impression of genetic variability, for those varieties are often simply the manifestation of recombinations within a limited gene pool. Conservation of recombinations by vegetative propagation has the effect of slowing down the rate of change. The sweet potato case from my data (1974b), however, seems to demonstrate the founder effect. Positing a small population originally from South America, and insignificant contributions from outside since (although there were some), over a wide range of characters studied such as root colors, internal and external, stem length, plant pubescence, the pooled Polynesian data showed narrow genetic bases compared with the Asian, Melanesian, and American collections. The latter, of course, represent the center of origin for the plant, and exhibited the maximum variability in most of the 42 plant characters assessed. The Asian and Melanesian were surprisingly variable, in some characters fully as variable as the South American. It was soon learned during field collection that there had been spasmodic but significant infusions of new varieties from unspecified overseas sources in recent times, while in historic times the opportunities of such occurrences were legion.

There was one example from New Guinea, where a variety *konime*, and variants on that name, were widespread throughout the highlands in 1963. It was said to be brought by Japanese soldiers, and spread from the lowlands, but there were so many forms (varieties) called by that name that the chances were that it had entered the gene pool through hybridizing with the local varieties, and its real identity lost.

The introduction of exotic germ plasm can happen in nature, but with agriculturists it takes its place with selection of varying degrees of intensity, and often in directions quite divergent from natural selection to produce useful or even novel variation. As Maynard Smith (1975, 130) says, "A domesticated population has been largely removed from the action of natural selection."

The one variety which showed significant variability outside the range of the American varietal population was from the northern Marquesas, collected in 1963 when the islands were depopulated and subsistence agriculture was at a low ebb. It was shown to produce the lowest specific gravity of the mature tuber in any variety tested. This is the closest to a potentially new variation arising through the random drift effect that the study of the sweet potato collection produced. It is, however, a negative one that would not be sought in purposeful selection of a starchy root crop.

Conclusion

The story of crop plant history in the Pacific is hardly near completion yet. In this paper I have tried to review what we have done. It seems little enough. In reaching into the past, we have gotten our models from history and the legacy of the European explorers; we have elaborated them with ethnographic fieldwork, and with collections for which we are heavily indebted to a disappearing breed, the subsistence farmer; we have cast eclectic nets of collaboration—archaeology, anthropology, taxonomy, cytology, palynology—to test these models. Sites like those of Kirch in Mussau are rare, but give us hope for further macrofossil remains, but over how wide an area can we expect that? But there is a new breed coming up fast, the new technologists to whom I have briefly referred. DNA analysis may give us a phylogenetic window on the basic units of evolution, and to a further dimension on the relationships of the Melanesian, Indonesian and Asian rice, *Canarium*, bananas, and sugar, using contemporary plant material. For the artifacts excavated from the soil and their past, the analysis of residues of plants and animals holds out the best prospects to fill out the detailed picture that we could not achieve.

Literature Cited

Allen, J., J. Specht, W. Ambrose, and D. Yen. 1984. *Lapita Homeland Project: Report of the 1984 Field Season.* Canberra: Piranha Publications, Australian National Univ.

Amherst of Hackney and B. Thomson, trans. and ed. 1901. *The Discovery of the Solomon Islands by Alvara de Mendaña in 1568.* 2 vols. London: Hakluyt Society.

Barrau, J. 1956. *L'agriculture vivrière autochone de la Nouvelle-Caledonie.* Noumea: Commission du Pacifique Sud.

———. 1957. L'arbre à pain en Océanie. *J. Agr. Trop. Bot. Appl.* 4:117–123.

———. 1958. *Subsistence agriculture in Melanesia.* Bernice P. Bishop Mus. Bul. 219.

———. 1959. The sago palms and other food plants of marsh dwellers in the South Pacific islands. *Econ. Bot.* 13:151–162.

———. 1961. *Subsistence agriculture in Polynesia and Micronesia.* Bernice P. Bishop Mus. Bul. 223:1–94.

———. 1965. Histoire et préhistoire horticoles de l'Océanie tropicale. *J. Société Océanistes* 21:55–78.

Beaglehole, J. C., ed. 1955. *The Journals of Captain James Cook.* Vol. 1, *The Voyage of the Endeavour, 1768–1771.* Cambridge: Hakluyt Society.

———, ed. 1961. *The Journals of Captain James Cook.* Vol. 2, *The Voyage of the* Resolution *and* Adventure, *1772–1775.* Cambridge: Hakluyt Society.

———, ed. 1962. *The* Endeavour *Journal of Joseph Banks, 1768–1771.* 2 vols. Sydney: Angus and Robertson.

Bellwood, P. 1979. *Man's Conquest of the Pacific.* New York: Oxford Univ. Press.

———. 1985. *Prehistory of the Indo-Malaysian Archipelago.* Sydney: Academic Press.

Benedict, P. K. 1975. *Austro-Thai Language and Culture*. New Haven: HRAF Books.

Blust, R. A. 1976. Austronesian culture history: some linguistic inferences and their relations to the archaeological record. *World Archaeology* 8:19–43.

Brandes, E. W. 1958. Origin, classification and characteristics. In *Sugarcane (*Saccharum officinarum *L.)*. Eds. E. Artschwager and E. W. Brandes. USDA Agr. Handbook 122:1–35.

Brown, A. D. H., and J. J. Burdon. 1987. Mating systems and colonizing success in plants. In *Colonization, Succession and Stability*. Eds. A. J. Gray, M. J. Crawley, and P. J. Edwards. Oxford: Blackwell. 115–131.

Brown, A. H. D., and D. R. Marshall. 1981. Evolutionary changes accompanying colonization of plants. In *Evolution Today*. Eds. G. G. E. Scudder and J. L. Reveal. Proceedings of the Second International Congress of Systematic and Evolutionary Biology. 351–363.

Buck, P. H. [Te Rangi Hiroa]. 1938. *Vikings of the Sunrise*. New Zealand ed., 1954. Christchurch: Whitcombe and Tombs.

Burney, J. 1803. *Chronological History of Voyages and Discoveries in the South Seas or Pacific Ocean*. Vol. 1. 1967 printing. Amsterdam: N. Israel.

Burrows, E. G. 1938. *Western Polynesia: A Study in Cultural Differentiation*. Goteburg: Gothenburg Ethnographical Mus.

Coates, D. J., D. E. Yen, and P. M. Gaffey. 1988. Chromosome variation in taro, *Colocasia esculenta:* implications for origin in the Pacific. *Cytologia* 55:551–560.

Conklin, H. C. 1961. The study of shifting cultivation. *Current Anthr.* 2:27–61.

Craib, J. L., and N. L. Farrell. 1981. On the question of prehistoric rice cultivation in the Mariana Islands. *Micronesica* 17:1–9.

Ferdon, E. N. 1988. A case for taro preceding kumara as the dominant domesticate in ancient New Zealand. *J. Ethnobiology* 8:1–5.

Forster, G. 1786. *De Plantis Esculentis Insularum Oceani Australis*. Halae ad Salam: Typis Franckianis.

Golson, J. 1971. Australian Aboriginal plants: some ecological and culture-historical implications. In *Aboriginal Man and Environment*. Eds. D. J. Mulvaney and J. Golson. Canberra: Australian National Univ. Press. 196–238.

———. 1977a. The making of the New Guinea highlands. In *The Melanesian Environment*. Ed. J. Winslow. Canberra: Australian National Univ. Press. 45–56.

———. 1977b. No room at the top: agricultural intensification in the New Guinea highlands. In *Sunda and Sahul*. Eds. J. Allen, J. Golson, and R. Jones. London: Academic Press. 601–638.

Golson, J., and P. J. Hughes. 1980. The appearance of plant and animal domestication in New Guinea. *J. Société Océanistes* 69:294–303.

Golson, J., R. J. Lampert, J. M. Wheeler, and W. R. Ambrose. 1967. A note on carbon dates for horticulture in the New Guinea highlands. *J. Polynesian Society* 76:369–371.

Gorecki, P. P. 1986. Human occupation and agricultural development in the Papua New Guinea highlands. *Mountain Research and Development* 6:159–166.

Green, R. C., and J. M. Davidson, eds. 1969. *The archaeology of Western Samoa*. Vol. 1. Auckland Institute Mus. Bul. 6.

Guiart, J. 1958. *Espiritu Santo (Nouvelles Hebrides0*. Paris: Libraire Plon.

Handy, E. S. C. 1923. *The native culture in the Marquesas*. Bernice P. Bishop Mus. Bul. 9.

———. 1940. The Hawaiian planter. Vol. 1, His plants, methods and areas of cultivation. Bernice P. Bishop Mus. Bul. 161.

Haudricourt, A. G., and L. Hedin. 1943. *L'homme et les Plantes Cultivées*. Paris: Gallimard.

Hoare, M. E., ed. 1982. *The* Resolution *Journal of Johann Reinhold Forster, 1772–1775*. Vol. 2. London: Hakluyt Society.

Irwin, G. 1988. Review of Feathered Gods and Fishhooks; An introduction to Hawaiian archaeology and prehistory by P. V. Kirch. *Archaeology in Oceania* 23:116–118.

King, R. C. 1968. *A Dictionary of Genetics*. New York: Oxford Univ. Press.

Kirch, P. V. 1978. Indigenous agriculture on Uvea (western Polynesia). *Econ. Bot.* 32:157–181.

_____. 1984. *The Evolution of the Polynesian Chiefdoms.* Cambridge: Cambridge Univ. Press.

_____. 1985. *Feathered Gods and Fishhooks.* Honolulu: Univ. of Hawaii Press.

_____. 1988a. Circumscription theory and sociopolitical evolution in Polynesia. *Amer. Behavioral Scientist* 31:416–427.

_____. 1988b. The Talepakemalai Lapita site and Oceanic prehistory. *Natl. Geogr. Res.* 4:328–342.

Kirch, P. V., and R. C. Green. 1987. History, phylogeny and evolution in Polynesia. *Current Anthr.* 28:431–456.

Kirch, P. V., and D. E. Yen. 1982. *Tikopia: the prehistory and ecology of a Polynesian outlier.* Bernice P. Bishop Mus. Bul. 238.

Lebot, V. 1991. Kava (*Piper methysticum* Forst. f.): the Polynesian distribution of an Oceanian plant. In *Islands, Plants, and Polynesians.* Eds. P. A. Cox and S. A. Banack. Portland, Oregon: Timber Press, Dioscorides Press.

Leenhouts, P. W. 1955. *The genus* Canarium *in the Pacific.* Bernice P. Bishop Mus. Bul. 216.

_____. 1959. *A monograph of the genus* Canarium. Leiden: Ijdo.

Loy, T., M. Spriggs, and S. Wickler. N.d. Evidence for the use of aroids in the Northern Solomon Islands from 28,000 years ago. Manuscript.

Malo, D. 1951. *Hawaiian antiquities.* Bernice P. Bishop Mus. Special Publication 2.

Markham, C., trans. and ed. 1904. *The Voyages of Pedro Fernandez Quiros, 1595 to 1606.* 2 vols. London: Hakluyt Society.

McCoy, P. C., and P. C. Cleghorn. 1988. Archaeological excavations on Santa Cruz (Nendo), southeast Solomon Islands: summary report. *Archaeology in Oceania* 23:104–115.

Merrill, E. D. 1917. *An Interpretation of Rumphius's Herbarium Amboinense.* Manila: Bureau of Printing.

Ochse, J. J., with R. C. Bakhuisen van den Brink. 1977. *Vegetables of the Dutch East Indies.* Eng. ver. of *Indische Groenten* (1931). Canberra: Australian National Univ. Press.

Oka, H. I., and W. T. Chang. 1960. Survey of variations in photoperiodic response in wild *Oryza* species. *Bot. Bul. Acad. Sin.* 1:1–14.

_____. 1961. Hybrid swarms between wild and cultivated species of rice. *Evolution* 15:418–430.

Oliver, D. L. 1974. *Ancient Tahitian Society.* 3 vols. Honolulu: Univ. of Hawaii Press.

Parkinson, S. 1784. *A Journal of a Voyage to the South Seas in His Majesty's Ship the* Endeavour. Rpt. 1984. London: Caliban.

Pawley, A., and R. (C.) Green. 1973. Dating the dispersal of Oceanic languages. *Oceanic Linguistics* 12:1–67.

_____. 1985. The Proto-Oceanic language community. In *Out of Asia.* Eds. E. Kirk and E. Szathmary. Canberra: J. Pac. History. 161–184.

Pollock, N. J. 1983. The early use of rice in Guam: the evidence from the historic records. *J. Polynesian Society* 92:509–520.

Powell, J. M. 1982. Plant resources and palaeobotanical evidence for plant use in the Papua New Guinea highlands. *Archaeology in Oceania* 17:28–50.

Safford, W. 1905. *The Useful Plants of Guam.* Washington, DC: Smithsonian Institution.

Sahlins, M. D. 1972. *Stone Age Economics.* Chicago: Aldine.

St. John, H. 1953. Origin of the sustenance plants of the Polynesians. In *Proceedings of the Seventh International Botanical Congress.* Stockholm.

Sauer, C. O. 1952. *Agricultural Origins and Dispersals.* New York: American Geographical Society.

Serpenti, L. M. 1965. *Cultivators in the Swamps.* Assen: Gorcum.

Sharp, A. 1960. *The Discovery of the Pacific Islands.* Oxford: Clarendon Press.

Skelton, R. 1969. *Magellan's Voyage: A Narrative Account of the First Circumnavigation.* New Haven: Yale Univ. Press.

Small, C. A. 1972. *Atoll Agriculture in the Gilbert and Ellice Islands.* Tarawa: Department of Agriculture.

Smith, J. Maynard. 1975. *The Theory of Evolution.* Rpt. 1985. Harmondsworth: Penguin Books.

Spriggs, M. 1981. *Vegetable Kingdoms: Taro Irrigation and Pacific Prehistory.* Ph.D. Thesis, Australian National Univ., Canberra.

_____ . 1982. Irrigation in Melanesia: formative adaptation and intensification. In *Melanesia Beyond Diversity.* Eds. R. J. May and H. Nelson. Canberra: Australian National Univ. Press. 309–324.

_____ . In press. Why irrigation matters in Pacific prehistory. In Pacific Production Systems: Approaches to Economic Prehistory.

Suggs, R. C. 1960. *The Island Civilizations of Polynesia.* New York: Mentor.

Telford, I. R. H. 1986. Dioscoreaceae. *Flora Australia* 46:196–219.

Thaman, R. R. 1975. *The Tongan Agricultural System.* Suva: Univ. of the South Pacific.

Tryon, D. T. 1985. The peopling of the Pacific: a linguistic appraisal. In *Out of Asia.* Eds. R. Kirk and E. Szathmary. Canberra: J. Pac. History. 147–160.

Whitmore, T. C., ed. 1981. *Wallace's Line and Plate Tectonics.* Oxford: Clarendon Press.

Wilder, G. P. 1928. *The breadfruit of Tahiti.* Bernice P. Bishop Mus. Bul. 50.

Yen, D. E. 1971. The development of agriculture in Oceania. In *Studies in Oceanic Culture History.* Vol. 2. Eds. R. C. Green and M. Kelly. Pac. Anthr. Rec. 21·1–12.

_____ . 1973a. Agriculture in Anutan subsistence. In *Anuta: A Polynesian Outlier in the Solomon Islands.* Eds. D. E. Yen and J. Gordon. *Pac. Anthr. Rec.* 21:112–149.

_____ . 1973b. Ethnobotany from the voyages of Mendana and Quiros in the Pacific. *World Archaeology* 5:32–43.

_____ . 1973c. The origins of Oceanic agriculture. *Archaeology and Physical Anthropology in Oceania* 8:68–85.

_____ . 1974a. Arboriculture in the subsistence of Santa Cruz, Solomon Islands. *Econ. Bot.* 28:247–284.

_____ . 1974b. *The sweet potato and Oceania.* Bernice P. Bishop Mus. Bul. 236.

_____ . 1980. The southeast Asian foundations of Oceanic agriculture. *J. Société Océanistes* 66–67:140–146.

_____ . 1982a. Ban Chiang pottery and rice. *Expedition* 24:51–64

_____ . 1982b. The southeast Solomon Islands cultural history programme. *IPPA Bul.* 3:52–66.

_____ . 1985. Wild plants and domestication in Pacific islands. In *Recent Advances in Indo-Pacific Prehistory.* Eds. V. N. Miscra and P. Bellwood. New Delhi: Oxford and IBH. 315–326.

_____ . In press. Agriculture and the colonization of the Pacific Islands. In *Pacific Production Systems: Approaches to Economic Prehistory.* Eds. D. E. Yen and J. M. J. Mummery. Canberra: Australian National Univ.

Yen, D. E., P. V. Kirch, P. Rosendahl, and T. Riley. 1972. Prehistoric agriculture in the upper valley of Makaha, Oahu. In *Makaha Valley Historical Project.* Interim Report no. 3. Eds. E. J. Ladd and D. E. Yen. Pac. Anthr. Rec. 18:59–94.

Yen, D. E., and J. M. Wheeler (Powell). 1968. Introduction of taro into the Pacific: the indications of chromosome numbers. *Ethnology* 7:259–267.

Yuncker, T. G. 1943. *The flora of Niue Island.* Bernice P. Bishop Mus. Bul. 178.

CHAPTER 5

Polynesian Plant Names: Linguistic Analysis and Ethnobotany, Expectations and Limitations

KARL H. RENSCH

Department of Linguistics
Australian National University
Canberra, Australia

The recording of vernacular plant names by botanists working in the field is a practice that has an old tradition in the discipline. The botanists who took part in the first scientific expeditions to the Pacific were no exceptions. Banks, Solander, and the Forsters took great pains to establish and to transcribe the native name of the plant specimen they had collected. The motive behind this linguistic interest is the expectation that a comparative study of their etymology and geographical distribution, combined with evidence from botany and other sciences, could shed light on the origin and diffusion pattern of a particular plant or botanical life form.

In most cases botanists are not trained linguists, and linguists seldom have a firm grounding in botany. This dilemma has caused problems in both disciplines. The possibility of so-called errors of the first degree (i.e., inaccurate recording of field data) is a constant worry to linguists, especially when analyzing older material. But this is not the only difficulty with which linguists contend. Working on plant names makes one painfully aware of how necessary it is to place the results of a linguistic analysis into the wider framework of ethnobotany and to cooperate with experts in prehistory, anthropology, and archaeology. The first step towards a fruitful cooperation is to get to know the methodology and theoretical orientation of the related disciplines to understand the constraints under which they operate.

Reflexes of kumara *in Tahiti*

In this paper I present the case for linguistics, and although the subtitle "Expectations and Limitations" may sound like an exercise in general didactics, I deal with a concrete example, a plant name that has stirred the imagination of scientists working in the Pacific like no other: *kumara,* the name of the sweet potato *Ipomoea batatas* (Convolvulaceae).

I shall restrict my discussion to Polynesia—more precisely to eastern Polynesia. I do not intend to go back to the question of whether the word *kumara,* which has reflexes in most Polynesian languages, is of South American Indian origin. The case for it has been proven beyond doubt (Yen 1974). I will instead deal with some linguistic oddities that the modern reflexes show in their phonological make-up, and that have not received the attention that a careful analysis based on a diffusionistic approach would require.

In modern Tahitian the generic term for the sweet potato is *'ūmara*[1]. As Proto-Polynesian (PPN) **k* changes in Tahiti to a glottal stop /ʔ/ quite regularly, *'ūmara* is what we expect from an older *kūmara*. In Tahitian the change **k* > /ʔ/ is without exception; /k/ has completely disappeared from the phoneme inventory.

Tahitian consonant phonemes

plosives	p	t	?
fricatives	f	v	h
nasals	m	n	
liquids	r		

The first European visitors commented on the inability of Tahitians to pronounce words containing *k,* noting that they replaced *k* occurring in foreign words simply by *t*. Captain Cook became known as *Tute,* Hicks as *Hite,* and Parkinson as *Patine*[2]. The *t* for *k* replacement is nothing extraordinary when we look at it from a phonological point of view. As Tahitian has only one non-peripheral oral plosive, namely /t/, (*p* and *?* are not made using the tongue as articulator), any other oral stop that they hear (e.g., a velar stop *k*) is mentally categorized and decoded as a variation of the phoneme /t/, and therefore likely to be reproduced in active speech as a [t]. In linguistic terms: the allophonic range of /t/ includes [k].

I have stated earlier that PPN **k* has become a glottal stop in Tahitian. This sound change had been completed at the time of European contact. If the speakers of Tahitian had still been aware of the /k/-/ʔ/ correspondence, Cook's name would not have ended up as *Tute,* but as [ʔuʔe], probably spelled *Ue* by the early European linguists who, as a rule, failed to identify the glottal stop as a distinctive element of the sound system and hence did not represent it in their transcriptions.

Linguistic Interpretation of Eighteenth Century Recordings for Sweet Potato

Having established that at the time of contact Tahitian no longer had a /k/ phoneme, we are somewhat puzzled by the form *cumala* "sweet potato" recorded by Banks in his Endeavour Journal (Beaglehole 1955, 36). We would have expected *umala* representing ['ūmala]. As we can safely exclude the possibility that the letter *c* is Banks' transcription for the glottal stop, we have to ask ourselves whether the *c* is just an error, another example of the unreliability of data collected by linguistic laypersons and therefore to be ignored, or whether Banks correctly transcribed what he heard.

When dealing with a printed source, as we do in the case of Banks' *Endeavour* journal, we have to consider a number of potential sources for error. The printer may have made a mistake, for example, inadvertently adding a *c* which did not exist in the manuscript. The possibility that this could have happened is not as unlikely as it might sound, as the Tahitian word is quoted in a comparative table side by side with the northern and southern New Zealand forms which are given as *cumala*.

The only way of finding out whether we are dealing with a printing error or not is to go back to the original manuscript. In the case of the *Endeavour* journal we are particularly lucky. The manuscript of the first published version is not only preserved but also easily accessible in a facsimile publication. The form *cumala* is not a printing error: it appears as such in the manuscript.

At this stage it would seem pedantic *in extremis* if one actively pursued the issue of a scribal or copying error any further. It was more by coincidence than by design that I got hold of a glossary of Tahitian words that Banks collected during his stay on the island. The manuscript is part of the Marsden collection in the library of the School of Oriental and African Studies, University College, London. To my delight I found among the 500 recorded words a listing for sweet potato, but surprisingly the vernacular form was not *cumala* but *umarrah* (i.e., a *k*-less form representing ['ūmara]). Instead of finding an answer to the question of *k* or glottal stop, our skepticism is increasing. Did two forms exist at the time of European contact, or is the linguistically unusual *k*-form an error which slipped into Banks' manuscript at the time of writing—which was presumably after his return from the voyage?

As far as the early visits by Europeans to Tahiti are concerned, we are in the fortunate position that quite a few members of the expedition had an interest in the fauna and flora of the South Pacific islands. They kept diaries recording faithfully what they saw and what they could learn from the indigenous populations. This allows us in many cases to cross-check information using notes from two or more observers.

The existence of the sweet potato in Tahiti is mentioned not only by Banks, but also by Solander (n.d.), his botanist friend from Sweden; by Sydney Parkinson (1773), the draughtsman; and by an anonymous person (possibly a crew member by the name of James Magra) who published the first account of the voyage of the *Endeavour* in 1771 without revealing his name. All of them recorded the vernacular name of the sweet potato. Solander's transcription from the manuscript in the British Museum was unfortunately not accessible to me[3]. Monkhouse, the surgeon of the *Endeavour*, also compiled a wordlist (Monkhouse n.d.), but the sweet potato is not mentioned in it. Below I have listed the forms that are known from various records of Cook's first voyage, to which I have added the forms that Forster and Pickersgill recorded on the second voyage (1772–1775).

cumala	Banks, *Endeavour* journal
umarrah	Banks
oomarra	Parkinson, journal, p. 38
tomalla	Magra?
goomarro	Forster (2nd voyage)
coomallo or *coomarro*	Pickersgill (2nd voyage,
	Beaglehole 1969, 360)

To use language data collected by people with no special training in linguistics is problematic, to say the least. While one can in most cases glean useful lexical and semantic information, one has to be careful when it comes to relying on their phonetic accuracy. In our case we can confirm, by looking at the various forms, that they all go back to the same etymon, but if we had expected to find an answer to the question of whether *kūmara* or *'ūmara* was the form used at European contact time, we seem to be further away from solving the problem than we were at the outset. Faced with what seem to be notorious examples of unreliable older source material we must ask ourselves whether there is any point in continuing the enquiry.

While it cannot be denied that people without any training in articulatory phonetics are likely to make mistakes when they are confronted with the problem of noting down words of a foreign language using the alphabet of their mother tongue, it is also true that many of the so-called mistakes turn out to be systematic rather than erratic. This means that it is not too difficult for a linguist who knows the phonological systems of both the naive transcriber's mother tongue and the target language to discover underlying patterns which allow the drawing of conclusions about the authenticity of the linguistic data. I am going to discuss this issue using Forster's form *goomarro* as an example.

There is no problem in finding out that the digraph *oo* represents the rounded high backvowel [u]. Forster himself explains in the introduction to his unpublished "Vocabularies" what phonetic value he assigns to the letters he is using for the transcription of Tahitian: "oo have the valour of oo in look, rook, u sounds like u in use, usurper."

The use of double *rr*—and of double consonants in general—does not refer to a quantity feature of the consonant in question, as it does, for instance, in Italian where *fato* "fate" and *fatto* "made" are pronounced the same except that in *fatto* the *t* is long (i.e., its release is delayed). In the transcription of Forster and other Anglophone explorers, the double consonant is an orthographic device to describe the preceding vowel as short.

In Polynesian languages, vowel length is phonemically relevant, that is, some words are distinguished solely on the basis of vowel length (minimal pairs), as for example, Tahitian *maha* "four" versus *māha* "to be satisfied." Although Forster and the other visitors who described Tahitian did not recognize the functional significance of vowel quantity, they nevertheless noticed that there were differences in vowel length. As only the shortness of a vowel has been orthographically marked, one has to conclude that vowels which are not followed by a double consonant did not attract any particular attention because they were close to the norm as far as quantity realization is concerned. The two transcriptions used by Banks (*cumala* and *umarrah*) show, however, that the marking of short vowels was not carried out in a very systematic fashion.

The use of *l, ll,* and *rr* in the above transcriptions seems to be rather puzzling and contradictory to people in whose native language *r* and *l* represent two different phonemes (e.g., in English where *light* is to be distinguished from *right*). In Polynesian languages, however, there is no phonological distinction between *r* and *l*.

The lack of an opposition between liquids is a phenomenon that is better known from Japanese. It causes difficulties not only for a Japanese person learning English, but also for a native speaker of English (or any language with an *r/l* distinction) who wants to learn Japanese. As Japanese does not use the difference between *r* and *l* to distinguish words, *r* and *l* are categorized as variations of the same functional unit: they are allophones of the same phoneme. This means that in Japanese one can shift pronunciation between *r* and *l* and *l* and *r* without causing lexical ambiguity. Native speakers of English listening to Japanese automatically try to assign the *r/l* variations to one of the two categories with which their native language has provided them: either /l/ or /r/. Failing to recognize the allophonic character of *r* and *l* will result in a useless discussion about whether the Japanese have an *r* or an *l* in their language.

What we have said about Japanese applies *mutatis mutandis* also to Tahitian and Polynesian languages in general. On purely phonological grounds both *r* and *l* are justifiable orthographic representations for the only liquid phoneme that occurs in Tahitian. James Michener in his novel *Hawaii,* describes in a delightful scene the difficulties the early missionaries had to come to grips with in a similar problem: the lack of a *t-k* distinction in Hawaiian. Keoki, the Hawaiian convert, Captain Janders, and the newly arrived Reverend Abner Hale have an argument about the correctness of Hawaiian spelling:

> "The way you Americans have decided to spell it is neither right nor wrong. My father's name you spell Kelolo. It would be just as right to spell it Teroro."
> "You mean the truth lies in between?" Janders asked . . .
> "Yes, Captain," the young man said happily. "In these matters the truth does lie somewhere in between."
> The idea was repugnant to Abner . . . "There is always only one truth" the young missionary corrected.
> Keoki willingly assented, explaining, "In matters of God, of course there is only one truth, Reverend Hale. But in spelling my father's name, there is no final truth. It lies between Kelolo and Teroro and is neither" (Michener 1960, 250).

Had Keoli been a linguist he could have added a few more examples from Hawaiian and other Polynesian languages to back up his argument about the relativity of "truth" in spelling. Not only do Polynesian languages lack an /r/-/l/ distinction, they also lack the opposition between voiced and unvoiced plosives. While English has minimal pairs in which the contrast between /p/ and /b/, /t/ and /d/, and /k/ and /g/ is used to distinguish meaning (pea/bee, tin/din, cut/gut), no such minimal pairs exist in any of the Polynesian languages. As far as the actual pronunciation of stop consonants is concerned, it means that the range of possible allophonic variance is much wider than in English, where /p/ and /b/ have to be distinguished; or in Thai, where a three-way phonemic distinction has to be observed between /p/, /ph/, and /b/ to prevent misunderstandings.

The spelling *g* in *goomarro* used by Forster is therefore—from a linguistic point of view—equivalent to the spelling *c* (i.e., [k]) used by Banks in *cumala*. Alternate *p/b* and *t/d* spellings are very common in all wordlists compiled by authors with an English or German background (Banks: *eiboo* "aipu", *midi* "miti"), but they are not found in words recorded by the early French and Spanish visitors to Tahiti, and this for a reason.

As in the case of the *r/l* dispute, we are once more not dealing with a question of absolute truth. The different spellings are the result of the different language background of the authors and are explainable by the different allophonic realization of /p/ and /t/ in the Germanic and Romance languages. The variants of the Tahitian plosive phonemes are pronounced as unaspirated stops (i.e., in the same way as the unvoiced stops in the Romance languages). The difference between /b/ and /p/, /t/ and /d/, and /k/ and /g/ in French or Spanish is one of absence/presence of voice. In English and German, however, the distinction between the /p,t,k/ and the /b,d,g/ stop phonemes in word initial, and also in most word medial positions, is of a duplex nature—based on the feature *voice* and the feature *aspiration*. (Technically speaking, aspiration is delayed voiced onset.) The auditorily most important cue for the recognition of /p/-/b/, /t/-/d/, and /k/-/g/ distinctions is, for English and German, the presence of aspiration. If this cue is absent, untrained listeners are likely to interpret unaspirated stops in a foreign language as /b/, /d/, and /g/. This explains the different spellings of Tahitian words in our wordlists and in those collected by speakers of Romance languages, such as Bougainville and Boenechea.

It was only decades after European contact, when the missionaries from the London Missionary Society had gained a more profound knowledge of the Tahitian language, that the *p/b* and *t/d* issue was finally decided in favor of an orthographical representation by the letters *p* and *t*, albeit not as a result of a deeper linguistic insight into the problem, but as a pragmatic response to the frustration felt over the inability to establish the ultimate truth[4].

So far we have not mentioned the spelling *-ah* and *o* in Banks' *umarrah*, Forster's *goomarro,* and Pickersgill's *coomallo/coomarro*. The spelling *-ah* representing final [a] is quite commonly used in Banks' unpublished "Collection of Vocabularies" (*meduah* "metua", *pootterah* "po'o te ra"). The final *-o* in Forster's and Pickersgill's transcriptions is unusual. As far as Forster is concerned we can exclude the possibility of a printing or copying error as the word appears in this form in the comparative table of his *Observations* and also in his "Vocabulary" manuscript. A possible explanation might be that we are dealing with a final vowel lacking in prominence due to the absence of stress and that the transcription *o* signals that its quality was different from that of an [a] in a stressed syllable[5].

We started our discussion with the intention of establishing whether the Tahitian word for the sweet potato started with *k* or a glottal stop, and so far we seem to have dodged the issue, dealing instead with diverging transcriptions that at first glance appear to have little bearing on the problem we were going to look at. The reason for dealing with the *k*—glottal stop problem after discussing the other spelling variations was to find out what degree of confidence we can have in the phonological accuracy of the recordings. It turned out that the *l/r* and *c/g* spellings, which on the surface appear to be glaring examples of linguistic dilettantism, can be explained in terms of the differences between the phonological systems of English and Tahitian. We are now in a position to back up the unusual spelling *cumala* found in Banks' *Endeavour* journal (Beaglehole 1962) and in Cook's account of the second voyage (Beaglehole 1969) by a second example. This is *goomarra*, recorded by Forster, whose ability to identify sounds one would have to rate fairly highly, as he had a reputation as a polyglot. It would now be difficult to deny that a pronunciation of the type [kūmara] existed, along-side with ['ūmara] and [tūmara].

We are now confronted with the problem of how to reconcile the three forms with the linguistic realities, that is, the stage of development in which the Tahitian language existed at the time of European contact. I have stated above that the form which causes no problem is *'ūmara,* as it shows the expected change of PPN **k* to glottal stop. We also mentioned earlier that this sound change was completed at the time of European contact as foreign *k*s were now converted to *t* (Cook to *Tute*). The form *tomalla* (representing [tūmara]) recorded by Magra is a reflex of this sound change[6] and provides evidence for the fact that a form *kūmara* had reached Tahiti after the completion of the earlier **k* > glottal stop change.

The irregular *k*-forms which are, as it were, exceptions twice over, defying not only the shift of PPN **k* > *?* but also the later one affecting *k* in loanwords, appear less mysterious when we treat them as local variations of the younger *t*-forms. A dialectal *k*-variation for /*t*/, well-known in the phonology of the Hawaiian and Samoan languages, is also attested for the Society Islands by Banks and Forster. Banks makes the following comments:

> All the Isles I was upon agreed perfectly as far as I could understand them; the people of Ulietea [Ulietea is the spelling for Raiatea used at the time of European contact] only chang'd the *t* of the Otahiteans to a *k*, calling *Tata* which signifies a man or woman *Kaka*, a circumstance which makes their language less soft. (Beaglehole 1962, 372).

The *Endeavour* stayed in Raiatea only for a few days. It is therefore more likely that Banks recorded the *k*-form aboard ship from Tupaia, an *ariki* and priest from Raiatea, who had been invited by Cook to visit England. Tupaia never made it to England. Like Parkinson and Monkhouse, he died on the return voyage in Batavia.

The *k*-variation, or *kappation* as it sometimes called, is also reported from Tahiti, and it is Forster (1774) himself who supplies the relevant information. While the explanation he gives for its existence is rather implausible—he believes that the alteration is due to an idiosyncratic inability of some persons to produce certain consonants—there can be no doubt that he actually observed *k*-variation. I quote from the introduction to his "Vocabulary":

> The inhabitants of the Isles are not all equally capable to pronounce all consonants, for at Otahitee 3 men, one of which was Orettee's Brother, the other Mahaina, Potatow's friend, who could not pronounce the *t* & always substituted to it a *k*; this must give a vast alteration to the language, & gradually form a new kind of dialect (Forster 1774).

Linguistic Evidence for Two Introductions of the Sweet Potato Into Tahiti

It would appear that the *t/k* variation existed as a regional phenomenon in Tahiti at the time of European contact. It is reasonable to assume that on the relatively big island which was politically divided into 14 *fenua* (i.e., more or less autonomous districts) and where the physical environment of high mountains, deep valleys, and subtropical forests was not conducive to islandwide communication, dialectal variations had developed. From the Cook and Forster account of the second voyage we know of *k* for *t* replacements in the district of Hitia'a[8].

The existence of this variation allows us to formulate an hypothesis which accounts for the phonological variations found in the early recordings of the name of the sweet potato in the following way:

The sweet potato was introduced to the Society Islands at least twice. In terms of relative chronology, the first introduction happened before or while PPN *k changed to /ʔ/. This explains the forms like *'ūmara*. The other introduction(s) took place after the conclusion of this shift, resulting in forms like *tūmara* in accordance with the new sound law which shifted [k] in loanwords to [t]. The *k*-forms are dialectal variations of these secondary *t*-forms, products of kappation, not remnants of an earlier borrowing, *kūmara*, which remained unaffected by the change PPN *k > glottal stop.

The weak point of this hypothesis is not one of linguistic methodology, but of general pragmatics. If there had been two introductions of the sweet potato, why should this have resulted into two phonologically different forms? If there existed an old established form *'ūmara<kūmara*, why not apply it unchanged to the same plant on its second introduction, even though this may have been centuries later? There are two answers to this question. The first one allows us to uphold the theory of two introductions separated by a time-gap long enough to obliterate in the minds of Tahitians the *k* > glottal stop shift. We would have to assume that the sweet potato had remained a marginal plant which did not play a major role in the economy and cultural life of Tahiti. The form *'ūmara* was not as firmly entrenched in the daily use of the language as not to allow the acceptance of *tūmara*, which shows the *t* for *k* replacement typical for the more recent phonological adaptation constraints on borrowings from other languages.

1st introduction *kūmara* > *'ūmara*
2nd introduction *kūmara* > *tūmara*
kūmara (kappation)

The emergence of phonological variation due to the infrequent use of a particular lexical item is a common phenomenon in all languages, particularly in nonstandardized languages that lack prescriptive guidelines.

The other answer would entail the abandoning of the supposition that the sweet potato was introduced before PPN *k had changed to /ʔ/ (i.e., at a relatively early point in time). We would have to assume that the /k/ > glottal shift happened outside Tahiti and that the imported word was *'ūmara*.

    a) *'ūmara*
    b) *kūmara* > *tūmara*
       kūmara (kappation)

We would still have to postulate more than one introduction of the sweet potato to account for the *t/k* reflexes, but instead of having to put them into a chronological sequence we could simply explain the Tahitian base forms *'umara* and *kumara* as borrowings from two different languages. This does not pose any problems as there are languages in eastern Polynesia which have preserved PPN *k (e.g., Paumotuan, Mangarevan, Rapanui, and some Marquesan dialects).

Linguistic Evidence for the Source of the Second Introduction of the Sweet Potato

Paumotuan as the donor language could be excluded on environmental grounds. The atolls do not provide the right soil conditions to make them a center of sweet potato production and diffusion. Ignoring the problem of distance, Easter Island would qualify both on linguistic and agricultural grounds as the source for at least one introduction: the Rapanui word is *kūmara,* and the sweet potato used to be the major staple diet, as evidenced by the great number of varieties that were found by the early explorers.

Taking into account geographical proximity and linguistic evidence, it is more reasonable to assume that the sweet potato was not imported directly from Easter Island but was first brought—probably via Mangareva—to the Marquesas, from where it reached Tahiti and the rest of the Society Islands. In the Marquesas the sound shift PPN *k* > glottal stop remained incomplete, with the northern islands Nuku Hiva, Ua Huka, and Ua Pou showing a smaller proportion of words affected by it than Tahuata, Hiva Oa, and Fatu Hiva in the southern group[8]. Consequently, both *'ūmara* and *kūmara,* which we posit as bases for the Tahitian variants, can be traced back to Marquesan models.

The modern vernacular forms for the sweet potato are *kūma'a* (Ua Pou, Nuku Hiva) and *'ūma'a* (Tahuata), and show the effect of the change of /r/ > /ʔ/ which is a characteristic of Marquesan. The forms recorded in Tahiti at the time of contact all show preservation of /r/. At first glance this seems to exclude Marquesan as the donor language. However, like the /k/ > /ʔ/ change, the development of /r/ to /ʔ/ took place over a period of time, spreading through lexical diffusion and progressing faster in some islands than in others. Lallour (1843–1848) recorded a *r*-preserving form *oumara* ['*ūmara*] as late as 1843. Elbert (1982) counted 108 /r/ - /ʔ/ doublets in Dordillon's Marquesan dictionary of 1904 whose data collection goes back to the 1870s. Tryon (1987), commenting on Elbert's research, informs us that "the sound change is now complete in the majority of cases," with Ua Pou and Fatu Hiva showing a higher retention rate than the other islands. On the evidence presented, the /r/ > /ʔ/ change appears to be a relatively late phenomenon. The Tahitian base forms *'ūmara* and *kūmara* had obviously been borrowed from the Marquesan before the change had come into effect.

Confirmation of a sweet potato connection between the Marquesas and Tahiti, with the Marquesas as the point of origin, is provided by forms like the Tahitian *umaa* ['*ūma'a*] quoted by Yen (1974, 339), for which he gives as his sources Churchill (1912) and Hornell (1946). How old these forms are is difficult to establish; they are not listed in Davies' Tahitian dictionary. Churchill mentions in the introduction that he relied on Jaussen's dictionary of 1889 for his Tahitian examples, but I was unable to find a listing for *umaa* in the 1889 edition and the revised edition of 1969 does not mention it either.

At this stage in our discussion, where I am trying to explain the diverging vernacular forms recorded by the early visitors as borrowings, it should be stated *expressis verbis* what linguistic borrowing entails in practical terms. Words denoting concrete things are not like labels that can be peeled off from an object at point A, transferred across the ocean, and reused again at point B. They are, as it were, an inalienable part of the object or product they stand for; in other words, if we can identify the source of the signifier, we can be reasonably sure that we have also established the provenance of the signified.

If the bond between signifier and signified, word and object, is as indissoluble as we have described it, it should be possible to reverse the logical argumentation of the statement by saying, "If we know that a particular object or product has come from a given place, we can be reasonably sure its name has also come from there." Again, the sweet potato can be cited as a case in point.

In the first half of the nineteenth century, sweet potato species were brought from Hawaii to Tahiti. The Hawaiian word for sweet potato is *'uala* or *'uwala*, and it comes as no surprise that Tahitian borrowed the word as *'uara*—with the predictable replacement of *l* by *r*—to refer to the newly introduced variety. The word is attested in Davies and in Jaussen, but has since disappeared.

Phonological Evidence for Two Introductions From Species Naming

According to Henry (1928, 38) six varieties of the sweet potato were known in Tahiti. Their vernacular names are given as *poheretetei, hererai, rau maire, mairi* (probably erratum for *maire*), *'umara vaihi,* and *rea moa.* With the exception of *poheretetei* and *hererai,* the names are straightforward, showing naming strategies which are common throughout Polynesia.

'Umara vaihi reveals its origin by the qualifier *vaihi* which means "Hawaii" in

Tahitian. It is likely that *'ūara* and *'ūmara vaihi* were both used to refer to the same variety imported from Hawaii.

The literal meaning of *re'a moa* is "egg yolk." The metaphorical basis for the name is the yellow color of this variety. It is interesting to note that Gayangos, who surveyed the coast of Tahiti in 1772, was presented in the district of Atehuru with "plantains, coconuts, roast eurus (breadfruit) and some sweet potatoes of the colour of yolk of egg" (Corney 1913, 321), a description which strikes me as a direct translation of *re'a moa*.

Maire is obviously a short form of *rau maire* and it is therefore doubtful whether the two names really refer to two different varieties. *Maire* is cognate with the Hawaiian *maile*, but in Tahitian *maire* designates not only *Alyxia stellata* (Apocynaceae) but also a fern, *Polypodium vitiense* (Polypodiaceae), and a species of breadfruit. It is the perceived similarity between the leaves of the fern and the particular variety of the sweet potato that has given rise to *rau maire* (literally "maire leaf"). In Hawaiian we find an another example of this kind of polysemy: *kihe* "small native fern" (*Polypodium*) is also the name of a variety of sweet potato.

The etymological perspicuity of these four names is an indication that we are dealing with varieties of sweet potato which are of rather recent origin. The etymologies of *hererai* and *poheretetei* are, however, quite obscure. Morphologically the two words consist of two lexemes each: *pohere* + *tetei* and *here* + *rai*, with *here* probably being a reduced version of *pohere*. A form *pohere* is not listed in Davies (1851). One could speculate that *pohere* is identical with *pohiri* (English spelling e for [i]?) whose meaning is given in Davies as "young shoots rising from the main stem," and with *poheri*, recorded by Jaussen (1889) with the same meaning. The name could then be a reference to the way the sweet potato is propagated; *tetei* appears to be a reduced form of *teitei* "tall," and *rai* could be a contraction of *rahai*, the popular pronunciation of *rahi* "big." The etymological obscurity of both forms reflects linguistic archaism and suggests that these varieties have been cultivated for a long time. The fact that there are older and younger vernacular names supports the hypothesis that the sweet potato was introduced to Tahiti more than once.

Hawaiian *'uala* Pointing to a Direct Link With South America

After subjecting the Tahitian word to a close scrutiny, it has to be pointed out that the Hawaiian word *'uala* is far more intriguing than the diverging old vernacular forms from the Society Islands. If we assume that *'uala* is derived from a protoform **kumara* or **kumala*, we are left with the problem of explaining the change of /m/ > 0, a change not attested in other Hawaiian words, or in other Polynesian languages[9]. One could, of course, explain it away as one of "those freak sound changes" that happen occasionally, but this would be tantamount to saying the regularity of Hawaiian sound changes is subject to the whims of Pele: sometimes she interferes, sometimes she does not. While I do not doubt for one minute that Pele's powerful *mana* makes volcanoes erupt and the earth tremble, I think there may be another way of explaining the *m*-less Hawaiian forms.

If there is no support from other Polynesian languages for a /m/ > 0 shift, it must be assumed that the Hawaiian reflexes go back to a protoform which was borrowed from outside Polynesia and which lacked *m* right from the beginning (i.e., a form like **kuara* or **kuala*). The existence of such a form is attested for the homeland of the sweet potato, South America, more precisely for the Cuna language spoken in northern Colombia[10].

It is interesting to note that Carter (1963), discussing the presence of American plants in Hawaii, identifies the same area as the most likely center of a South America–Hawaii–Asia linkage on extralinguistic grounds. I quote:

> Could Hawaii at some past time have been a staging point for people maintaining a trans-Pacific contact? That is, could Hawaii at some time have been an equivalent of Guam? If so, then the plant evidence would suggest that the American end of this connection lay somewhere on the northwest coast of South America. This is precisely the area that Heine-Geldern's study of South American metal techniques (1954) points to as having come under Asiatic influence about 500 B.C. It is in this area that strongly Asiatic pottery forms have been reported, dating back to about 250 B.C. This is near the homeland of the Cuna, who possessed writing with at least two or three signs identical in form and meaning with early Chinese forms (Heine-Geldern 1938). And this is the area to which the Andean element the flora of Hawaii points (Carter 1963, 17).

Concluding Observations

In my introductory remarks I commented on the need for linguists to cooperate with experts in other disciplines. The discussion of the vernacular names of the sweet potato in Tahiti and Hawaii, our attempt to explain their phonological variation, has led us to set up hypotheses which account for the linguistic facts, but rely heavily on evidence from related disciplines for the conclusions we have drawn regarding the spread of the plant in Eastern Polynesia. Carter's arguments provide the kind of collateral support that linguists are looking for. We are now more confident to promote the hypothesis that the sweet potato reached Polynesia at least twice: once via a northern route through Hawaii under the guise of **kuara/*kuala,* and once via a southern route under the guise of **kumara,* with Easter Island as its point of entry. In both places a great number of varieties of the sweet potato is attested. As Polynesians propagated the sweet potatoes through cuttings, the new varieties came about through a very slow process of vegetative mutation, pointing to antiquity of cultivation[11].

Returning to the theme of this paper—"linguistic analysis, expectations and limitations"—it would perhaps be too much to expect that a linguistic study of species names and the naming strategies can supply the definite answer to the question of long-dating cultivation and the spread of the sweet potato into Polynesia. It will, however, within the constraints of its analytical approach, arrive at an explanatory hypothesis which can be critically evaluated against evidence from other ethnobotany-related disciplines and thus contribute to the advancement of our knowledge about the issue.

Notes

1. The glottal stop [ʔ] is represented by ' in the orthography of modern Tahitian.
2. "The natives could not repeat, after us, the sounds of the letters, *Q, X,* and *Z,* without great difficulty; *G, K,* and *S,* they could not pronounce at all" (Parkinson 1773, 65).
3. The vocabulary in Lanyon-Orgill (1979, 6) which has an entry for sweet potato (*cumala*), has been erroneously attributed by the author to Solander. It was in fact collected by Banks.
4. [B]ut what is remarkable in the pronunciation of the Tahitian consonants, is, the universal practice of confounding *b* and *p, d* and *t,* and it is a fact, that scarce a Tahitian can be found, who is able to distinguish between them. In spelling or pronouncing the letters singly, they run all the *p*s into *b,* and all the *t*s into *d;* but in speaking, they immediately turn most of them into *p* and *t,* and there is hardly a Tahitian word, in which it can be said, that *b* and *d* are universally used. These two letters *b* and *d* have therefore been rejected from the Tahitian alphabet (Davies 1851, 2).
5. The transcription *o* for pretonic [u] in *tomalla* (Magra) reflects English spelling as in "tomorrow" and needs no further discussion.
6. I am using the term *sound change* in a wider sense including what is, strictly speaking, a case of phonological adaptation.
7. "Mr. Pickersgill having expended his stock in trade, put off from Aitepeha in the afternoon, and came the same evening to Hiddea (Hitia'a), the district of O-Rettee (Reti) where M. de Bougainville lay at an anchor in 1768. Here he was hospitably entertained by the worthy old chief, who is so justly celebrated by that gallant French navigator; and the next morning his brother Tarooree embarked with our officer, in order to visit the ships which they saw in offing. When he came on board we found he had a kind of impediment in his organs of speech, by which means he substituted a *K* wherever the language required a *T;* a fault which we afterwards observed in several other individuals" (Cook and Forster, 1777, 3:259).
8. [T]here is also considerable variation in the reflexes of PCE [Proto-Central Eastern Polynesian] *k. While MQN [Northern Marquesan] most commonly retains PCE *k as /k/, it is commonly reflected as /ʔ/ in MQS [Southern Marquesan]. However, there are numerous cases where MQS retains PCE *k as /k/ and where MQN reflects it as /ʔ/ for the same item . . . Note, too, that the same speaker will use a form with or without /k/ indifferently where two competing forms exist in the one dialect." (Tryon 1987, 675).
9. The forms *uara* in Mkin (Gilbert Islands) and *uara/kuara/ku'ara* in Magaia, *kuara* in Aitutaki and Rarotonga quoted by Yen (1974, table B1 and table E1) from various sources are clearly Hawaiian borrowings or blends. Williams (1839, 578) specifically mentions that the sweet potato was introduced to the Cook Islands by missionaries (cf. Dixon 1932, 48).
10. "In various Quechua dialects of Peru and Ecuador the sweet-potato is known under the name *Kumara, Kumara, Umar', Umar', Kumal,* and in Colombia as *Umala* and *Kuala,* the latter name extending as far north as in Cuna dialect' (Heyerdahl 1952, 429).
11. Yen (1974) has argued that the possibility of natural seeding cannot be excluded (i.e., the varieties could have developed in a relatively short period of time as a result of sexual hybridization).

Literature Cited

Banks, J. N.d. Vocabulary of the language of Otaheite. School of African and Asian Studies Library, University College, London. Manuscript.

———. 1980. *The Journal of Joseph Banks in the* Endeavour. Facsimile ed. Surrey, England: Genesis Publications.

Barrau, J., ed. 1963. *Plants and the Migrations of Pacific Peoples.* Honolulu: Bishop Mus. Press.

Beaglehole, J. C., ed. 1955. *The Journals of Captain James Cook.* Vol. 1, *The Voyage of the* Endeavour, *1768–1771.* Cambridge: Hakluyt Society.

––––––, ed. 1969. *The Journals of Captain James Cook.* Vol. 2, *The Voyage of the* Resolution *and* Adventure, *1772–1775.* Cambridge: Hakluyt Society.

––––––, ed. 1962. *The* Endeavour *Journal of Sir Joseph Banks, 1768–1771.* 2 vols. Sydney: Angus and Robertson.

Carter, F. C. 1963. Movement of people and ideas across the Pacific. In *Plants and the Migrations of Pacific Peoples.* Ed. J. Barrau. Honolulu: Bishop Mus. Press. 7–11.

Churchill, W. 1912. *Easter Island: The Rapanui Speech and Peopling of Southeast Asia.* Washington, DC: Carnegie Institute.

Cook, J., and G. Forster. 1777. *A voyage round the world performed in His Brittanic Majesty's Ships the* Resolution *and* Adventure *in the years 1772, 1773, 1774 and 1775 written by James Cook, Commander of the* Resolution, *and Georg Forster, F.R.S.* Dublin: Printed for W. Whitestone.

Corney, G. C., ed. 1913. *The Quest and Occupation of Tahiti by Emissaries of Spain During the Years 1772–1776.* London: Hakluyt Society.

Davies, J. 1851. *A Tahitian and English Dictionary.* Tahiti: London Missionary Society Press. Rpt. Papeete, Tahiti: Haere Po No Tahiti, 1985.

Dixon, R. B. 1932. The problem of the sweet potato in Polynesia. *Amer. Anthr.* 34:40–66.

Dordillon, R. I. 1931. *Grammaire et Dictionnaire de la Langue des Îles Marquises, Marquisien-Français.* Paris: Institut d'Ethnologie.

Elbert, S. H. 1982. Lexical diffusion in Polynesia and the Marquesan-Hawaiian relationship. *J. Polynesian Society* 91:499–517.

Forster, J. R. 1774. Vocabulary of the language spoken in the isles of the South-Sea. Staatsbibliothek Preussischer Kulturbesitz, Berlin. Manuscript.

––––––. 1778. *Observations Made During A Voyage round the World on Physical Geography, Natural History and Ethnic Philosophy.* London: G. Robinson.

Henry, T. 1928. Ancient Tahiti. Bernice P. Bishop Mus. Bul. 48.

Heyerdahl, T. 1952. *American Indians in the Pacific.* London: Allen and Unwin.

––––––. 1966. Discussions of transoceanic contacts: isolationism, diffusionism, or a middle course. *Anthropos* 61:689–707.

Hornell, J. 1946. How did the sweet potato reach Oceania? *J. Linn. Soc., Bot.* 53:41–62.

Jaussen, T. 1889. *Grammaire et Dictionnaire de la Langue Maori, Dialecte Tahitien.* Paris: Bélin.

––––––. 1969. *Grammaire et Dictionnaire de la Langue Tahitienne.* Cinquième édition revue par Mgr Mazé et le R. P. H. Coppenrath. Paris: Musée de l'Homme.

Lallour, V. 1843–1848. Îles Marquises et notes sur les Marquises. A. Turnbull Library, Wellington. Manuscript.

Lanyon-Orgill, P. A. 1979. *Captain Cook's South Sea Island Vocabularies.* London: P. A. Lanyon-Orgill.

[Magra, J.?] 1771. *Journal of a Voyage round the World in His Majesty's Ship* Endeavour, *In the Years 1768, 1769, 1770, and 1771; Undertaken in pursuit of Natural Knowledge, at the Desire of the Royal Society: containing All the various occurrences of the Voyage, with descriptions of several new discovered Countries in the Southern Hemisphere; and Accounts of their Soil and productions; and of many Singularities in the Structure, Apparel, Customs, Manners, Policy, Manufactures, &c. of their Inhabitants, to which is added a Concise Vocabulary of the Language of Otahitee.* London: T. Becket and P. A. De Hondt.

Merrill, E. D. 1954. The botany of Cook's voyages and its unexpected significance in relation to anthropology, biogeography and history. *Chron. Bot.* 14(5/6).

Michener, J. 1960. *Hawaii.* London: Secker and Warburg.

Monkhouse, W. B. N.d. Otahite words. School of African and Asian Studies Library, University College, London. Manuscript.

Parkinson, S. 1773. *A Journal of a Voyage to the South Seas in His Majesty's Ship the* Endeavour. *Faithfully Transcribed from the Papers of the Late Sydney Parkinson, Draughtsman to Sir Joseph Banks Esq. on his Late Expedition with Dr. Solander, round the World.* London: S. Parkinson.

Solander, D. C. N.d. Taitian vocabulary. School of African and Asian Studies Library, University College, London. Manuscript.

Tryon, D. 1987. The Marquesan dialects: a first approach. In *A World of Language.* Eds. D. Laycock and W. Winter. Canberra: Pacific Linguistics. 669–681.

Williams, J. 1839. *A Narrative of Missionary Enterprises in the South Sea Islands.* London: John Snow.

Yen, D. E. 1974. The sweet potato and Oceania. Bernice P. Bishop Mus. Bul. 236.

CHAPTER 6

Polynesian Agricultural Systems

PATRICK V. KIRCH

Department of Anthropology
University of California, Berkeley
Berkeley, California 94720

Despite common origins that can be traced back to the Lapita culture of the second millennium B.C., the agricultural systems of Polynesia were strikingly diverse and varied. Any effort to synopsize this diversity can be dangerous, for not only must one consider the complexity of ethnographically documented systems, there is also the matter of historical process. In this treatment, I limit consideration as much as possible to systems as they operated at the time of early European contact, and in prehistory. The post-European modification of Polynesian agricultures—through the adoption of new crops, new tools, and new agronomic concepts, and also as a result of rearrangement of social and economic contexts—is an area that must be excluded for limitations of space, and because it lies beyond my particular expertise. I will concentrate on the islands of "triangle Polynesia" (the triangle subtended by New Zealand, Easter Island, and Hawaii), for the most part excluding the widely scattered "Polynesian outliers" lying within Melanesia and Micronesia. (The justification for this exclusion lies in the particular sequences of historical process in outlier Polynesia, where external relationships with non-Polynesian systems led to agricultural practices not present within triangle Polynesia.)

The primary sources concerning Polynesian agriculture are many and varied, with those cited in the body of the text representing only a sampling. Descriptions by early European explorers of Polynesian agricultural landscapes, and of the preparation and consumption of food, provide important texts. However, the tasks of ferreting out, evaluating, and synthesizing such accounts are formidable, and have been systematically attempted only in a few instances (e.g., Oliver's brilliant account of Tahiti, 1974). Early nineteenth-century accounts by resident missionaries and others (e.g., Henry 1928), and by literate Polynesians (e.g., Malo 1951; Kamakau 1976) add considerably to this record. Although the "salvage" ethnographies of the 1920s and 1930s (e.g., Handy 1923; Aitken 1930; Buck 1930, 1938; Metraux 1940) generally provide brief summaries of food plants and agricultural practices, detailed ethnographic studies of Polynesian agricul-

ture (and subsistence in general) are surprisingly few. The few notable exceptions are Best (1925) on Maori agriculture, Handy (1940; Handy and Handy 1972)
on Hawaii, Christiansen (1975) and Yen (1973a) on the outliers of Bellona and
Anuta, Fox and Cumberland (1962) on Western Samoa, and the shorter treatments of Barrau (1963) and Kirch (1975, 1978) on Wallis and Futuna. The
botanists have added a few contributions, such as Wilder's study of Tahitian
breadfruit (1928), and that by MacDaniels (1947) on the *fe'i* banana. In writing this
essay, of course, I am mindful of working in the shadow of Barrau's masterful overview (1961), and of Yen's insightful contributions (1971, 1973b, 1974b).

In addition to these historical and ethnographic sources, Polynesian
archaeologists have—since the early 1970s—begun to contribute significantly to
our understanding of the region's prehistoric agricultural systems. Indeed, it
could be fairly claimed that archaeological efforts to track the development and
intensification of Polynesian production systems have infused new life into the
study of what had become a rather neglected area of research. To date, this
archaeological work has been most intensive in Hawaii (e.g., Yen et al. 1972; Riley
1975; Kirch 1977, 1979, 1985; Earle 1978, 1980; Tuggle and Tomonari-Tuggle
1980; Schilt 1984; Allen 1987) and New Zealand (e.g., Leach 1979, 1984). It is, of
course, the archaeological approach which dominates my own perspective on
Polynesian agriculture.

In this paper, my concern is with agricultural systems which, as Yen observes,
extend beyond "the cultivation of plants" to "encompass animal production,
concepts and methods of tillage, and relationships to the natural environment"
(1973b, 68; see also Conklin 1963; Brookfield 1968). I will extend the notion of
system yet further to include some consideration of the social relations of agricultural production. A further aim of this essay is to treat Polynesian agricultures not
as static forms, to be described solely on the basis of the ethnohistoric endpoints,
but as dynamic systems that were continuously evolving and transforming.

Polynesian Agricultural Environments

The diversity of Polynesian agricultural systems is closely tied to the great
variety of environments for which the region is noted. Here I can touch upon only
a few key variables, among which are climate, soils, rainfall, topography,
hydrology, island size, and isolation. We must also briefly consider temporal
variability, both stochastic and directional; of the latter sort, the role of humans is
especially critical.

The core of Polynesia—from Samoa and Tonga in the west to the Societies
and Marquesas in the east—lies within the humid tropics, with uniform and
equable temperatures averaging 70–80° F. Thus climate posed no barrier to the
prehistoric transferral of an adventive, tropical cultigen inventory with origins in
island southeast Asia and Melanesia (see Yen, this volume). The periphery of
eastern Polynesia, however, presents a range of subtropical to temperate climates
which, at the least, acted as selective agents mitigating against particular crop
species, and—particularly in the New Zealand case—required drastic adaptation
of agronomic practice.

Oceanic islands are classically arrayed into three types—volcanic or "high," makatea or upraised limestone, and atolls—each with its own characteristic soil forms (see Fosberg, this volume). The volcanic islands tend to have young but fertile soils, formed on weathered flow slopes and alluvially deposited in valley bottoms. Makatea islands can also have deep and fertile soils, as in the case of the Tongan group (where enrichment with volcanic ash fall has played a role), but may in some cases lack any soil development at all (as with Henderson Island). Atolls consist primarily of late Holocene unconsolidated, calcareous sediments, with only the thinnest organic soil horizons. Indeed the richest soils on atolls usually prove to have resulted from anthropogenic enrichment through human occupation (i.e., midden soils formed on old occupation sites). New Zealand, as always, stands as an exception to the above, with an edaphic diversity reflective of its ancient, plate-margin geological history.

The agronomically significant variables of rainfall, topography, and hydrology tend to be complexly linked with topographic forms, partly controlling or at least influencing both rainfall patterns and stream development. On high islands, volcanic ridges orographically induce precipitation, with high rainfall on the windward sides, usually falling off steeply to quite arid conditions on the leeward sides. On the island of Molokai, for example, the windward valleys of Halawa and Wailau receive an annual average of more than 250 inches (6250 mm) at their headwaters, while the coastal Kaluakoi lands, only a few miles distant, barely receive 10 inches (250 mm). Stream patterns are not exclusively dependent upon rainfall and topography, however, as geological age is also a factor. Thus, most of the large island of Hawaii lacks surface watercourses, and its history of indigenous agricultural development as a consequence followed quite different pathways from that of the older, western islands of Kauai and Oahu. In the cases of matakea islands and atolls, rainfall tends toward uniformity, and surface flow is wholly absent. Atolls, however, contain unique freshwater aquifers (the Ghyben-Herzberg lens; see Wiens 1962) which, when tapped by excavation of pits, provide suitable microenvironments for aroid cultivation.

Isolation and distance might not normally be included in a list of agriculturally significant variables, but these cannot be ignored in our investigation, for they influenced the abilities of Polynesian colonists to transfer planting stocks. The west-to-east reduction in numbers of cultigens, particularly marked at the margins of eastern Polynesia, certainly reflects the hazards of long-distance transport of seedlings or rootstock. Isolation too, as in the case of Easter Island, lessened the chance of long-distance social exchange and later introduction of new cultigen varieties or technological innovations from other islands.

Polynesian environments vary not only in space, but also in time. Three sorts of temporal change may be distinguished: (1) seasonal rhythms, with a high degree of predictability; (2) longer-term stochastic perturbations, especially induced by drought and cyclones; and (3) directional change, whether natural or human-induced. Within tropical Polynesia, a wet-dry seasonality is typical, and is reflected in the agricultural calendar, especially in yam planting and harvesting. The temperate climate of New Zealand imposed another kind of seasonality on agricultural production, necessitating adaptations to over-winter storage of tubers (Yen 1974b, 1961). Stochastically recurring environmental hazards also played a major role in island agricultural systems, with drought and cyclonic damage periodically devastating local production systems (see Kirch 1984, 127–135 for further discussion of hazards). Finally, island ecosystems also underwent long-term directional changes, many of these initiated by human colonization and land-use practices. Among such anthropogenic changes were forest clearance, alteration of indigenous biotic communities, erosion, siltation, and other forms of physical modification of landscapes (Kirch 1982b, 1984). Some of these changes evidently had dramatic consequences for island agricultural systems, including the erosion of fragile soil horizons on steep volcanic slopes (e.g., on Mangaia, Mangareva, Futuna, and other islands), and the deposition of highly productive alluvium in valley bottoms (as demonstrated by Spriggs's geoarchaeological work on the island of Aneityum in eastern Melanesia [1981, 1986]). It is no exaggeration to state that the historical development of Polynesian agricultural systems was intimately bound up—as both cause and consequence—with the cultural modification of island landscapes.

The Cultigen Inventory

The indigenous Polynesian cultigen inventory comprised approximately 25 species, and with one exception (the sweet potato), all of tropical southeast Asian and Melanesian derivation (see Yen, Whistler, Rensch, this volume). Since European contact, a large number of new species has been added to this cultigen roster, and some, such as manioc (*Manihot esculenta*, Euphorbiaceae) and *Xanthosoma sagittifolium* (Araceae), have become staple dominants. The principal indigenous cultigens are itemized in Table 1. Barrau (1961, 35–66) discussed both indigenous and historically introduced crops in considerable detail, and Massal and Barrau (1956) provided further details on principal cultigens. The following notes will be limited to the five main groups of starch staples that dominated indigenous cultivation systems: aroids, yams, bananas, breadfruit, and sweet potatoes.

Taro (*Colocasia esculenta*, Araceae) was cultivated throughout Polynesia, although in New Zealand it was restricted to the more northerly parts of North Island. Although often regarded as a hydrophile, the plant's ecological tolerance is actually fairly broad, and dryland plantings doubtless vastly exceeded those in irrigated fields. However, the higher yields and reduced maturation time for taro grown in wet conditions were well understood by Polynesians, who developed various irrigation and drainage strategies for *Colocasia* production; these are described in detail below.

A second aroid, *Alocasia macrorrhiza* (Araceae), although widely distributed in Polynesia, was of major importance only in the western island groups (Tonga, Samoa, Futuna, Uvea). Not irrigated, *Alocasia* is a dominant of shifting cultivations.

A third species, *Cyrtosperma chamissonis* (Araceae) or giant swamp taro, was of relatively minor significance in Polynesia, although its tolerance of stagnant, brackish water accounts for its importance in certain atoll systems, where it was grown in pits excavated to the Ghyben-Herzberg aquifer. On the Polynesian outlier of Tikopia, a particular cultivar of *Cyrtosperma* is adapted well beyond its usual swampy template, and assumes the status of a dominant in a perennial, orchard-gardening system on steep hill slopes (Kirch and Yen 1982, 39).

Five species of yam, all members of the genus *Dioscorea* (Dioscoreaceae), were cultivated in Polynesia, but were dominant components of cultivation systems only in western Polynesia (Barrau 1961, 45). The most important species is *D. alala,* the greater yam, which remains a key element in Tongan, Futunan, and Uvean agriculture today (Kirch 1975, 1978). The species is tropophytic, with the tuber lying dormant during the dry season. West Polynesian agricultural calendars are strongly oriented around the scheduling of the yam crop. A second species of some importance in western Polynesia is *D. esculenta.* Two species, *D. pentaphylla* and *D. bulbifera,* are fairly widespread in Polynesia, but were only rarely cultivated, occurring more frequently as feral components of second-growth vegetation. *Dioscorca bulbifera,* for example, is widely distributed through-out the second growth of Hawaiian valleys. The presumption is that these species must have been of greater significance during the colonization phase of Polynesia (cf. Barrau 1965a, 1965b). A fifth yam, *D. nummularia,* seems not to have extended beyond western Polynesia.

Table 1. Major Polynesian Cultigens

Botanical Name	Common Name	Type[1]	Use[2]
DICOTYLEDONEAE			
Moraceae			
Artocarpus altilis	Breadfruit	FF	MS, C
Broussonetia papyrifera	Paper mulberry	O	B
Piperaceae			
Piper methysticum	Kava	O	N, M
Leguminosae			
Inocarpus fagifer	Tahitian chestnut	NF	NS
Anacardiaceae			
Spondias dulcis	Vi apple	NF	NS
Convolvulaceae			
Ipomoea batatas	Sweet potato	FT	MS, SS
MONOCOTYLEDONEAE			
Taccaceae			
Tacca leontopetaloides	Arrowroot	FT	SS
Dioscoreaceae			
Dioscorea alata	Greater yam	FT	MS
Dioscorea esculenta	Lesser yam	FT	MS
Gramineae			
Saccharum officinarum	Sugar cane	O	NS
Palmae			
Cocos nucifera	Coconut	NF	NS, C
Araceae			
Alocasia macrorrhiza	Elephant ear	FT	MS
Colocasia esculenta	Taro	FT	MS
Cyrtosperma chamissonis	Swamp Taro	FT	SS
Musaceae			
Eumusa hybrids	Banana	FF	MS

1. FT = farinaceous tuber or corm; FF = farinaceous fruit; NF = nonfarinaceous fruit; O = other.
2. MS = major staple; SS = secondary staple; NS = nonstaple food; C = construction; N = narcotic; B = bark cloth; M = medicinal.

Bananas formed a third major component of Polynesian cultivation systems, where they were treated both as field crops in shifting cultivation, and as perennial herbs in orchard gardens. There was a range of cultivars, in both the sections Eumusa and Australimusa. The latter, termed *fehi* or *fe'i* in Polynesian, and characterized by an upright inflorescence with orange-red fruit (the color is passed on into the urine after eating), were of particular importance in central eastern Polynesia, especially Tahiti (MacDaniels 1947).

Breadfruit (*Artocarpus altilis,* Moraceae) was the focus of arboricultural production, and assumed great importance as a dominant staple starch in certain island groups, such as the Marquesas (see Ragone, this volume). Both seeded and seedless forms are found in western Polynesia, but the former disappear in eastern Polynesia, and the tree is "propagated by shoots or root cuttings" (Barrau 1961, 61). Barrau noted that the "fruit is seasonal, with the main harvest during the southern summer, followed by a secondary fruit-bearing season in July to August" (1961, 51). This pronounced seasonality in fruiting required the development of ensilage techniques in those islands where it was a dietary staple; these storage techniques are discussed further below.

The sweet potato (*Ipomoea batatas,* Convolvulaceae) was a major component of certain marginal eastern Polynesian cultivation systems, especially those of Hawaii, Easter Island, and New Zealand, but seems not to have been present in western Polynesia prior to European contact (Yen 1974b). This peculiar marginal, eastern distribution pattern is in keeping with the South American origin of the plant, which must have been introduced fairly early into central eastern Polynesia. The dominance of the species in the cultivation systems of New Zealand, Easter Island, and Hawaii is explained by the plasticity of the plant's ecological requirements, and by its relatively high yields in environments that were marginal to many of the tropical Polynesian cultigens.

Tools

The Polynesian cultivator worked with a very simple set of tools. This set shows hardly any variation from archipelago to archipelago. The digging stick of sharpened hardwood was the primary instrument used in field preparation, planting, and harvesting (see Buck 1930, 545 and 1957, 12–13 for typical descriptions). For the heavier work of planting tubers in clay or rocky soils, a heavy planting pole was used. In Futuna, the digging stick (*koso*) also serves as a carrying pole, and is carefully stored in the cookhouse between trips to the gardens. Planting poles (*koso lasi*), however, are made on the spot as required, and discarded after use (Kirch 1975, 113–114).

The New Zealand Maori uniquely developed the wooden spade for use in sweet potato cultivation. Ethnographic collections display a striking range of variation in blade form and handle ornamentation (Best 1925, 45–70). Another Maori innovation was the addition of a footrest to the digging stick, thus allowing increased mechanical leverage.

Steel axes and bush knives were so eagerly adopted by Polynesians following initial contact with Europeans that early accounts are virtually mute concerning stone tools. On archaeological evidence, stone adzes were the primary tool used to clear mature forest, with particular forms of large, heavy adzes presumably designed expressly for this purpose. However, fire may be presumed to have played a major role in the clearing and preparation of land for gardens.

Tools used in harvesting and transporting of crops were also simple. The digging stick was again used in extracting tubers from their earthen matrix. Forked poles, sometimes with small net bags attached (Buck 1938, 116–118), were used to pluck breadfruit. Crops were transported back to settlements in a variety of baskets or bags, with the aid of carrying poles.

Major Polynesian Agricultural Subsystems

As noted earlier, an agricultural system at a given point in time consists of a complex set of interrelated components, including the cultigen set, tools, agronomic concepts and practices, conditions and constraints of the local environment, and the social context of labor and land, among others. For purposes of description and comparison, however, it is useful to segregate these larger systems into several key classes of subsystem. In Polynesia, five major agricultural subsystems can be delineated: (1) shifting cultivation; (2) intensive dryfield cultivation; (3) irrigation and drainage; (4) arboriculture; and (5) animal husbandry. Any particular system thus consists of the integration of several of these subsystems along with environmental and social variables.

Shifting Cultivation

Shifting cultivation (also known as swidden cultivation, or bush-fallow rotation) may be minimally defined as "any continuing agricultural system in which impermanent clearings are cropped for shorter periods in years than they are fallowed" (Conklin 1963, 1). It is an extremely widespread and highly variable type of cultivation in the Indo-Oceanic tropics (Spencer 1966), with origins presumably in the early Holocene.

Where it is still practiced, such as in Futuna, Uvea, and Samoa, Polynesian shifting cultivation usually focuses on an initial planting phase of aroids (*Colocasia* and *Alocasia*) and yams (*Dioscorea alata* and *D. esculenta*), followed by a second phase of bananas. Other secondary crops may be included. A swidden plot is first cleared and the cut vegetation allowed to dry sufficiently (usually 3–4 weeks) before firing. Yams are harvested first, after 7–9 months, followed by the aroids (12–24 months), while bananas extend the productive life of the plot up to 36 months or more. New swiddens are cut each year (during the yam planting season), so that each household will normally have several swidden plots representing various successional stages. (See Kirch 1975, 1978 for more detailed descriptions of Futunan and Uvean shifting cultivation.)

At the time of early European contact, and into the present era, shifting cultivation in Polynesia has been practiced primarily on the larger high islands, where substantial tracts of primary and secondary forest exist, and where the ratio of population to arable land is relatively low. Shifting cultivation continues to be important on such islands as Futuna (Kirch 1975), Upolu, and Savaii (Fox and Cumberland 1962) in western Polynesia, and was certainly a major subsystem as late as the early nineteenth century in Tahiti and the Hawaiian Islands.

We may suppose, however, that shifting cultivation was formerly a major agricultural subsystem on virtually every high island (and the large makatea islands) during initial periods of colonization and agricultural expansion. This hypothesis was advanced by Barrau, who proposed that the initial emphasis on shifting cultivation, utilizing burning for forest clearance, led to "deterioration of both vegetation and soils on the majority of high islands," in turn necessitating development of "semi-permanent forms of agriculture" (1961, 18; see also Yen 1973b, 78). His hypothesis has received some support from archaeological and geomorphological studies in various parts of Polynesia and Melanesia (e.g., Riley 1975; Spriggs 1981, 1986). Such a sequence has been archaeologically documented for Tikopia, for example, with the initial emphasis on shifting cultivation giving away to extensive arboriculture and limited field rotation (Kirch and Yen 1982, 351–352).

On many of the Polynesian high islands, shifting cultivation in earlier periods of prehistory evidently led to the degradation of substantial areas, now characterized by terminal vegetative associations of *Dicranopteris* fern (Gleincheniaceae), scrub *Pandanus* (Pandanaceae), *Casuarina* (Casuarinaceae), and a few other species on lateritic or saprolitic soils. Such conditions exist on Uvea, Futuna, Mangaia, Atiu, Mangareva, and other islands (see Kirch 1984, 139–146).

Intensive Dryfield Cultivation

The distinction of intensive dryfield cultivation from shifting cultivation can be drawn on two primary criteria: (1) a fallow length shorter than or equal to the cropping period; and (2) the permanent demarcation of plots. In terms of historical process, however, intensive dryfield cultivation in most cases (at least within Polynesia) develops out of the intensification of shifting cultivation. Such a developmental sequence has been archaeologically demonstrated for the Kohala Field System on Hawaii Island (Rosendahl 1972; Tuggle and Griffin 1973). Ethnographically, we have relatively little information on the operation of intensive dryfield cultivation subsystems, a reflection of the disintensification of Polynesian agriculture in most islands following European contact and population decline. The isolated small high island of Anuta, however, retains a highly intensive dryfield subsystem, with rotation of taro and manioc (a recent replacement for yams), in a grass-sedge fallow regime of 0–3 years. This system was studied in detail by Yen (1973a), who documented the heavy labor inputs in weeding and mulching that are critical in the maintenance of soil fertility. Yen's calculations indicate a labor input of about 7000 man-hours per hectare per year (1973a, 139), more than twice the level indicated by Conklin for the Hanunoo, a classic shifting cultivator group (1957, 151). Yen also describes the permanent definition of field boundaries with stone alignments that function as soil-retention structures (1973a, 124).

Intensive dryfield cultivation generally (though not necessarily) involves the **permanent demarcation of plot boundaries with stone alignments, terraces, or** other permanent markers with archaeological visibility. Archaeological investigation of such field remains have been carried out extensively in both the Hawaiian Islands (Rosendahl 1972; Tuggle and Griffin 1973; Schilt 1984; Kirch 1984, 181–192; Kirch 1985) and New Zealand (Leach 1979, 1984). In Hawaii, these subsystems evidently centered on sweet potato, taro, and banana, whereas the New Zealand case involved a dominance on sweet potato. As noted earlier, the Hawaiian systems clearly display a developmental sequence out of an earlier phase of more extensive shifting cultivation. Indeed, the historical processes appear to have had both temporal and spatial axes, with the lateral (marginal) expansion of cultivation involving shifting cultivation even as core areas were undergoing intensification and permanent definition of plot boundaries. Though not well studied archaeologically, dryfield plot boundaries are also recorded on Alofi Island in western Polynesia (Kirch 1975). Prehistoric cultivation on Easter Island also involved a form of intensive dryfield cropping (Metraux 1940, 151–2), although curiously without permanent field demarcation.

Water Control: Irrigation and Drainage

A wide variety of intensive water control technologies were applied in Polynesia for the purpose of providing suitable microenvironments for *Colocasia* culture. Those methods generally described as irrigation, and usually involving pond-field cultivation, have attracted the most attention (e.g., Wittfogel 1957; Goldman 1970; Earle 1978), but other forms of water control—including drained "garden island" systems and atoll pit cultivation—also deserve consideration (Damm 1951; Spriggs 1981). All these techniques reflect a thorough understanding by Polynesian cultivators of the ecological requirements of *C. esculenta*, and of the response of the species to favorable hydrologic conditions.

Upon first consideration, atolls might appear the least likely of island environments to support taro culture, yet this was successfully achieved through the excavation of pits that tapped the thin freshwater aquifer present in larger atoll islets. The addition of organic debris to these pits provided nutrients otherwise lacking in the unconsolidated, calcareous, sand matrix. In the northern Cook Islands of Pukapuka and Manihiki-Rakahanga (Beaglehole 1938, 40–41, 87–90; Buck 1932, 96–98), *Cyrtosperma*, as well as *Colocasia*, was cultivated in these pits, whereas in the Tuamotu group of eastern Polynesia, only *Colocasia* appears to have been present. Chazine (1977) has reported on archaeological remains of taro pits on Takapoto, and their presence on uninhabited Howland atoll is recorded by Emory (1934, 4). However, a detailed survey of such pits for all Polynesian atolls has yet to be undertaken.

A second strategy for creating suitable hydromorphic conditions for taro cultivation is the drainage of naturally swampy coastal flats, and the creation of slightly raised "garden island" beds between a reticulated network of drains. The aim of the drains in these systems is not the wholesale removal of ground water, but the increase of its circulation. Generally these garden bed systems were constructed on low-lying alluvial flats, with springs issuing at the base of steeper hillsides. Such systems have been ethnographically documented by Barrau (1963) and Kirch (1975, 1978) in Uvea, and are reported by Handy (1930) in the Society

Group, though they doubtless occurred in other islands as well. Ishizuki (1974) describes archaeological remains of reticulate ditches in the interior Falefa Valley of Upolu, Western Samoa.

The most important strategy for wet taro cultivation, however, was the construction of inundated pond-fields, usually by terracing, although occasionally by excavation of sunken fields. Pond-field systems in Polynesia exhibit considerable variation in technique of construction, scale, and complexity of water reticulation, and several schemata have been proposed for their classification (Riley 1975; Kirch 1977; Earle 1980; Allen 1987). The simplest systems are barrage walls across intermittent stream channels. More complex systems involve irrigation canals to transport water flow from stream channels to the field complex. The largest recorded systems, in the Hawaiian Islands and Futuna (Kirch 1975), may cover areas of up to 10–15 hectares with as many as 350 individual fields.

Ethnographic studies of Polynesian irrigation are limited (Handy 1940, Handy and Handy 1972; Allen 1971; Barrau 1963; Kirch 1975), although extant systems in Futuna, Rapa, Mangaia, and Rarotonga could repay intensive fieldwork. In Hawaii, substantial archaeological attention has been paid to the physical remains of irrigation systems (Yen et al. 1972; Riley 1975; Kirch 1977, 1979; Earle 1978, 1980; Tuggle and Tomonari-Tuggle 1980; Allen 1987), and a radiocarbon-based chronology for the expansion and intensification of such systems is now emerging. In other island groups, such as the Marquesas and Societies, the presence of stone terrace systems in interior valleys has been reported (e.g., Suggs 1961; Bellwood 1972), but intensive mapping and excavation programs focused on these structures remain to be carried out.

Wet cultivation of taro is known to produce among the highest yields per unit area of any Polynesian agricultural subsystem (Massal and Barrau 1956; Spriggs 1981); estimates vary from 30 to 60 metric tons per hectare. Certainly the potential of such systems to produce a substantial surplus was understood by the Hawaiian chiefs, and probably by those of other island groups as well. The development and control of irrigation systems was an intricate part of the late prehistoric and early historic Hawaiian political economy (Earle 1978; Kirch 1985).

Arboriculture

Throughout much of lowland island Melanesia, arboriculture involving a mix of fruit- and nut-bearing species (*Canarium* [Burseraceae], *Barringtonia* [Barringtoniaceae], *Terminalia* [Combretaceae], *Artocarpus* [Moraceae], *Pometia* [Sapindaceae], *Burckella* [Sapotaceae], and others) is typical (Yen 1974a). Recent archaeological evidence suggests that such arboriculture was a part of the Lapita subsistence system, from which the founding Polynesian systems derived (Kirch 1988, 1989). In Polynesia, however, there is a substantial decline in the diversity of tree crops, matched by the development in particular localities of a virtual monocropping of breadfruit. Aside from *Artocarpus*, the only tree crops of any significance in Polynesia are *Cocos nucifera* (Palmae), *Spondias dulcis* (Anacardiaceae), and *Inocarpus fagifer* (Leguminosae), and the latter two are confined principally to the tropical islands of western and central eastern Polynesia.

As a major agricultural subsystem, breadfruit cultivation is restricted to the tropical core of Polynesia, and achieved its greatest dominance in the Society Islands (Wilder 1928), Mangareva (Buck 1938), and the Marquesas (Handy 1923). Breadfruit was cultivated in Hawaii, although it appears to have been a relatively minor crop, except perhaps in parts of Maui and Hawaii islands. Kelly (1983, 57–62), relying on historic sources, has identified a distinctive breadfruit zone within the Kona Field System on the island of Hawaii.

Animal Husbandry

The Polynesian domestic animal set consists of pig, dog, and chicken, all of original southeast Asian ancestry. All three species were not present in every island group, with, for example, the pig and chicken absent in New Zealand, and the pig and dog in Easter Island. Such absences are generally confined to marginal eastern Polynesia, or to atoll systems, so that the elimination of domestic species can be accounted for either by failure of initial transfer, or by selection in marginal environments. Despite the possibilities of ferality on large high islands, pigs were closely integrated into Polynesian agricultural systems, at least on the ethnographic evidence. As Yen notes, "apart from household waste, pig husbandry is mainly conducted by the feeding of coconut, breadfruit and sweet potato, with the support of foraging for natural products from the flora and sea-shore" (1973b, 71). Agricultural systems notable for intensive pig husbandry, such as Futuna, or the leeward part of Hawaii Island at European contact, were also centers of highly intensive agricultural production (valley irrigation and intensive dryfield cultivation, respectively). In most islands dogs appear to have occupied a scavenging niche, and were never present in large numbers. In Hawaii, however, dogs were husbanded much as hogs, and regularly fed on agricultural produce, including *poi* (Titcomb 1969, 6–8). A starchy diet for prehistoric Hawaiian dogs was confirmed on dental evidence by Svihla (1957). In most islands the chicken (actually a domesticated jungle fowl, *Gallus gallus* [Ball 1933]) was also a household scavenger, but in remote Easter Island became the focus of intensive husbandry, presumably a reflection of the scarcity of other flesh foods. Chickens were kept in special stone houses (*hare moa*), with carved human ancestral skulls to ensure fertility (Metraux 1940); the extent to which they were fed on agricultural produce appears uncertain.

Agricultural Systems: Two Examples

Having reviewed the major Polynesian agricultural subsystems, I now briefly summarize two individual cases as examples of the integration of subsystems into large operating systems. The Futunan system lies in western Polynesia, with the largest cultigen inventory of any Polynesian system. The Marquesas are part of eastern Polynesia, with a more restricted cultigen inventory. Both are high islands within the tropical core of Polynesia.

Futuna

Futunan agriculture was first systematically described by Burrows (1936), and more recently by Barrau (1963) and Kirch (1975). Yen (1974b, 136–138) offers a useful summary account of agriculture. The description presented here is of the system operating in Singave District, a group of permanent stream valleys along the southwestern side of Futuna Island. (Alo District and nearby Alofi Island present certain contrasts; see Kirch 1975 for details.)

In terms of the subsystems reviewed above, Futunan agriculture integrates shifting cultivation, intensive pond-field irrigation, arboriculture, and animal husbandry. The principal crops are *Colocasia* taro, *Alocasia*, yams (*Dioscorea alata* and *D. esculenta*), bananas, breadfruit, and coconut, but a wide range of other species are cultivated, both as field crops and perennial plantings.

The system can best be described in terms of the spatial zonation of its components. The narrow coastal plain, with individual hamlets strung out linearly behind the beach, is the primary arboricultural zone, with coconut along the strand, and breadfruit and other fruit and nut trees (e.g., *Barringtonia, Spondias,* and *Inocarpus*) interspersed among dwellings and cookhouses. Some breadfruit plantings continue inland on the less steep ridge slopes and spurs. Pigs, of which there are large numbers, are confined to this village arboricultural zone by a continuous stone wall running inland of the dwellings and seaward of the cookhouses.

The alluvial valley bottoms inland of the coastal plain are extensively terraced for the pond-field cultivation of *Colocasia esculenta*. The Singave pond-field systems are among the largest and most complex of Polynesia; the Nuku system, for example, includes about 350 individual fields, with two separate irrigation ditch systems (Kirch 1975; forthcoming). Terracing extends a short distance up the adjacent ridges, and abandoned terrace sets in the valley interiors indicate a contraction of pond-field cultivation in the historic period.

The steeper valley walls and inland ridges are the setting for the third major subsystem, shifting cultivation. Vegetation on these slopes comprises a mosaic of grassland, second growth, and climax forest, with second growth the preferred choice for cutting new swiddens. Grassland is generally avoided because of the low fertility of the underlying soils, and climax forest poses heavier labor costs in tree felling and clearing, although swiddens cut in climax forest are known to be especially productive. Swiddens are planted either in a mix of yams and aroids (especially *Alocasia*), or in aroids exclusively, with a later replanting in bananas. In addition to owning several irrigated pond-fields, each household also cuts and plants at least one new swidden (usually more) each year.

As Yen observed, "pigs are of greatest moment to the Futunans as stock-raisers, calculated spontaneously in an individual's enumeration of wealth after taro fields" (1974b, 137). The antiquity of this emphasis on pigs is revealed in the journal of Schouten and LeMaire (Villiers 1906) on their voyage of discovery in 1616. Though prevented from intruding into the inland pond-field and swidden zones, pigs are an integral part of the agricultural system, being fed daily on coconut, bananas, and taro tubers (Kirch 1975, 141). Pork is consumed by most households at least once a week, but is especially important during village or district level feasts (*katoanga*), at which displays of anywhere from 50 to 250 whole, baked hogs are common.

The Marquesas Islands

Handy (1923, 181–202) provided the best general summary of indigenous Marquesan agriculture (see also Yen 1974b, 140–144). Recent archaeological surveys provide additional information on the extent of taro terracing (e.g., Kellum-Ottino 1971; Bellwood 1972).

As in Futuna, Marquesas agriculture integrated shifting cultivation, pond-field terracing for *Colocasia*, arboriculture, and animal husbandry. The particular combination of subsystems, and the relative emphasis accorded them, differed strikingly, however. The orchard gardening of breadfruit dominated Marquesan agriculture, with most of the valley floors given over to breadfruit plantings. Coconut (especially nearer the coast) and bananas were lesser but important elements in this perennial cropping system. Residence was not concentrated in coastal villages, as in Futuna, but rather consisted of dispersed hamlet groups throughout the valley interiors. Early historic descriptions describe small garden plots of annual plants, and stands of paper mulberry (*Broussonetia papyrifera*, Moraceae) close to these hamlets.

The emphasis on breadfruit, a seasonal crop, is reflected also in the elaboration of technology for semi-anaerobic fermentation and pit ensilage of the fruit. Preserved breadfruit (*ma*) provided the mainstay of the Marquesan diet, and a wide variety of recipes for the preparation of breadfruit paste is reported by Handy (1923, 189–195).

Handy (1923, 184–186) indicated that by the time of his fieldwork in 1920–21, terraced cultivation of taro had been practically abandoned, and that he could obtain little information on taro cultivation practices. However, he noted the "general distribution" of abandoned taro terrace systems, and recent archaeological surveys have confirmed that most Marquesan valleys have significant areas in stone-faced terrace systems. It thus appears that pond-field cultivation of *Colocasia* was formerly a major component of Marquesan agriculture. This is not surprising in light of the evident late prehistoric population levels (Suggs 1961), and intense competition between local polities (Kirch, forthcoming). Such demographic as well as socio-political pressures could be expected to favor the expansion of intensive, wet taro cultivation.

The extent of shifting cultivation in the Marquesas is not entirely clear, but Yen observed that "small swiddens may be cut from secondary bush of valley areas or grassland" (1974b, 143). The archaeologically attested sequence of production system development over approximately 2000 years (Suggs 1961; Kirch 1984, 156–159) hints at the rise of the dominance of breadfruit orchard-gardening (manifested by shell peelers and storage pits) in the Expansion and Classic periods. In the preceding Colonization and Development periods, the role of shifting cultivation was presumably much greater.

Pigs, dogs, and chickens were all introduced into the Marquesas by the Polynesian initial colonizers, although the dog is generally reported as absent by early European voyagers. The husbandry of pigs was a major aspect of later prehistoric subsistence, and Marquesan sites of the Expansion and Classic periods yield large numbers of pig bones (Suggs 1961; Kirch 1973; Rolett 1989). Handy (1923, 198) describes the cultural significance of pigs in feasting, but fails to discuss the integration of pig husbandry in agricultural production. We can only surmise that a significant percentage of the crop yield must have gone toward the maintenance of large pig herds.

Seasonality and Perturbations

Agricultural systems vary not only in space, but also in time, and the temporal dimension includes both seasonal rhythms and more irregular responses to stochastic environmental perturbations. The literature on Polynesian agriculture gives little consideration to seasonality and the annual agricultural calendar of most islands. Perhaps the only thorough ethnographic account of a full agricultural year is that presented in Sir Raymond Firth's several volumes on Tikopia (1936, 1939, 1967), even though his primary interest was the ritual cycle, rather than agriculture per se. (Firth's *Work of the Gods in Tikopia* was focussed on the Tikopian ritual year, but as this is itself closely tied to the economic, and especially the agronomic, calendar, it can be read as well for its agricultural information.) Indeed, in most island groups, the pre-Christian agricultural calendar seems to have been encoded in religious ritual, most of which was lost with the introduction of Christianity.

Several kinds of recurring environmental "hazards" or perturbations occur in Polynesia, but the most widespread and destructive of agricultural production are cyclones and drought. Cyclones are especially prevalent in western Polynesia, decreasing in frequency as one moves into central eastern Polynesia. Drought was an environmental hazard found in virtually every island group. Both kinds of hazard result both in a reduction in food supply, and potentially longer-term debilitation of the system itself (e.g., through destruction of perennial crops, and infrastructure such as ditches and terracing). Not surprisingly, famine (marked by the Polynesian term *onge* or *honge*) was a recurrent problem in most Polynesian societies (Currey 1980; Kirch 1984, 131).

Social Relations of Agricultural Production and Distribution

The crops, fields, and tools which are the "stuff" of agriculture are situated within a complex social and economic fabric. As the Marxist anthropologists have stressed, the means of production (including land) are linked in a complex dialectic with the social relations of production. Any attempt to understand Polynesian agricultural systems is incomplete without at least some consideration of these social relations. In particular, we need to consider the control of land and gardens, the organization of labor (including gender aspects), and the control and distribution of agricultural products.

Throughout most of Polynesia, land and most production apparatus (e.g., tools, nets, canoes) were held as common property of a minimal ramage group, a descent group organized around a common ancestor. Such groups tend to be patrilineal in ideological bias, although ambilineal affiliation is not uncommon. Affiliation is also strongly conditioned by residence; as Firth notes, "land rights established by descent-group membership tend to remain operational only through residence" (1957, 7). Minimal ramages (often organized as extended households) are generally linked at a higher level into more extensive conical clans (Kirchoff 1955), in theory descended from a common ancestor, although precise genealogical links may not be known. Such conical clans usually control a larger territory, and are headed by a hereditary chief who is the titular head of all ramages within the clan. Such chiefs were usually due first-fruits tribute, but in effect rarely concerned themselves with agricultural production on the ramage level.

The fundamental control over land and agricultural production was generally based at the level of the ramage or minimal descent group. The allocation of particular garden land, and decisions concerning clearing, planting, and harvest were therfore made at this level. Polynesian agricultural economy can thus be characterized by what Sahlins (1972) has termed the "domestic mode of production." In the domestic mode of production, each extended household or local descent group is concerned primarily with meeting its own self-contained needs, and thus tends toward an overall strategy of "underproduction," as Sahlins has termed it, an "anti-surplus" economy (1972, 82).

For the most part, agricultural labor was also organized at the local descent group or household level. Few tasks required labor parties larger than that which could be mobilized by the ramage. Tasks requiring extra-ramage organization, such as maintenance of communal irrigation networks, or the clearing of large communal plantings in primary forest (as in Futuna), were initiated or controlled by the territorial chiefs. For the most part, however, the household acted as a self-contained unit of labor organization.

Little information exists on the sexual division of agricultural labor in traditional Polynesian societies. One gets the impression that most agricultural labor was male, with assistance from females in the tasks of field maintenance (weeding, mulching), and at harvest (especially in transporting crops back to the residence). However, there are hints that the respective roles of male and female labor in agriculture were not uniform in Polynesia, and that particular kinds of systems may have led to a substantially increased demand for female labor. Intensive dryland field systems, especially, required substantially higher labor inputs than either shifting cultivation or wet taro cultivation. (The latter had high initial requirements in field construction, and thus could be considered a male activity, but relatively low maintenance requirements.) The Anutan field system documented by Yen (1973a) operated on a labor input level twice that of Philippine swidden cultivators, and much of this labor was provided by females. Similarly, Kamakau (1961, 239) remarks that in Hawaii and Maui islands, "women worked outside as hard as the men." This emphasis on female agricultural labor may be explained by the dominance in Maui and Hawaii of intensive dryland field systems (whereas the other islands had greater areas in taro pond-fields). Spriggs, drawing upon the work of Modjeska (1977), has suggested that "the limits of agricultural intensification were largely set by the amount of garden labor women could be forced to undertake" (1981, 179). Certainly, the subject of relative gender contributions to agricultural labor in relation to intensification is one that would repay further study.

Given that the means of production were largely in the hands of local descent groups, and that labor was organized on the same level, it follows that the control of the agricultural product was also dominantly within the domain of the "domestic mode of production." However, as is characteristic of chiefdoms generally, Polynesian societies also possessed a political economy that extended beyond the household level. In the majority of Polynesian societies, this political economy was rather underdeveloped, with chiefs receiving annual presentations of first-fruits, but in effect exercising little direct control over production or distribution. The main role of chiefs in such societies was probably in the organization of community response to periodic environmental disasters, as ethnographic data from Tikopia and Anuta have suggested (Firth 1936; 1939).

There are, however, a few Polynesian societies in which political development advanced beyond the level of simple chiefdoms, with several levels of chiefly hierarchy. In these, the production of a true surplus was applied specifically to fuel a political economy of the dominant elites. The most complex, hierarchical, and centralized of these societies were Hawaii, the Society Islands, and Tonga, although the Marquesas, Easter Island, Mangareva, and the southern Cooks show less marked tendencies in this direction. Not surprisingly, in many of these cases the dominance of chiefs over agricultural production was maintained specifically by control over stored food reserves, especially fermented breadfruit paste (Cox 1980) (but also yams, in the Tongan case).

In Hawaii (and probably also in Tonga) chiefly control over agriculture had progressed to the point of a true structural transformation in the system, for the control of land itself had shifted from the local descent group to the chiefs. With the means of production in direct chiefly control, Hawaiian economy was no longer at the level of the "domestic mode of production." Territory itself was the object of political intrigue and conquest, and improved, terraced taro land was particularly sought after in frequent territorial wars between rival chiefs. Lacking a storage economy, however (taro does not lend itself particularly well to storage), the chiefs adopted a peripatetic pattern of movement from territory to territory.

Historical Process: Differentiation and Intensification

I have already raised, in earlier sections of this paper, several questions of historical process; for example, the hypothesized changing dominance on shifting cultivation in most systems over time, and the transformation, in some societies, from a simple "anti-surplus" domestic mode of production to a surplus-concentrating political economy. Underlying such specific themes is the broader issue of agricultural intensification, and its relations to environmental, demographic, and socio-political factors (Boserup 1965; Brookfield 1972; Kirch 1984). Within the constraints imposed here, I can no more than touch upon a few of the problems which an historical approach to Polynesian agriculture must address. Fortunately, the renewed interest of Polynesian archaeologists in production systems has made many of these problems the foci of current research programs.

In approaching historical process in Polynesian agricultural systems, it may be useful to distinguish between the differentiation of systems occasioned by adaptation to a varied range of environmental conditions and constraints, and change due to the expansion and intensification of systems in response to demographic and socio-political factors. Yen (1973b, 76–80) has commented insightfully on the "adaptation of agriculture on transfer," and I can add little to his discussion. As he notes,

> the portable features of agriculture [plants, tools, and concepts] have to undergo a reassortment or resegregation as a first step in the colonization of a new island as an Introductory-Developmental sequence whose progress is dictated by the ultimate constraints offered by the new environment and the genetic flexibility of the introduced species (1973b, 76).

The "portable features" themselves may be subject to intense selection or reduction in variability as a result of cultural "founder effect" (Vayda and Rappaport 1963). Particular plant materials or animals may not have been loaded into colonizing canoes, may have perished during the voyage, or may have failed to survive initial establishment attempts. Likewise, a colonizing party may not have fully represented the agronomic knowledge and lore of the parent group. Either or both of these selective factors likely account for the trend of west-to-east reduction in numbers of cultivated and husbanded species of plants and animals, although this west-to-east reduction also occurs in the indigenous floras and faunas.

Within the tropical high-island core of Polynesia, there was probably relatively little environmentally induced reassortment of agricultural systems upon colonization. Movement from a high island to an atoll, however, would always require drastic adaptation. And, colonization extending beyond the tropical core region to subtropical or temperate climatic regimes (as in the case of New Zealand), certainly necessitated dramatic adaptations. Most of these adaptations or reassortments, as Yen terms them, were probably accomplished relatively rapidly after colonization. Thus, the initial diversification of Polynesian agricultural systems was essentially coeval with the process of colonization and settlement itself.

There is no reason, however, to postulate that agricultural systems ceased to change following initial adaptation upon transfer. Rather, the archaeological records of production systems in all islands which have been studied suggest that these systems were marked by phases of both expansion and intensification, frequently leading to European-contact period endpoints quite different from their prior configurations.

Conclusion

Without implying that these operated as separate processes, it may be useful to distinguish the expansion of agricultural systems from the intensification of production. (In actual developmental sequences, of course, expansion and intensification often occur simultaneously as part of historical process.)

The expansion of agricultural systems occurred throughout Polynesia in what are usually characterized by prehistorians as Developmental or Expansion phases—for example, between ca. 500–1400 A.D. in the Marquesas. The expansion sequence in Hawaii has been most thoroughly investigated, especially due to the impetus of Hommon's "inland expansion" model (1986). This phase in Hawaii is marked by a very rapid spread of population out of ecologically core areas into leeward valleys and slope regions. The driving engine of expansion was clearly demographic increase. In Yen's terms, it was probably in these expansion episodes that the transformation was made from horticulture to agriculture.

The intensification of agricultural systems in Polynesia, however, cannot be so simply linked to a demographically deterministic model. With late prehistoric Polynesian populations burgeoning and frequently pushing the limits of their island carrying capacities, the demographic factor was clearly omnipresent. But we are also dealing with socio-political formations that in many islands were themselves entering new structural forms in later prehistory. If the development of the extensive Hawaiian taro irrigation systems was simply a response to population pressure, we should expect those systems to have proliferated across the landscape at a somewhat earlier date than the archaeological chronologies are indicating. Rather, the most elaborate systems appear to be very late prehistoric developments, indeed, closely tied to the political and economic aspirations of the increasingly status-conscious and competitive chiefs. I need only mention as well the parallel development of fishpond aquaculture, which Kikuchi's work (1976) has shown to be closely linked to the rise of the chiefly hierarchy. And as Yen (this volume) has pointed out, the social selection process acted as well even upon the genetic component of agricultural systems.

To the prehistorian, it is these historical processes of differentiation, expansion, and intensification that are of the greatest moment in our understanding of Polynesian agriculture. For it is in this area of research that the contribution of ethnobotany (or paleoethnobotany) will extend beyond the descriptive cataloging of plant uses, and contribute to the wider understanding of human cultural and social systems throughout Polynesia.

Literature Cited

Aitken, R. T. 1930. Ethnology of Tubuai. Bernice P. Bishop Mus. Bul. 70.

Allen, B. 1971. Wet-field taro terraces on Mangaia, Cook Islands. J. *Polynesian Society* 80:371–378.

Allen, J. 1987. Five Upland 'Ili: archaeological and historical investigations in the Kane'ohe Interchange, Interstate Highway H-3, Island of O'ahu. Bernice P. Bishop Mus., Dept. Anthr. Report 87-1.

Ball, S. C. 1933. Jungle fowls from Pacific islands. Bernice P. Bishop Mus. Bul. 108.

Barrau, J. 1961. Subsistence agriculture in Polynesia and Micronesia. Bernice P. Bishop Mus. Bul. 223:1–94.

————. 1963. L'agriculture des îles Wallis et Futuna. *J. Société Océanistes* 19:157–171.

————. 1965a. Histoire et préhistoire horticoles de l'Océanie tropicale. *J. Société Océanistes* 21:55–78.

————. 1965b. Witnesses of the past: notes on some food plants of Oceania. *Ethology* 4:282–294.

Beaglehole, E., and P. Beaglehole. 1938. Ethnology of Pukapuka. Bernice P. Bishop Mus. Bul. 150.

Bellwood, P. 1972. Settlement pattern survey, Hanatekua Valley, Hiva Oa, Marquesas Islands. Pac. Anthr. Rec. 17.

Best, E. 1925. *Maori Agriculture*. Rpt. 1976. Wellington: Government Printer.

Boserup, E. 1965. *The Conditions of Agricultural Growth: The Economics of Agrarian Change Under Population Pressure*. London: Allen and Unwin.

Brookfield, H. C. 1968. New directions in the study of agricultural systems in tropical areas. In *Evolution and Environment*. Ed. E. T. Drake. New Haven: Yale Univ. Press. 413–439.

_____ . 1972. Intensification and disintensification in Pacific agriculture: a theoretical approach. *Pac. Viewpoint* 13:30–48.

Buck, P. H. [Te Rangi Hiroa]. 1930. Samoan material culture. Bernice P. Bishop Mus. Bul. 75.

_____ . 1932. Ethology of Manihiki and Rakahanga. Bernice P. Bishop Mus. Bul. 99.

_____ . 1938. Ethnology of Mangareva. Bernice P. Bishop Mus. Bul. 157.

_____ . 1957. Arts and crafts of Hawaii. Bernice P. Bishop Mus. Special Publication 45.

Burrows, E. G. 1936. Ethnology of Futuna. Bernice P. Bishop Mus. Bul. 138.

Chazine, J. M. 1977. Prospections archéologiques à Takapoto. *J. Société Océanistes* 56–57:191–214.

Christiansen, S. 1975. Subsistence on Bellona Island (Mungiki). Folia Geographica Danica 13. Copenhagen.

Conklin, H. C. 1957. Hanunoo agriculture. FAO Forestry Development Paper 12.

_____ . 1963. *The Study of Shifting Cultivation*. Washington, DC: Union Panamericana.

Cox, P. A. 1980. Masi and tanu 'eli: ancient Polynesian technologies for the preservation and concealment of food. Pac. Trop. Bot. Garden Bul. 10(4):81–93.

Currey, B. 1980. Famine in the Pacific. *GeoJournal* 4:447–466.

Damm, H. 1951. Methoden der Feldbewesserung in Ozeanien. In *South Seas Studies in Memory of Felix Speiser*. Basel. 204–234.

Earle, T. K. 1978. Economic and social organization of a complex chiefdom: Halelea District, Kauai, Hawaii. Univ. Michigan Mus. Anthr. Paper 63.

_____ . 1980. Prehistoric irrigation in the Hawaiian Islands: an evaluation of evolutionary significance. *Archaeology and Physical Anthropology in Oceania* 15:1–28.

Emory, K. P. 1934. Archaeology of the Pacific equatorial islands. Bernice P. Bishop Mus. Bul. 123.

Firth, R. 1936. *We, the Tikopia*. London: Allen and Unwin.

_____ . 1939. *Primitive Polynesian Economy*. London: George Routledge and Sons.

_____ . 1957. A note on descent groups in Polynesia. *Man* 57:4–8.

_____ . 1967. *The Work of the Gods in Tikopia*. New York: Humanities Press.

Fosberg, F. R. 1991. Polynesian plant environments. In *Islands, Plants, and Polynesians*. Eds. P. A. Cox and S. A. Banack. Portland, Oregon: Timber Press, Dioscorides Press.

Fox, J. W., and K. B. Cumberland, eds. 1962. *Western Samoa: Land, Life, and Agriculture in Tropical Polynesia*. Christchurch: Whitcombe and Tombs.

Goldman, I. 1970. *Ancient Polynesian Society*. Chicago: Univ. of Chicago Press.

Handy, E. S. C. 1923. The native culture of the Marquesas. Bernice P. Bishop Mus. Bul. 9.

_____ . 1930. History and culture in the Society Islands. Bernice P. Bishop Mus. Bul. 79.

_____ . 1940. The Hawaiian planter. Vol. 1, His plants, methods and areas of cultivation. Bernice P. Bishop Mus. Bul. 161.

Handy, E. S. C., and E. G. Handy, 1972. Native planters in old Hawaii: their life, lore, and environment. Bernice P. Bishop Mus. Bul. 233.

Henry, T. 1928. Ancient Tahiti. Bernice P. Bishop Mus. Bul. 48:1–651.

Hommon, R. 1986. Social evolution in ancient Hawaii. In *Island Societies: Archaeological Approaches to Evolution and Transformation*. Ed. P. V. Kirch. Cambridge: Cambridge Univ. Press. 55–68.

Ishizuki, K. 1974. Excavation of site SU-Fo-1 at Folasa-a-lalo. *Auckland Institute Mus. Bul.* 7:36–57.

Kamakau, S. M. 1961. *Ruling Chiefs of Hawaii.* Honolulu: Kamehameha Schools.

———. 1976. The works of the people of old. Bernice P. Bishop Mus. Special Publication 61.

Kelly, M. 1983. Na Mala o Kona: gardens of Kona. A history of land use in Kona, Hawaii. Bernice P. Bishop Mus., Dept. Anthr. Report 83–2.

Kellum-Ottino, M. 1971. Archeologie d'une vallée des îles Marquises. Publication Société Océanistes 26.

Kikuchi, W. K. 1976. Prehistoric Hawaiian fishponds. *Science* 193:295–299.

Kirch, P. V. 1973. Prehistoric subsistence patterns in the northern Marquesas Islands, French Polynesia. *Archaelogy and Physical Anthropology in Oceania* 8:24–40.

———. 1975. *Cultural Adaptation and Ecology in Western Polynesia: An Ethnoarchaeological Study.* Ann Arbor, Michigan: University Microfilms.

———. 1977. Valley agricultural systems in prehistoric Hawaii: an archaeological consideration. *Asian Perspectives* 20:246–280.

———. 1978. Indigenous agriculture on Uvea (western Polynesia). *Econ. Bot.* 32:157–181.

———. 1979. Late prehistoric and early historic settlement-subsistence systems in the Anahulu Valley, Oahu. Bernice P. Bishop Mus., Dept. Anthr. Report 79–2.

———. 1982a. Ecology and the adaptation of Polynesian agricultural systems. *Archaeology in Oceania* 17:1–6.

———. 1982b. The impact of the prehistoric Polynesians on the Hawaiian ecosystem. *Pac. Sci.* 36:1–14.

———. 1984. *The Evolution of the Polynesian Chiefdoms.* Cambridge: Cambridge Univ. Press.

———. 1985. Intensive agriculture in prehistoric Hawaii: the wet and the dry. In *Prehistoric Intensive Agriculture in the Tropics.* Ed. I. S. Farrington. BAR International Series 232, Oxford. 435–454.

———. 1988. The Talepakemalai Lapita site and Oceanic prehistory. *Natl. Geogr. Res.* 4:328–342.

———. 1989. Second millennium B.C. arboriculture in Melanesia: archaeological evidence from the Mussau Islands. *Econ. Bot.* 43:225–240.

———. In press. Chiefship and competitive evolution: the Marquesas Islands of Eastern Polynesia. In *Economy, Ideology, and Power in Chiefdoms.* Ed. T. Earle. Cambridge: Cambridge Univ. Press.

———. Forthcoming. *The Wet and the Dry: Irrigation and Intensification in Tropical Polynesia.* Cambridge: Cambridge Univ. Press.

Kirch, P. V., and D. E. Yen. 1982. Tikopia: the prehistory and ecology of a Polynesian outlier. Bernice P. Bishop Mus. Bul. 238.

Kirchoff, P. 1955. The principles of clanship in human society. *Davidson J. Anthr.* 1:1–10.

Leach, H. 1979. Evidence of prehistoric gardens in eastern Palliser Bay. National Mus. New Zealand Bul. 21:137–161.

———. 1984. *1,000 Years of Gardening in New Zealand.* Wellington: A. H. and A. W. Reed.

MacDaniels, L. H. 1947. A study of the fe'i banana and its distribution with reference to Polynesian migrations. Bernice P. Bishop Mus. Bul. 190.

Malo, D. 1951. *Hawaiian Antiquities.* Honolulu: Bishop Mus. Press.

Massal, E., and J. Barrau. 1956. Food plants of the South Sea islands. S. Pac. Comm. Tech. Paper 94.

Metraux, A. 1940. Ethnology of Easter Island. Bernice P. Bishop Mus. Bul. 160.

Modjeska, N. 1977. *Production Among the Duna.* Ph.D. Dissertation, Australian National Univ., Canberra.

Oliver, D. 1974. *Ancient Tahitian Society.* 3 vols. Honolulu: Univ. of Hawaii Press.

Ragone, D. 1991. Ethnobotany of breadfruit in Polynesia. In *Islands, Plants, and Polynesians.* Eds. P. A. Cox and S. A. Banack. Portland, Oregon: Timber Press, Dioscorides Press.

Rensch, K. H. 1991. Polynesian plant names linguistic analysis and ethnobotany, expectations and limitations. In *Islands, Plants, and Polynesians.* Eds. P. A. Cox and S. A. Banack. Portland, Oregon: Timber Press, Dioscorides Press.

Riley, T. 1975. Survey and excavations of the aboriginal agricultural system. Pac. Anthr. Rec. 24:79–115.

Rolett, B. 1989. *Hanamiai: Changing Subsistence and Ecology in the Prehistory of Tahuata (Marquesas Islands, French Polynesia)*. Ph.D. Dissertation, Yale Univ.

Rosendahl, P. H. 1972. *Aboriginal Agriculture and Residence Patterns in Upland Lapakahi, Island of Hawaii*. Ph.D. Dissertation, Univ. of Hawaii, Honolulu.

Sahlins, M. D. 1972. *Stone Age Economics*. Chicago: Aldine.

Schilt, R. 1984. Subsistence and conflict in Kona, Hawai'i. Bernice P. Bishop Mus., Dept. Anthr. Report 84-1.

Spencer, J. 1966. Shifting cultivation in southeastern Asia. Univ. California Publication Geography 19.

Spriggs, M. J. T. 1981. *Vegetable Kingdoms: Taro Irrigation and Pacific Prehistory*. Ph.D. Dissertation, Australian National Univ., Canberra.

———. 1986. Landscape, land use and political transformation in southern Melanesia. In *Island Societies: Archaeological Approaches to Evolution and Transformation*. Ed. P. V. Kirch. Cambridge: Cambridge Univ. Press. 6–19.

Suggs, R. C. 1961. Archaeology of Nuku Hiva, Marquesas Islands, French Polynesia. Anthr. Paper, Amer. Mus. of Natural History 49(1).

Svihla, A. 1957. Dental caries in the Hawaiian dog. Bernice P. Bishop Mus. Occ. Paper 22:7–13.

Titcomb, M. 1969. Dog and man in the ancient Pacific. Bernice P. Bishop Mus. Special Publication 59.

Tuggle, H., and P. Griffin (3 eds.). 1973. *Lapakahi, Hawaii: Archaeological Studies*. Asian and Pacific Archaeology Series 5. Honolulu: Social Science Research Institute, Univ. of Hawaii.

Tuggle, H., and M. Tomonari-Tuggle. 1980. Prehistoric agriculture in Kohala, Hawaii. *J. Field Arch.* 7:297–312.

Vayda, A. 1962. Expansion and warfare among swidden agriculturalists. *Amer. Anthr.* 63:346–58.

Vayda, A., and R. Rappaport. 1963. Island cultures. In Man's Place in the Island Ecosystem. Ed. R. Fosberg. Honolulu: Bishop Mus. Press. 133–142.

de Villiers, J. A. J. 1906. *The East and West Indian Mirror*. Hakluyt Society, Second series no. 18.

Whistler, W. A. 1991. Polynesian plant introductions. In *Islands, Plants, and Polynesians*. Eds. P. A. Cox and S. A. Banack. Portland, Oregon: Timber Press, Dioscorides Press.

Wiens, H. 1962. *Atoll Environment and Ecology*. New Haven: Yale Univ. Press.

Wilder, G. P. 1928. The breadfruit of Tahiti. Bernice P. Bishop Mus. Bul. 50.

Wittfogel, K. 1957. *Oriental Despotism*. New Haven: Yale Univ. Press.

Yen, D. E. 1961. The adaptation of kumara by the New Zealand Maori. J. *Polynesian Society* 70:338–348.

———. 1971. The development of agriculture in Oceania. *Pac. Anthr. Rec.* 12:1–12.

———. 1973a. Agriculture in Anutan subsistence. In *Anuta: A Polynesian Outlier in the Solomon Islands*. Eds. D. E. Yen and J. Gordon. Pac. Anthr. Rec. 21:112–149.

———. 1973b. The origins of Oceanic agriculture. *Archaeology and Physical Anthropology in Oceania* 8:68–85.

———. 1974a. Arboriculture in the subsistence of Santa Cruz, Solomon Islands. *Econ. Bot.* 28:247–284.

———. 1974b. The sweet potato and Oceania. Bernice P. Bishop Mus. Bul. 236.

———. 1991. Polynesian cultigens and cultivars: the questions of origin. In *Islands, Plants, and Polynesians*. Eds. P. A. Cox and S. A. Banack. Portland, Oregon: Timber Press, Dioscorides Press.

Yen, D. E., P. V. Kirch, P. Rosendahl, and T. Riley. 1972. Prehistoric agriculture in the upper valley of Makaha, Oahu. In *Makaha Valley Historical Project*. Interim Report no. 3. Eds. E. J. Ladd and D. E. Yen. Pac. Anthr. Rec. 18:59–94.

CHAPTER 7

Polynesian Uses of Seaweed

ISABELLA A. ABBOTT

Dept. of Botany, 3190 Maile Way
University of Hawaii
Honolulu, Hawaii 96822

Most coastal peoples in the Pacific are familiar with seaweeds, or marine algae, as food, whether eaten raw (most Polynesians), cooked (Chinese), or pickled (Japanese), and in a variety of ways by Koreans, Malaysians, and others. Although there are records of food uses by French, Welsh, Irish, and Chileans, they are not well known. Polynesians, like the Maori of New Zealand and the Hawaiians, use seaweeds ceremonially as well.

The Hawaiian use of seaweeds as food was the best known in the Pacific (Abbott and Williamson 1974; Abbott 1984) until Xia and Abbott (1987) established for the Chinese the most diverse list of seaweeds (74 species) used for food. The Japanese, however, have been influential in introducing at least two species of algae, *Laminaria japonica,* or *kombu,* and *Porphyra* species, or *nori,* to the Western world as ingredients in instant soup mixes and in sushi or flavored rice rolls, respectively; their stock of edible algae consists of 52 species.

A survey of the marine algae of Indonesia (Weber van Bosse 1913–28) and Melanesia (Womersley and Bailey 1970) and a brief investigation into uses of seaweeds as food by Indonesians (Heyne 1922; Zaneveld 1959; Soegiarto 1979) to trace aboriginal uses shows that the early European discovery of Indonesia and subsequent settlement have obscured native uses as food. If the early pathway of Lapita folk started in Indonesia, leading to extensive travels throughout Melanesia, we are not able to follow their pathways through their use of seaweeds as food, although this would be a very conservative (but abundant) food resource. We are therefore forced to examine uses within Polynesia as if the choice of seaweeds as food arose *de novo,* which is probably incorrect since the marine algae of Melanesia (Womersley and Bailey 1970) are largely similar to those of central and western Polynesia.

Limu is the Hawaiian word used here used for algae. I usually restrict the usage of this word further, in accordance with local tradition, to edible algae. Hawaiians discriminated between edible and inedible algae (Abbott 1984). In the second group, it was acknowledged that some were edible but not eaten because of local preference, whereas there were others that were inedible because of texture, coarseness, bitterness, and so forth. The most recent edition of the Hawaiian dictionary (Puku'i and Elbert 1986) lists under the word *limu* "plants under water (both fresh and salt), lichens, liverworts, mosses and animals known generally as soft corals." The best known of the soft corals is a species of *Palythoa* called "limu make o Mu'olea" (the deadly *limu* of Mu'olea) which contains a potent toxin. The word *limu* is used in the same general way in Tahiti, Tonga, and Samoa; in the Marquesas the word *imu* is used, and in New Zealand, *rimu*.

In Hawaii, there are approximately 86 names that apply to these nonalgae, or to algae for which no edible use has been ascribed (Abbott 1984). On the other hand, there are 63 Hawaiian names that are thought to apply to edible plants of the sea, freshwater in taro patches or *lo'i*, or in streams or brackish water ponds. Of these, 30 Hawaiian names can be linked to a specific binomial (Abbott 1984).

Traditional Hawaiian preparation of *limu* always had salt added to it, if for no other reason than to preserve it. The Hawaiian word *lipa'akai* refers to *limu* preserved for future consumption by heavy salting (Abbott 1984). So far as is known, this practice was limited to two species of brown algae, *Dictyopteris australis* (Dictyotaceae) and *D. plagiogramma*. The most valued of all Hawaiian *limu*, the red alga *Asparagopsis taxiformis* (Bonnemaisoniaceae) (Fig. 1), was called *lipehu* when heavily salted. Other algae could have been treated in the same way, but these taxa are the only ones that have survived with this practice to modern times. In fact, it is probably as much for the salt as for the different flavors that *limu* were items treasured by Hawaiians for consumption with dried or raw fish and other kinds of seafood. The *Dictyopteris* species were called *limu lipoa* by Hawaiians and *limu kohu* was the name given to *Asparagopsis*. Both these seaweeds were frequently eaten alone with taro *poi* and formed a welcome piquancy to the relatively bland *poi*. A meal of either of these *limu* and *poi* both was a treat and filling, satiating the desire for fish or other things to eat.

Other than Hawaii, only scanty information may be found in the literature or is at present known about Polynesian seaweed uses, either for food or other cultural uses. In the islands nearer the equator than Hawaii, seaweed or *limu* is usually eaten raw, and dressed or sauced with coconut cream or grated fresh coconut. The

Figure 1. *Asparagopsis taxiformis*, present in every island group in Polynesia which has been studied for marine algae, but known to be eaten in Hawai'i only.

preparation of *limu* with grated fresh coconut or coconut cream (which is expressed from grated coconut), was unknown to both ancient and modern Hawaiians. Yet of the nine Polynesian locations reported upon here, six of them—Tonga, Tahiti, Tokelau, the Cook Islands, Samoa, and Fiji—use either coconut cream or grated fresh coconut with their seaweed. Although there are records of seaweeds being eaten in the Marquesas Islands (B. Meilleur, per. com. 1988), the algal species are not known. Finally, in eastern Polynesia, a Chilean colleague saw Easter Islanders gathering a brown alga, *Dictyopteris repens,* for food (B. Santelices, per. com. 1983). Metraux (1971) cited one of the officers in the La Perouse visit to Easter Island in 1797 as saying that a species of brown alga was gathered on the shore and that the names of edible seaweeds were *miritonu, miritonbu mama, auke,* and *ringaringa-pea.* Metraux himself noted that "nowadays only children enjoy eating seaweed."

A survey of seaweeds in Easter Island, Samoa, the Marshall Islands, Enewetak, Vietnam, Tahiti, and Moorea (Abbott and Santelices 1985) showed that each of these places had at least 40 percent of the species in common with each of the other locations. If Hawaii were to be included in such comparisons, there would be that kind of similarity, also. Of the most common species, however, only one of them (*Asparagopsis taxiformis*) is known to be eaten (only in Hawaii), although several others are edible (*Enteromorpha clathrata* (Ulvaceae), *Cladophora socialis* (Cladophoraceae), *Cladophoropsis sundanensis* (Valoniaceae), and *Valonia ventricosa* (Valoniaceae)).

In warm parts of Polynesia and outside Hawaii, only four species of marine algae, and no freshwater algae, are known to be eaten at this time. In my literature survey, I found no written record of seaweed consumption in Samoa, Tonga, Tahiti, Mangareva, the Cook Islands (Aitutaki), or the Marquesas Islands.

However, despite omission from the older literature, at the present time some seaweeds are consumed in Tonga, Tahiti, the Cook Islands, Samoa, the Tokelau Islands, and Fiji. In these six places, a green alga, *Caulerpa racemosa* (Caulerpaceae) (Fig. 2), is chopped and thick coconut cream is added; in Tonga this is called *limu fuofua* and sometimes hot chilies and chopped onions are also added (M. Buelow, per. com. 1982). In Samoa, this same species is eaten raw,

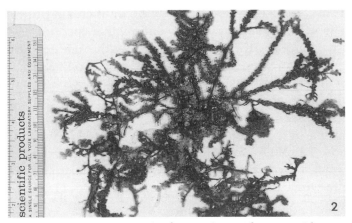

Figure 2. *Caulerpa racemosa,* common in the tropics, and eaten with grated coconut or with coconut cream in central and western Polynesia.

without salt or coconut cream (R. Annesley, per. com. 1981). Although this species is known in Hawaii, it is not as common there as in islands closer to the equator, or islands having lagoons. *Caulerpa racemosa* is called *lelatu* in Indonesian, and *limu eka* in the Cook Islands (Arasaki and Arasaki 1983). This species has a peppery flavor, and is well known in the Philippines as *araucip*.

A species of *Halymenia* (a red alga, Halymeniaceae) (Fig. 3) recently has been collected in Western Samoa where it is baked in coconut cream (G. Yamasaki, National Marine Fisheries, per. com. 1988). Two recipes were given by Mafi Buelow from Tonga, but it was not possible to identify with certainty the seaweed used. Both recipes used coconut cream, and both were cooked, and thus may be relatively new innovations. One of them was called *limu tanga'u,* and may be a species of *Gracilaria* (Gracilariaceae), which are known to be eaten in many parts of the Pacific. "Plant gelatin" (agar) is produced on cooking *Gracilaria,* which when combined with coconut cream makes a coconut pudding similar to the Hawaiian *haupia.* Species of *Gracilaria* (Fig. 4) are the favorites of all fresh seaweeds used by all racial groups living in Hawaii at the present time.

In the opinion of Handy and Handy (1972), the coconut may have been introduced late to Hawaii. The late introduction was speculated upon because (1) the coconut was not used as widely in food or for cultural purposes as elsewhere in southern Polynesia; (2) the plants were not grown as densely as in those southern islands, even in dry, leeward places where it would have been a useful resource; (3) there were only two varieties in Hawaii—*niu hiwa,* used ceremonially, medicinally, and for cooking; and *niu lelo,* used for religious purposes, sometimes as a substitute offering. Women were not permitted to use coconuts because the tree was the body of the god Ku (Handy and Puku'i 1958).

The *niu lelo* was further forbidden to women (Kamakau 1964, 64) because it was used as an offering in the temples. In contrast to the two Hawaiian varieties, there were 16 varieties of coconut recognized in Tahiti (Henry 1928). Other primary uses of coconut in southern Polynesia included the extensive use of coconut cordage and rope. In Hawaii, coconut cordage for fishing nets was supplanted by cordage made of the Hawaiian endemic, *Touchardia latifolia* (Buck 1957; Summers, in press), a superior cordage that was also used as the basis for the Hawaiian feather cloaks (Buck 1957).

These points may be used to explain why coconut cream or grated coconut were not used as food with *limu* in Hawaii—simply that coconut was not widely used with any sort of food. The three Hawaiian dishes that use coconut—*haupia* (a coconut pudding), *kulolo* (a taro and coconut pudding), and *ko'ele palau* (a mixture of coconut cream and mashed sweet potatoes)—could have been introduced in the last century, or during the time of the Tahitian arrivals. In precontact times, only men could have been served these dishes, probably made of the *niu hiwa* variety. Combinations or mixtures very close to these are known in the southern Polynesian islands. Although my Hawaiian mother and grandmother were familiar with these uses of coconut, their ages would have taken them back only to the mid 1800s, some time after the religion was overthrown (1819) and accounts of precontact times are sparse.

The knowledge of seaweeds as food has apparently been lost in most of Polynesia. Seaweed species formerly were more widely recognized and used than

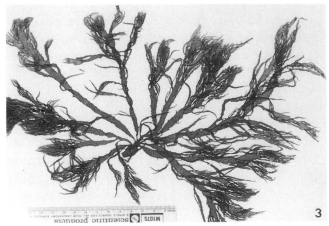

Figure 3. *Halymenia species,* baked with coconut cream in modern Samoa.

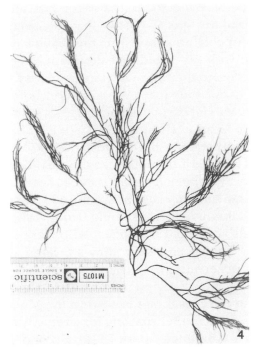

Figure 4. *Cracilaria coronopifolia,* a common Hawaiian species and currently most favored of edible algae in Hawai'i, used elsewhere in the Pacific for its "plant gelatin" or agar.

now, and with no large legacy of folk taxonomy remaining, it would be impossible to produce a list of seaweeds greater than the 63 attributed to the Hawaiians. From my own seaweed research, it is clear that most, if not all, of the species of marine algae that the Hawaiians used as food can also be found in southern Polynesia (excepting Easter Island and New Zealand). What, then, could be the reason for Hawaiians to focus on seaweed as food?

Food habits by precontact Hawaiians were determined (as was all else) by a very strictly enforced male-dominated religion (Valeri 1985). The kapu system that evolved governed not only societal behavior, including the establishment and maintenance of a caste system, but individual behavior as well. Among the most strictly enforced kapu was *'aikapu* which regulated who might eat together (sexes ate separately, and different ranks within each sex were also segregated), and what they might eat. This was carried to an extreme with respect to the taro plant, which represented the god Kane; thus only men could take part in the planting and caring of this sacred plant, to the extent that its final product, taro *poi*, was only made by men (Handy and Handy 1972), although a portion could be given to women to eat. Similarly, the pig represented the body of the god Lono, and women were prohibited from eating pork. Many fish, especially red-colored fish, could not be eaten by women because such fish were frequently used in sacrificial offerings in temples where women were excluded (Valeri 1985).

There were no invertebrates or plants of the sea that women were prohibited from eating, and it is not surprising that they were the ones (Titcomb 1978) who became the experts in recognizing and understanding the habits of *limu*, snails, shrimp, limpets, crabs and sea urchins, while men became the fishing—especially deep-sea fishing—experts. Even today the older Hawaiian women know the names, and can describe the species, better than the men. Women, then, were probably responsible for obtaining food from the shallow reef flats and tide pools, which when prepared with salt could be eaten with sweet potato or breadfruit (neither of which was denied them) or with taro *poi* if they were given this choice food. I know from my own family that seafoods were choice *ko kula kai* exchanges with taro in *ko kula 'uka*, the Hawaiian exchange system between *'ohana* in the same *ahupua'a* or geographic location (Handy and Puku'i 1958). Although we do not know who collected and prepared the shellfish, Kirch (1979) records very large quantities of shells of a variety of molluscs whose soft parts were presumably consumed (or taken away to be consumed later) at Kalahuipua'a, Hawaii Island. This site was a fishing settlement, in use between 1400 and 1750 A.D. (Kirch 1979). The quantities of invertebrates collected would strongly suggest to me that marine algae were probably also collected by women who were present at this periodic settlement. The shore habitat currently shows a large variety of edible algal species (Abbott, pers. observation).

Finally, in including New Zealand in Polynesia, two uses of the brown alga, *Durvillea antarctica* (Durvilleaceae), are known to the Maori. First of the uses of *rimurapa* was eating the blades after roasting for a remedy against skin infections, and eating the tips as a vermifuge (Stark 1979). Second, the Maori perfected a practice of preserving cooked or salted mutton birds (*titi* or sooty shearwater, *Puffinus griseus*) that is unmatched anywhere else in the world. It is also a very different use of seaweeds than known in other parts of Polynesia. (*Durvillea* species also occur in Chile and southern Australia. In Chile, *cochayuyo* [an Araucanian Indian name] is dried to be incorporated into stews. It was and is sold along the streets of the cities by vendors.) In New Zealand, the seaweed is sometimes called New Zealand bull kelp. It is a large plant about 10 m long that favors rough-water coasts. Off Stewart Island, on the south coast of South Island, thousands of shearwater arrive near the end of October and have their chicks, which are fed until about the beginning of May when the parents leave and the chicks are large enough to fly. Beginning on April 1, only Maori people may catch these fledgling birds which are killed, plucked, cleaned, cooked or salted, and placed in bags made from the blades of this seaweed. The central parts of the blades have a tissue that is like honeycomb, which can be forced apart to accommodate the birds. Outside of the *poha,* another bag made of New Zealand flax (*Phormium tenax*) is tied securely. Thus prepared, the *poha titi* can be kept for two years or more.

Cultural Uses

In Polynesia, the greatest use for seaweeds was, and is, as food, with the Hawaiians using the largest number of species and having more names for species than any other area in this geographic region. Only the Hawaiians have important cultural uses on record. Species of *Sargassum* (Sargassaceae), a brown seaweed (Fig. 5), are used in the important forgiveness ceremony known as *ho'oponopono,* and in purification ceremonies. Both ceremonies are thought to be the basis for the folk name of *limu kala* in which *kala* means "to forgive."

A certain species (Fig. 6) of *Ulva* (Ulvaceae), the genus to which "sea lettuce" belongs, is thought to represent the green "clothing" surrounding a baby shark, which may serve as a family god or *'aumakua.* Those who have the shark as an *'aumakua* do not eat this *limu.* Another species of *Ulva, U. fasciata,* (Fig. 7) was used at Polihale on Kaua'i Island in a special hula. If similar cultural uses were known to other Polynesians, this information is not readily available, and should be sought.

Seaweeds are also portions of the specific items mentioned in the Kumulipo, the Hawaiian creation story in which, for organisms that originated in the sea,

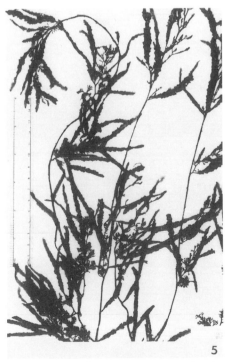

5

Figure 5. *Sargassum,* or *limu kala,* used by Hawaiians in the forgiveness ceremony called *ho'oponopono.*

Figure 6. One of the species of *Ulva,* a green alga commonly called "sea lettuce," which was thought to be a wrapping for baby sharks. Sharks are gods for certain Hawaiian families.

Figure 7. *Ulva fasciata,* used in earlier times at Polihale, western Kaua'i Island, for a special hula dance.

there was a "twin" on land with a similar sounding name. "Born was the *'Ekaha* moss living in the sea, guarded by the *'Ekahakaha* fern living on land" is a couplet from the Beckwith (1972) translation. *'Ekaha,* I believe, is a species of *Grateloupia* (Halymeniaceae) (Fig. 8) which grows on high-energy basalt shores in the Hawaiian Islands; this species grows in upright tufts that are frequently green owing to bleaching of the red pigment, and that resemble the tufted habit of the "Bird's nest fern," *Asplenium nidus* or *'ekaha.*

The clustering habit of species that seem to nestle in small irregularities of the substratum, such as old sea urchin holes, is shown by *Laurencia dotyi* (Rhodomelaceae) (Fig. 9) and *L. succisa.* On account of their secretive nature, these seaweeds are shunned by hula dancers because learning and exhibiting hula movements is explanatory and open. The two species are called *lipe'epe'e* in Hawaiian, and are liked for their crunchiness.

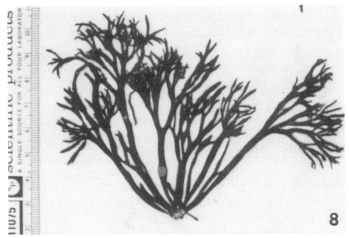

Figure 8. *Gratelopuia phuquoensis* called *'ekaha* by Hawaiians, a marine plant that is matched with the terrestrial *Asplenium nidus* (bird's nest fern) called *'ekahakaha* by Hawaiians.

Figure 9. *Laurencia dotyi,* called *lipe'epe'e* by Hawaiians, and not eaten by hula dancers (see text).

Conclusion

It is suggested that a male-dominated religion which exercised many prohibitions, including food prohibitions, against women literally drove women into the sea to seek out edible non-kapu foods. These were mostly invertebrates and *limu* or seaweed. Incidentally, the addition of vitamins and minerals available in seaweeds and not present in the terrestrial plants that formed the main Polynesian vegetable staples probably contributed to the general good health of the Hawaiian people in precontact times.

Nonetheless, the use of a green alga, *Caulerpa racemosa*, by many other Polynesians brought other quality vitamins (Vitamin A) and minerals (e.g., calcium, iron) in excess of those occurring in other indigenous foods, and coupled with the use of coconut cream provided a quantity of fat that was ordinarily in short supply (and from which Hawaiian women would have profited had they not been restricted from using coconut).

The use by the New Zealand Maori of only one seaweed, *Durvillea antarctica*, is probably an incomplete record. Of all Polynesians, the Maori had the largest number of seaweed species to choose from (probably about 500 edible species), and a larger number of uses would be expected.

Handy and Handy (1972, 236) stated that

> to give botanical identification, habit, dietary and medicinal uses, and ceremonial uses and significance of these plants [seaweeds] would require almost a life's work.

Dr. Handy was correct, but the time may already have passed when such information could be obtained. Dr. Handy did his fieldwork in the 1920s and 1930s when the Marquesas Islands and Hawaii were not as Westernized as they are now, and at a time when there were many more who had information on ancient ways than there are at present. It has been very difficult and discouraging to try to obtain information on seaweeds in Tahiti and Samoa in recent years. It may be too late.

Acknowledgments

I thank Dr. Murray Parsons, DSIR, Christchurch, New Zealand, for the information on the *poha titi*, and Mafi Buelow, Maile Drake (both from Tonga), Rhonda Annesley, Gordon Yamasaki (both from Western Samoa), Anouk Hunter (from Raiatea, French Polynesia), and Bernabe Santelices (from Chile) for information on Tongan, Samoan, Tahitian and Easter Island uses of seaweeds.

Literature Cited

Abbott, I. A. 1984. *Limu. An Ethnobotanical Study of Some Hawaiian Seaweeds.* Lawai, Hawaii: Pac. Trop. Bot. Garden.

Abbott, I. A., and B. Santelices. 1985. The marine algae of Easter Island (eastern Polynesia). In *Proceedings of the Fifth International Coral Reef Congress, Tahiti* 5:71–75.

Abbott, I. A., and E. H. Williamson. 1974. *An Ethnobotanical Study of Some Edible Hawaiian Seaweeds.* Lawai, Hawaii: Pac. Trop. Bot. Garden.

Arasaki, S., and T. Arasaki. 1983. *Vegetables From the Sea.* Tokyo: Japan Publications.

Beckwith, M. 1972. *The Kumulipo. A Hawaiian Creation Chant.* Honolulu: Univ. of Hawaii Press.

Buck, P. H. [Te Rangi Hiroa]. 1957. Arts and crafts of Hawaii. Bernice P. Bishop Mus. Special Publication 45.

Handy, E. S. C., and E. G. Handy. 1972. Native planters in old Hawaii: their life, lore, and environment. Bernice P. Bishop Mus. Bul. 233.

Handy, E. S. C., and M. K. Pukui. 1958. *The Polynesian Family System in Ka'u, Hawai'i.* Wellington: The Polynesian Society

Henry, T. 1928. Ancient Tahiti. Bernice P. Bishop Mus. Bul. 48:1–651.

Heyne, K. 1922. Algen. In *De Nüttige Planten van Nederlandisch Indie.* Dept. Landb. Nijverh. Hand., Buitenzorg. A:33–38.

Kamakau, S. M. 1964. Ka Po'e Kahiko. Bernice P. Bishop Mus. Special Publication 51:1–165.

Kirch, P. V. 1979. Marine exploitation in prehistoric Hawaii. Archaeological investigations at Kalahuipua'a, Hawai'i Island. Pac. Anthr. Rec. Bernice P. Bishop Mus. No. 29.

Metraux, A. 1971. Ethnology of Easter Island. Bernice P. Bishop Mus. Bul. 160.

Parsons, M. J. n.d. *Durvillea antarctica* and traditional poha titi or kelp bags.

Pukui, M. K., and S. H. Elbert. 1986. *Hawaiian Dictionary.* Honolulu: Univ. of Hawaii Press.

Soegiarto, A. 1979. Indonesian seaweed resources: their utilization and management. In *Proceedings of the International Seaweed Symposium.* Eds. A. Jensen and J. R. Stein. 9:463–471.

Stark, R. 1979. Maori Herbal Remedies. Christchurch: Viking Sevenseas.

Summers, C. C. In press. Hawaiian cordage. Bernice P. Bishop Mus. Occ. Paper.

Titcomb, M. 1978. Native use of marine invertebrates in old Hawai'i. Pac. Sci. 32:325–391.

Valeri, V. 1985. *Kingship and Sacrifice. Ritual and Society in Ancient Hawai'i.* Chicago: Univ. of Chicago Press.

Weber van Bosse, A. 1913–1928. Liste des Algues du Siboga. 1–5. Mongr. Siboga Exped. 59a-d. Leiden: E. J. Brill.

Womersley, H. B. S., and A. Bailey. 1970. Marine algae of the Solomon Islands. *Phil. Trans. Roy. Soc. London B. Biol. Sci.* 259:257–352.

Xia, B., and I. A. Abbott. 1987. Edible seaweeds of China and their place in the Chinese diet. Econ. Bot. 41:341–353.

Zaneveld, J. S. 1959. The utilization of marine algae in tropical South and East Asia. Econ. Bot. 13:89–131.

CHAPTER 8

Polynesian Herbal Medicine

PAUL ALAN COX

Department of Botany and Range Science
Brigham Young University
Provo, Utah 84602

The Polynesians showed a remarkable ability to use indigenous plants through-out their island homes. Early European explorers were deeply impressed with Polynesian agricultural plants, and indeed the ill-fated expedition of H.M.S. *Bounty* to Tahiti was launched to collect a Polynesian tree-crop, *Artocarpus altilis* (Moraceae) or breadfruit, for use in the Caribbean. Roggeveen was very impressed with the technological skill displayed in the construction of the Samoan oceangoing vessels he encountered, since these boats "were not hollowed-out trees, but made of planks and inner timbers and very neatly joined together, so that we supposed that they must have some tools of iron" (Roggeveen 1771–1772, 151).

Ornamented bark cloth, collected from various islands, was made into books by some of the enterprising crew of Cook's voyages and sold at a premium in London. Few European expeditions returned without at least some of their crew being tattooed by Polynesian artists working with ink made from the kukui tree, *Aleurites moluccana*. And the intricate Maori meeting houses, ornamented with beautifully carved timbers and woven panels, captured the imagination of European architects. Yet one of the uses of plants by Polynesians merited scant mention by the first European visitors, even though paradoxically it is regarded by many modern Polynesians as the most impressive use of plants by their ancestors. This is Polynesian herbal medicine.

The practice of Polynesian herbal medicine continues today throughout Polynesia, despite subtle and occasionally overt discouragement from island governments, educational institutions, and medical establishments. Practicing Polynesian herbalists can be found not only throughout the islands, but also in expatriate populations of Polynesians living in Auckland, Sydney, Honolulu, San Francisco, and Los Angeles.

Studies of Polynesian herbal medicine as it is practiced today raise a number of intriguing questions. What were the historical antecedents of Polynesian herbal medicine? Is Polynesian herbalism a tradition beginning long before European contact, or is it, as some have suggested, much like Christianity—a European introduction that has subsequently been embraced by the Polynesians? Does Polynesian herbal medicine have an empirical basis, or is it solely rooted in the legends and animism of former years? Does Polynesian herbal medicine constitute a consistent body of theory and practice throughout Oceania, or does it differ greatly from island to island? What are the intrinsic differences between Western and Polynesian medicine, and must these disparate traditions be unavoidably and unalterably in conflict? And finally, what is the efficacy of Polynesian herbal medicine? Do sick people treated by it get better, and if so, why?

Ethnomedicine

To approach these questions, it is first necessary to view Polynesian herbal medicine within the broader context of ethnomedicine. Nearly all cultures, including Western culture, have developed ways of dealing with disease and treating the sick. While these traditions differ dramatically, there are three features that unite them. All ethnomedical traditions have (1) a collection of cosmological beliefs that attempt to explain the cause, nature, etiology, and treatment of disease; (2) a group of substances or compounds, usually derived from plants, which are believed to be efficacious in treating the sick; and (3) a health care delivery system, or cultural context in which various treatments are provided to the sick and afflicted.

All three of these features differ from culture to culture, but are so deeply imbedded within a culture that it is sometimes difficult for members of a particular culture to even conceive of any different way of viewing these three different features of ethnomedicine. For example, modern Western cultures teach that (1) most infectious disease is caused by microorganisms that have invaded the body. They believe that unless the body's immune system is successful in overcoming this microbial challenge, it may be necessary (2) for the sick person to take, either orally or by injection, antibiotic substances usually derived originally from molds or other lower plants, but sometimes produced synthetically. In Western cultures, these substances are (3) provided on the advice of a physician, frequently dressed in white clothing, who is paid both money and cultural respect for his or her services.

Few Western people would feel comfortable being treated by Navajo healers, yet to Navajo culture, Western medicine is equally alien. To the Navajos many diseases (1) are caused by disharmony between the sick person and nature, possibly as the result of violating a cultural prohibition, such as entering the hogan of a dead person in the wrong fashion. In such cases it may be necessary (2) for the person to ingest medicinal plants and undergo ritual purges, possibly in combination with a sweat bath. The treatment is guided (3) by a healer, who sings traditional songs with the afflicted person's kin, while making a sand painting that is later destroyed, taking with it the vestiges of the disease.

Polynesian ethnomedicine also differs significantly from Western medicine, yet appears to its adherents as a logical and sensible way of treating the sick, as do indeed most ethnomedicinal traditions appear to those who rely upon them. As

Reid pointed out in her seminal study of ethnomedicine in North Arnhem land, Australia, "Yolngu beliefs about causality in illness are not illogical superstitions. Sickness, sorcery and social events are linked in a logical structure which is comparable to a Western scientific theory" (Reid 1983, xx).

In this sense, Polynesian ethnomedicine can be seen as a scientific paradigm (see Kuhn 1962). A paradigm, according to Kuhn, is a model of theory and application "from which springs particular coherent traditions of scientific research" (Kuhn 1962, 10). A paradigm is therefore a way of viewing the world so that scientists who share a paradigm are "committed to the same rules and standards for scientific practice" (Kuhn 1962, 11). Examples of different paradigms include Copernican astronomy, Newtonian mechanics, or Aristotelian dynamics. Such paradigms, when viewed from within, have logical consistency, reasonable fit of theory to observed data, and offer the means and hope to solve questions of interest.

One of the major triumphs of historians of science in recent years has been to explain previous scientific paradigms from within the context of the paradigms; that is to say, historians of science now attempt to explain previous modes of science on the basis of the world views, questions, methods, and approaches that seemed reasonable at the time of their practitioners. By so doing, historians of science have forced us to expand our definition of what science is. Simply put, we might broadly define science as the attempt to systematize observations about the world, ask meaningful questions about those observations, and make predictions based on those observations.

Since ethnobotany is a branch of ethnoscience its task is to explore indigenous approaches to plants within indigenous paradigms. Can Polynesian healers therefore be considered in some sense scientists? In the schemes of Kuhn (1962) and Feyerabend (1978) they can, for Polynesian healers have developed a systematized group of observations about the world, they have theories explaining these observations, and their theories have predictive value about future events.

To facilitate discussion of Polynesian ethnopharmacology, I will examine Polynesian ethnomedicine in terms of the three broad ethnomedicinal categories that I have outlined. I will: (1) explore Polynesian explanations for disease causation, etiology, and treatment, (2) describe the Polynesian repertoire of plant-derived substances believed to be efficacious in healing, and, (3) seek to explain the distinctive patterns of traditional health care delivery systems in Polynesia. I will then conclude with a few thoughts on the origin of Polynesian herbalism.

Polynesian Theories of Disease Causation

In Polynesian cultures, much more than in European cultures, an individual is a part of a highly defined and important social context. An individual is deeply identified within a kinship network consisting of departed ancestors and current, extended family groups descended from a single ancestor, or extended family groups entered into by marriage or tied together by other bonds of consanguinity. In contrast to modern Western societies, where individuals are frequently isolated from their extended families and where even nuclear families are increasingly ephemeral in nature, the *'aiga*, or extended kinship group of Polynesians, is extremely important, and extends far beyond household units to encompass entire clans and village or multivillage units.

Many of the ambiguities of social life found in European cultures are absent in Polynesia because of the precise hierarchical structure that is the warp and woof upon which the Polynesian cultural fabric is woven. Polynesian rhetoric, ceremonial activities, political structures, and village life constantly reinforce and confirm the hierarchical social structure. For example, on ceremonial occasions, *kava* (a water-based infusion of the rhizomes of *Piper methysticum* [Piperaceae]) (see Lebot's chapter, this volume) is distributed to the assembled chiefs in decreasing order of rank. Even among children, a strict hierarchy based on age occurs. As Kirch argues (this volume) and to which I have alluded (Cox 1980a), this hierarchical structure of Polynesian societies may have been culturally adaptive in that it allowed communal control of crucial resources during time of scarcity or famine. But regardless of its genesis, the hierarchical nature of Polynesian societies has directly influenced patterns of illness and healing.

This highly articulated cultural structure places many duties and responsibilities upon its participants. Membership within a kinship group carries with it responsibilities to both the living and the dead, and an individual has responsibilities to the village and chiefdom in which he or she resides as well. In Polynesian belief, violation of these responsibilities may result in illness.

Thus, in contrast to Western theories of disease causation, Polynesians believe that abrogation of familial responsibilities as well as interpersonal hostility may result in illness. To Tongan healers, *monitonu* (healthiness) depends on how well an individual meets his or her familial and social responsibilities (George 1989). Covert or direct hostility against unrelated individuals may also result in illness. In Samoa, *nifo loa*, a serious disease whose symptoms resemble osteomyelitis, is said to occur in individuals who have given offense to a resident of Falelima village. However, unlike some Melanesians, who believe that sorcerers may deliberately cause disease (Spencer 1941), Polynesians generally believe that such ailments are not caused as retribution by living individuals, but are the natural consequence of straining the social fabric or violating *tapu*. Even in Tuvalu, where some illness is attributed to the use of sorcery, such illness is frequently believed to result from inappropriate use of magical powers (Chambers and Chambers 1985).

Polynesian healers also believe that illness may occur without the agency of any supernatural forces in individuals who harbor hostile thoughts, for the simple reason that such individuals estrange themselves from their familial and social bonds. Being alone and without companionship of friends or family, either as the result of irresponsible behavior, or by something as simple as traveling alone to the forest, is not viewed as a healthy circumstance by Polynesians. Neither is living in strained familial or social environments. As a result, Polynesian healers are very sensitive to circumstances that may have induced a sense of isolation in a sick individual and frequently seek to resolve such difficulties by reducing tensions and reintroducing the sick individual into his or her normal social context. This is a very different approach than that of Western medicine which frequently removes sick individuals from their normal social context, and places them in a completely new environment, such as a hospital, that has a completely different hierarchy and novel patterns of social interaction.

The attempt by Polynesian healers to reintroduce a sick individual to a normal social context can be seen by the way in which Samoan healers treat the disease called *musu*. An adolescent girl who becomes increasingly estranged from her family may eventually manifest the symptoms of *musu*, a psychological malady characterized by near autistic withdrawal from all social interaction, inability to speak, and in severe cases partial paralysis. All these symptoms mimic those of spiritual possession, but there is a subtle difference: a possessed person is not aware of his or her identity but a person with *musu* remains aware of their own identity (Kinloch 1985b). Samoan techniques in dealing with *musu* differ somewhat from healer to healer, but all approaches have a similar objective—reduction of the familial tensions that led to *musu* in the first place. As several healers have confided to me, they do not regard *musu* as a genuine case of spiritual possession, but rather the result of a strained familial environment. Thus, healers usually initiate a rather elaborate treatment with incantations and seemingly ritual gestures quite uncharacteristic of other Samoan medicinal practices (but see Moyle 1974). This treatment invariably culminates in the afflicted person speaking in a slow and sonorous voice about perceived inequities in the familial structure. Since family members believe the person speaking in such a manner to be spiritually possessed, his or her utterances are regarded as privileged speech not subject to censure. After the possessed person delivers a long and frequently harsh discourse, the "spirit" usually leaves the afflicted person, who is then "cured."

Other supernatural agents that may cause illness in Polynesian cultures include spirits, *aitu* or *atua*, which Feinberg (1979) appropriately glosses as "spooks". Ellis reported in Hawaii that healers who successfully treated spiritual possession gained a good deal of repute, such as Oronopua and Makanuiairono "who were deified after death, particularly because they were frequently successful in driving away the evil spirits by which the people were afflicted and threatened with" (Ellis 1826; Chun 1986). Spooks occur in the forest or in lonely places at nighttime, and may cause disease or even possession to the unwary. *Aitu*-caused diseases in Polynesia have received a great deal of attention by cultural anthropologists, and, interestingly, by the early Christian missionaries (for reasons discussed below), but such diseases and possessions are relatively infrequent among modern Polynesians.

Improper diet is also seen by Polynesian healers as an important cause of disease. Much time is spent by Polynesian healers in counselling patients, particularly pregnant women, about diet. In Samoa, healers frequently counsel individuals to avoid fatty, sweet, or refrigerated foods. Special foods, such as *vaisalo* (a porridge made from *Manihot esculenta* [Euphorbiaceae] tubers, *Spondias dulcis* (Anacardiaceae) fruits, and coconut milk) are given to mothers immediately after childbirth. Polynesian herbal treatments frequently include dietary restrictions for the afflicted person.

Healers also name inadequate hygiene as a cause of disease. High standards of personal cleanliness in most Polynesian societies merited comment by early European visitors to Polynesia.

Other sources of disease in Polynesian ethnomedicine include organic trauma, such as breaking a leg or stepping on a sea urchin. In addition, most modern Polynesian healers believe in some form of the germ theory of disease causation. As a result, Polynesian healers do not see their beliefs and treatments as being inimicable to Western medicine. Most have a pluralistic view, believing that some diseases are best treated by Western medicine while others would most quickly be resolved by traditional remedies. Both Parsons (1985) and George (1989) record distinct partitioning of diseases by Tongan healers into *mahaki fakapalagi* (Western diseases) or *mahaki fakatonga* (Tongan diseases); the choice of Western or Tongan therapy is determined by the disease category.

These different views of disease causation, however, compound the problem of relating Polynesian disease categories to Western categories. As a result, there are probably few linguistically competent ethnobiologists who have not agonized over the translation of indigenous disease categories into Western terms. Pharmacognosists and physicians properly expect us to translate into terms they understand the disease for which *Psychotria insularum* (Rubiaceae) is used. And yet I find myself as speechless in communicating the realities of the disease *oso fa puni moa* in Western terms as do my bilingual Samoan friends. This situation is particularly frustrating for ethnobotanists, as the frequent agreement between Polynesians and trained botanists on the limits and identities of plant species is extraordinary, yet there is frequently little correspondence between Polynesian and Western disease categories.

Some general patterns do, however, appear in the construction of Polynesian disease categories: (1) Polynesian diseases are usually labelled with a binomial composed of a generic term with a specific modifier; (2) classification rules uniting genera are unknown to informants; (3) disease categories above the generic level are not used; and (4) Polynesian disease taxonomies consist of unrelated generic terms of differing degrees of articulation.

As an example, the disease category *ila* is used throughout Polynesia. Several binomials for *ila* disease in Tahiti and Samoa are illustrated in Table 1. In both places, *ila* includes disease of childhood although some adult ailments are also included. What is striking here is the use of the same generic term with completely different specific modifiers between the islands. Healers are not able to delineate the specific reasons why all these disparate ailments are included within the *ila* category, nor are they able to describe how this category relates to other categories. This and similar examples throughout Polynesia suggest the possible existence of a proto-Polynesian disease classification system that through the years has been modified with concurrent loss of connections between different generic terms.

There are at least seven different ways in which generic-level terms for disease categories originate, as shown by an analysis of Samoan disease terms (Table 2). *Anufe*, for example, is the word for worms and means "worms," the disease taking its name from the cause. *Ate* or "liver" and *fefete* or "swollen" provide an anatomical origin for a disease name, while *malaga umete* is morphological, referring to the shape of certain head ulcerations. New mothers are vulnerable to *failele gau* while *fe'efe'e* summons the vision of an octopus crawling inside one's intestines. *Lepela* is a transliteration of the Western term "leprosy," while *lafa* is an irreducible moneme for ringworm.

Table 1. *Ila* Disease Types in Samoa and Tahiti

Name	Source	Symptoms
Ila a'ati	Samoa	red eyes, fevers
Ila fa'au tama	Samoa	birthmarks
Ila fale	Samoa	inflammation of buttocks
Ila mea	Samoa	unexplained crying
Ira miti	Tahiti	morning fever
Ira vaeha'a	Tahiti	pain on one side of face
Ira 'ahure	Tahiti	inflammation of urethra
Ira tui	Tahiti	pus from ears
Ira 'ute	Tahiti	painful lips
Ira ninamu	Tahiti	darkened lips

Tahitian data from Hooper 1985.

Table 2. Examples of Samoan Disease Categories

Type	Term	Meaning
Causal	*anufe*	worms
Anatomical	*ate fefete*	swollen liver
Morphological	*malaga umete*	bowl scabs
Personal	*failele gau*	sick mother
Symbolical	*fe'efe'e*	octopus
Foreign	*lepela*	leprosy
Irreducible	*lafa*	ringworm

Polynesian Pharmacological Materials

Upon diagnosis of a sickness, Polynesian healers have different sorts of therapies available, including therapeutic massage, physical therapy, and dietary and family counselling. However, in many cases the healer will decide to employ remedies prepared from natural products. Polynesian ethnomedicine relies almost exclusively upon preparations from vascular plants, even though many marine invertebrates and some fish species are known to be pharmacologically active. However in Hawaii, some species of the algal genus *Ulva* were used medicinally (Neal 1934).

The choice of plants to be used is constrained by the healer's personal repertoire of medicinal species. Several factors influence this repertoire. First, the composition of the local flora will influence a healer's familiarity with particular species, although some healers know and use medicinal plants found in areas distant to their home village. Consequentially, there is a small but significant traffic in medicinal plants within and between islands. For example, *faito'o*, or Tongan healers in Nukualofa on the island of Tongatapu, use many medicinal plants carried from the neighboring island of 'Eua by family members and friends. In many Polynesian markets a few common herbal remedies such as *lega* (dried and powdered rhizomes of *Curcuma longa*) can be purchased.

Second, knowledge systems concerning medicinal plants are strongly family based, and (particularly in Samoa) are frequently matrilineal. Thus ethnopharmacopoeias vary somewhat from healer to healer, based on the healer's familial affiliations and training.

Finally, Polynesian healers frequently have a sense of ownership of certain herbal formulations which approximates Western concepts of intellectual property rights as codified by copyright and patent law. However, where Western law seeks principally to protect financial benefits derived from intellectual property, Polynesian healers primarily seek to preserve efficacy of their herbal remedies. Thus, even though one healer may know the remedy used by another healer, he or she will not use the other healer's *vai* or remedy, not only out of a sense of propriety, but also because he or she knows that unauthorized use will not be efficacious in healing the sick. As Hooper found in Tahiti:

> *Ra'au* [herbal remedies], however, are regarded as personal property. Even though the prescription may be a simple one, learned and committed to memory within a matter of minutes, it remains the property of an owner . . . and should not be made except under his or her direction. Failure to do so is widely believed to result in that medicine being *ma'au* 'spoiled' and rendered ineffectual (Hooper 1985, 170; see also Hooper 1978).

In Tonga, George (1989) described a procedure called *fanofano'i* in which a healer bestows authority on an apprentice to prepare his or her remedies. Feinberg (1979) mentions a similar bestowal of "proprietary rights" to an herbal remedy in Anuta. Yet the authority to prepare a remedy does not imply that the healer claims ownership of the plants from which the remedy is formulated. Most Polynesian healers believe that the plants they use in their medicine are a gift of God. As Samoan healer Epenesa Mauigoa told me:

E tatau ona e manatua ae le'i	You should remember before
sau le palagi i Samoa sa le	Europeans came to Samoa that
maua tagata Samoa foma'i,	Samoans did not have doctors,
falema'i, tui o'ona, ma	hospitals, antibiotic shots,
le avanoa e faia tipiga.	or the ability to perform surgery.
Pau lava le mea sa maua	All that the people had was the
tagata o la'au i le vao	plants in the forest that God
sa alofa mai e le Atua.	had given them.

As I will later suggest, this belief, although expressed in Christian terms, may date from pre-European contact times since it occurs in different islands and among healers from a variety of religious persuasions.

In contrast to Chinese or Japanese herbal medicine, Polynesian herbal remedies are almost always formulated from fresh, rather than dry, plant materials. Healers are very specific as to the particular part of the plant used in formulation. As a result, Polynesian healers converse using a rich botanical terminology that has detailed terms describing such features of plant morphology as rhizomes, roots, shoots, internodes, apical meristems, petioles, and so forth.

Polynesian ethnotaxonomies are equally impressive, with the total Polynesian ethnopharmacopoeia probably being in excess of 500 species. This large number of species is partially due to the tremendous ecological diversity and the high rates of plant endemism of islands colonized by the Polynesians.

In a review of the literature, Zepernick (1972) found that 427 plant species from over 300 genera had been reported as being used in Polynesian medicine. Comparing these species to the pharmacopoeias of other geographical areas, Zepernick reported that 55 of these species were officinal in Western medicine, 1 was used in European folk medicine, 16 were used in Chinese and Tibetan folk medicine, and 72 were used in Melanesian folk medicine (excluding Fiji). Thus, according to Zepernick's data, 66 percent of the Polynesian ethnopharmacopoeia is used for medicine only in Polynesia (Fig. 1). This, Zepernick believed, suggests that Polynesian herbal medicine is a heritage from pre-European times. I will discuss a bit later in this essay Zepernick's hypothesis.

Although a few Polynesian healers indicate that they choose plants for their formulations based on dreams or other spiritual phenomena, the majority use only those in whose use they were instructed by their mentor during their apprenticeship. As a result, Polynesian herbal medicine is a strongly conservative tradition, with very little experimentation with new plants occurring. Polynesian healers claim that their choice of plants used in formulations is therefore ultimately based on efficacy, rather than on other considerations such as the Doctrine of Signatures (the utility of a plant can be deduced from its appearance) as developed in Western folk medicine.

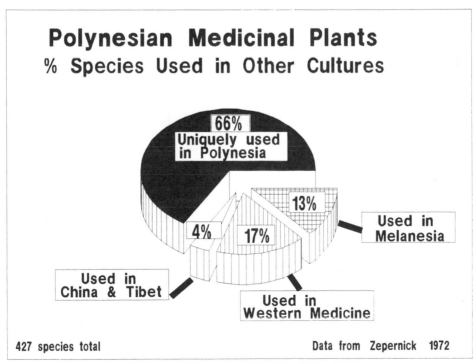

Figure 1. Polynesian Medicinal Plants

There are scientific reasons to believe that the plants used in Polynesian medicine may indeed be efficacious in treating disease. A recent survey of 74 plant species used in Samoan herbal medicine showed that 86 percent demonstrated pharmacological activity in either a broad *in vitro* or *in vivo* screen (Cox et al. 1989). The pharmacological activity of the Samoan ethnopharmacopoeia can also be inferred from different screening techniques. Norton et al. (1973) tested 24 of the same species for pharmacological activity; 63 percent were found to produce significant hypotensive effects in rats.

Plant families prominent in Polynesian healing (based on number of different species used) include Leguminosae, Euphorbiaceae, Polypodiaceae, Compositae, Rubiaceae, Gramineae, Verbenaceae, and Myrtaceae. Examples of individual species that are used widely for medicine throughout Polynesia include *Aleurites moluccana* (Euphorbiaceae), *Artocarpus altilis* (Moraceae), *Calophyllum inophyllum* (Guttiferae), *Casuarina equisetifolia* (Casuarinaceae), *Cocos nucifera* (Palmae), *Colocasia esculenta* (Araceae), *Curcuma longa* (Zingiberaceae), *Gardenia taitensis* (Rubiaceae), *Hibiscus tiliaceus* (Malvaceae), *Morinda citrifolia* (Rubiaceae), *Pandanus tectorius* (Pandanaceae), *Piper methysticum* (Piperaceae), *Premna taitensis* (Verbenaceae), *Solanum nigrum* (Solanaceae), *Syzygium malaccense* (Myrtaceae), *Thespesia populnea* (Malvaceae), and *Zingiber zerumbet* (Zingiberaceae).

Specific botanical details of plants used in Polynesian ethnopharmacology will appear in an upcoming survey of Polynesian herbal medicine by Whistler as well as in my intensive analysis of Samoan herbal medicine, *Samoan Ethnopharmacology: 'O Le Faiga Vai Samoa*. To give an indication of the amount of (or lack of!) ethnobotanical and pharmacological information known about some of these common Polynesian medicinal plants, brief synopses are given of three species. The pharmacological activity of the first species, *Aleurites moluccana*, has been somewhat investigated, while the second species, *Zingiber zerumbet*, has received only cursory attention, and the third species, *Gardenia taitensis*, has not been studied at all by Western pharmacologists and chemists.

Aleurites moluccana (L.) Willd. (Euphorbiaceae)

This large tree of secondary forests was introduced throughout Polynesia during the early Polynesian voyages of discovery (see Whistler, this volume). It has different names in the different Polynesian groups—in Hawaii it is called *kukui*; in Tahiti, Rurutu, and Rimatara *tutui*; in Tonga, Makatea, Uvea, Futuna, Tubuai, and Niue *tuitui*; in Mangareva, *rama*; in the Marquesas, *'ama*; and in Samoa it is called *lama*. The Polynesian roots of all these words mean "light" because, as its English name implies, the candlenut tree was used in ancient times to provide light. The oil derived from the nut was burned by the Hawaiians in stone lamps. In Samoa, the nuts were strung together on the midribs of coconuts and would give light all night to a darkened hut. In fact, the word for nighttime fishing in Samoa is *lama*, because candlenut torches were used in the canoes to provide illumination for spear fishermen.

In Samoa the oil is used in ointments and as a mild purgative. In Tahiti, a water infusion of a mixture of plants including the seeds of *A. moluccana* is given to a child to drink as a remedy for urethritis. A boiled extraction of a mixture of plants, including the grated bark of *A. moluccana,* is bathed in daily for hemorrhoids (Grepin and Grepin 1984). In the Cook Islands, a medicine made from the crushed seeds, formulated with grated limestone, is used in a massage for *tui*—an ear infection oozing pus—and *tui kai roro*—severe headache, sometimes with nausea and high temperature (possibly meningitis) (Whistler 1985). In Tahiti the nuts are used in medicines for the same ailment (Whistler 1985). In Hawaii the leaves were used for poultices for deep contusions and swellings (Handy et al. 1934).

Aleurites moluccana is used medicinally in regions outside of Polynesia as well. In New Guinea the oil is used as a contraceptive (Holdsworth 1977). In Indonesia the bark is used to treat dysentery and thrush (De Clercq 1927). In Malaysia the pulped kernels or boiled leaves were applied to treat headaches, ulcers, and swollen joints (Burkill and Haniff 1930). In the Philippines the fresh leaves are used as a treatment for rheumatism and the seeds are considered mildly purgative (Guerrero 1921; Quisumbing 1951). However, Soriano (1940) reported that they must be used in small doses, as accidents have occurred in their use as treatment for cholera. The fresh, oiled leaves are indicated as a treatment for rheumatism. Fruits, thrown into rivers, are said to stupefy fish.

As with many other Polynesian medicinal plants, *A. moluccana* has other uses as well. An indelible dye made from the seeds is used to color mats and bark cloth, and was used in tattooing. The beautiful polished seeds are strung together throughout Polynesia to make lovely leis. The candlenut trees themselves are beautiful and strong, with fragrant white flowers. Indeed, their scientific name, *Aleurites,* is the Greek word for "flowery." Today, the candlenut tree is the state tree of Hawaii because of "the multiplicity of its uses to the ancient Hawaiians for light, fuel, medicine, dye, and ornament, as well as the distinctive beauty of its light-green foliage which embellishes many of the slopes of our beloved mountains" (Neal 1965, 506).

Broad pharmacological screens show *A. moluccana* to be pharmacologically active (Cox et al. 1989). Chemical analyses indicate a variety of active compounds (Duke 1985). Contact with the latex can cause acute dermatitis, as part of the tree contains a saponin and phytotoxin. Symptoms from eating the seeds are severe stomach pain, vomiting, diarrhea, debility, slowed breathing, poor reflexes, and possibly death. Toxic components include quercitrin, rutin, and saponin (Duke 1985). The oil cake, containing approximately 46.2 percent protein, 4.4 percent P_2O_5 and 2.0 percent K_2O, is said to be poisonous. A toxalbumin and HCN have been suggested. Extracts from the dried seeds exhibit antitumor activity in the P388 mouse leukemia cell line (Ferrigni et al. 1982). Several different triterpenes and steroids have been isolated from *A. moluccana* seeds, and currently the oil from the seeds is being commercially extracted and used in the cosmetic and natural pharmaceutical industries.

Zingiber zerumbet (L.) Smith. (Zingiberaceae)

Zingiber zerumbet is a small, perennial, herbaceous plant with fragrant inflorescences borne terminally on leafless shoots arising directly from the subterranean rhizome. Within the succulent inflorescence, numerous delicate, white flowers are borne in the axils of red bracts. In Samoa, it is called *'ava pui*; in Hawaii, *'awapuhi*; in the Marquesas, *kokpuhi*; in Raivavae, *opuhi*; in Tahiti, *rea moru*; in the Cook Islands, *kopi'enua*; and in Tonga, *angoango*. The fluid from the inflorescence has been traditionally used throughout Polynesia as a hair balm; this use continues in modern-day Samoa.

In Tonga, the rhizomes of *Z. zerumbet* are used for a variety of ailments of the mouth, including *pala ngutu* (sores of the mouth), *pala fefie* (oral thrush), *kiaotolu nifo* (swollen gums) (Bloomfield 1986; George 1989), and for *kahi* (internal blockage) (Singh et al. 1984; George 1989), while the grated bark was used in an infusion to treat infertility (Singh et al. 1984). In Samoa, it is formulated with the macerated stems of *Homalanthus acuminatus* to treat *tulita* (abdominal distress). In the Cook Islands, the rhizome is used internally or rubbed onto hemorrhoids and prolapsed rectums (Whistler 1985). In Fiji (Singh et al. 1984) and Hawaii (Oliveros and Cantoria 1982) the rhizome was used in an oral infusion for coughs and colds.

The rhizome of *Z. zerumbet* was also used medicinally in other parts of Oceania and southeast Asia. Stopp (1962) reported that the rhizome is used in New Guinea for burns or cuts and for toothache. In Indonesia the rhizomes are considered as a stimulant to the mucous membrane of the stomach and bowels, and to externally relieve pain (Van Steenis 1953), while in the Philippines, the pulverized rhizome is administered as antidiarrheic (Guerrero 1921). In the Philippines a decoction is given to treat asthma, and applied as an embrocation for rheumatism (Quisumbing 1951). In Indo-China the rhizome, macerated in alcohol, is regarded as a tonic, stimulant, and depurant, and is administered for postpartum illness; the rhizome is also applied to the head of children in convulsions (Menaut 1929) and to the head and stomach of feverish children; it also is a component in suppositories to treat constipation of babies (Vidal 1959). In China, the rhizome pounded with other spices is ingested to relieve stomachache (How et al. 1956).

Pharmacological analyses of extracts of *Z. zerumbet* show the rhizomes to be cytotoxic (Matthes et al. 1980) and antibacterial but not mutagenic (Ungsurungsie at al. 1982). A number of monoterpenes and sesquiterpenes have been isolated from the rhizomes (Matthes et al. 1980; Oliveros and Cantoria 1982).

Gardenia taitensis de Candolle (Rubiaceae)

Gardenia taitensis is a large shrub or small tree with pleasant-scented, pale white flowers and dark green foliage. In Tahiti, Hawaii, the Marquesas, and the Cook Islands it is called *tiare,* while in Tonga it is called *siale tonga,* and in Samoa it is called *pua samoa.* The flowers are used to scent coconut oil throughout the Pacific.

In Samoa, it has numerous uses. The sterile fluid from unopened flowers is used to treat eye infections. The leaves are used to treat *mumu tatau* (high fevers and paralysis of limbs in infants) while the bark is used for *ila fa'au tama* (birthmarks). Kramer (1903) also recorded that the leaves were used to regulate menstruation.

Gardenia taitensis is used medicinally throughout Polynesia. In Tubuai, the floral buds are used to treat inflammation of the urogenital tract, and the meristems are used to treat inflammation of the urogenital tract and testicular swelling due to gonorrhea, as well as pain or irritation in the chest (Zepernick 1972). In Tahiti the floral buds are used to treat abscesses, and an infusion of the flowers is used for certain headaches. In Niue the roots are used to treat headache (Yuncker 1943). In Tonga, bark infusions are used to treat morning sickness in pregnant women and hallucinations (Weiner 1971). It is also used medicinally in Tokelau (Whistler 1988). Despite indications of its usefulness, no pharmacological or phytochemical analyses have been made of this species.

Similar analyses could be provided for many other medicinal plants, some of which show promise of yielding new and important pharmaceutical compounds. An example is *Homalanthus acuminatus* (Euphorbiaceae) in Samoa, which has yielded a phorbol ester that exhibits anti-AIDS activity *in vitro* (Gustaffson et al. 1990).

Although Polynesian herbal remedies may one day yield new pharmaceutical compounds to Western medicine, in a traditional context they usually are administered internally as water or oil infusions, or externally through massage with coconut oil. Some remedies are administered as eye, nose, or ear drops or introduced into the vagina, while others are inhaled in steam baths, or in the smoke from their combustion. In some remedies for infants, smoke from the combustion of the plant is actually blown onto the afflicted area.

Although some Polynesian medicinal plants are used singly, it is much more common for them to be administered as mixtures. The precise formulations, often known as *vai* or a cognate, are considered proprietary information. Transcriptions of such formulations appear in Kramer (1903), Hooper (1978, 1985), George (1989), and Cox (1990). Formulations tend to be quite precise on the details of the plants and plant parts to be used. As an example, I here reproduce a remedy told to me by healer Lelea'i Silia, of Falealupo village, Savaii, Western Samoa.

Vai a Tamaiti Mama'i	Remedy for Sick Children
'O le matalafi, lau nonu, moemoe seasea; e fai soa ia lau nonu ma lau matalafi ae faatele lau seasea. Tātā ia mālū ona sui lea i se u'u. Aua le tele le u'u. Ona fusi lea i se ie ma fa'alo'ilo'i i ai le vai i le mata o le ma'i. Aua ne'i nofo to'atasi. E aogā fo'i i le sila'ilagi e fusi ai ta'ele i le sami. Aua le alu to'atasi. O le lau nonu lau u'umi ona	Use *Psychotria insularum*, *Morinda citrifolia*, and very young leaves of *Syzygium corynocarpum*; use the *M. citrifolia* leaves and the *P. insularum* leaves in pairs, but use many more of the *S. corynocarpum* leaves. Pound them until soft and then add them to some coconut oil. Don't use a lot of oil. Wrap them in a cloth and drip the remedy onto the head of the sore. Don't leave the patient alone. This remedy is also useful for boils by wrapping it on [like a plaster] and bathing in the sea. Don't let them go alone. The *S. corynocarpum* to use is

lau. E aoga fo'i i
le matolu o tamaiti.
E milia'i fo'i i le
ma'i so'o se ma'i
lava e aoga i ai.

the one with long leaves. The
remedy is also useful for head
scabs in children. It can be
rubbed on any type of ailment
that it is used for.

Cultural Context of Polynesian Herbal Medicine

In Polynesia there are two domains of healing knowledge. There is a general domain, shared by most individuals, of simple remedies for common maladies. For example, many people working in gardens will use a natural astringent, such as the leaves of *Mikania micrantha,* to treat a superficial wound, and most mothers know of a few herbal remedies, such as an infusion of *Psidium guajava* (Myrtaceae) to treat diarrhea in infants. But within Polynesian societies there are individuals with specialized and extensive knowledge of herbal medicine. Such healers are called *faito'o* in Tonga and Futuna; *tufuga, tohunga, ta'unga,* and *tahu'a* in Tuvalu, Aotearoa, Rarotonga, and Tahiti, respectively; and *kahuna* in Hawaii. Although most do not accept payment for their services (see Parsons 1985 for a summary of healing practices in the Pacific), such individuals are highly valued members of their societies.

The importance of healers in Polynesian societies can be illustrated by examining their role in Samoa. There, healers are called *fōfō,* although four specialties occur:

(1) *Fōfōgau* (bone-setters) deal with sprains, muscle tears, and broken bones. They are almost always men and are in high demand throughout Samoa, particularly in areas where Western remedies are not available.

(2) *Fa'atosaga* are midwives and are always women. Although I do not have detailed statistics, it would be a safe guess that they deliver the majority of children born outside the town areas (see Kinloch 1985a).

(3) *Fōfō* are healers who use massage in therapy. Although most Samoans know some therapeutic massage techniques, they frequently seek the specialized skills of *fōfō.*

(4) *Taulāsea* are herbalists who provide treatment from a pharmacopoeia of nearly 150 species of flowering plants. This is perhaps the most important of the four healing specialties.

Before the introduction of Christianity in 1830, an additional specialty could be found. *Taulā'aitu* or "ghost doctors" dealt with spiritual afflictions (Stair 1897). Some Samoan herbalists still occasionally use "ghost remedies" (*vai aitu*).

Except for *fōfōgau* (bone setters) who are usually men, the majority of Samoan healers are women. Partially as a result, Samoan ethnopharmacology is matrilineal in character. A practicing healer usually first learns her skills by apprenticing with her mother. Sometimes, though, a healer may choose an unrelated girl as an apprentice if the girl shows a particular interest in healing.

The apprenticeships are lengthy, often lasting up to seven years, but very informal in nature. Usually a healer will pick a particular daughter to assist in locating plants, preparing the formulations, or administering the treatment. As the daughter progresses in her apprenticeship, her knowledge of diagnostic techniques and herbal remedies continues to grow (Cox 1990).

The skills of a completely qualified *taulasea* are impressive. A healer usually can diagnose over 200 diseases that she treats with a repertoire of over 120 medicinal plants in 150 formulations. Not only must extensive diagnostic and therapeutic protocols be memorized, but a healer must also assume the role of physician, pharmacist, pharmaceutical manufacturing firm, and botanical explorer. Since only fresh preparations are used in Samoan ethnopharmacology, a healer must make frequent journeys into the forest to search for needed medicinal plants. Formerly, some healers even climbed the interior volcanoes of Savaii to mine sulfur for use in antifungal remedies.

Given the length and difficulty of the apprenticeship and the tremendous responsibilities of a Samoan healer, the lack of compensation or overt cultural recognition for healers is striking. Samoan healers routinely refuse all compensation for their efforts. Healers believe that the plants they use are a gift of God. They fear that if they were to accept payment for their services their remedies would cease to work. Particularly noticeable in the highly stratified Samoan society is the complete absence of respect terms or considerations for healers. Thus, when a village divides a cooked pig, the ribs go to the high chiefs, the loins are given to the village orators, the head is presented to the untitled men, and so forth, but no portion is reserved for the healers.

Healers participate in the aspects of village life that their regular status (such as being the wife of a high chief) would ordinarily afford them. Since they receive no payment from their vocation, most healers support themselves (as do most Samoans) through traditional subsistence agriculture and reef foraging. Truly, Samoan ethnopharmacology is a labor of love.

Polynesian healers can be found even in expatriate populations far from their island homes. Samoan healers, for example, can be found in Auckland, Honolulu, Los Angeles, and San Francisco. Practicing herbal medicine far from their plant sources obviously creates some difficulty in obtaining ethnobotanical materials, but the frequent air travel of modern Polynesians tends to alleviate this problem. As a Samoan healer residing in Honolulu told me,

> There really isn't much of a problem. If I need a plant indigenous to Samoa, I merely telephone my family in Samoa. They send a kid out in the forest to find the plant and then ask somebody at the airport (in Samoa) to slip it in their bag. I get it the next morning.

Polynesian herbalism in general is suffering a decline. Indeed, with the increasing Westernization of Polynesia, most of the plant lore discussed in this book is rapidly disappearing. Ethnopharmacology appears to be particularly vulnerable. Training in Polynesian ethnopharmacology is lengthy and offers little prospect of financial reward to young people in the increasingly monetized cultures of Polynesia. Western educational systems do little to affirm the value of traditional knowledge systems, and overt hostility from Western medical practitioners may have also deterred some from learning or practicing Polynesian herbal medicine.

Yet a few farsighted programs, such as collaborations between Western psychiatrists and traditional healers in the treatment of expatriate Polynesians in New

Zealand (Kinloch 1985b), promise to utilize traditional healing knowledge in modern contexts. Other signs of cooperation emerge, particularly since the World Health Organization (WHO) began emphasizing the use of traditional medicine in the primary health care schemes of developing countries. Partially as a result of this WHO initiative, the Western Samoan government has provided short courses in Western medical practices to traditional midwives (Kinloch 1985a). The study of traditional Polynesian plant remedies with the tools of modern pharmacology and structural chemistry promises to provide scientific confirmation of the pharmacological activity of many Polynesian medicinal plants (Cox et al. 1989).

Origins of Polynesian Herbalism

Many Pacific anthropologists assume that Polynesian herbal medicine did not exist prior to European contact. In making this assertion they are on firm scholastic ground, because the earliest written accounts, particularly those by missionaries, appear to discount the existence of Polynesian herbalism. Thus, to argue that Polynesian herbalism was practiced in precontact times requires an explanation of not only the silence of the early Christian missionaries on Polynesian herbalism, but also of their denigration of Polynesian ethnomedicine in general. In addition to explaining missionary accounts, any argument for the existence of precontact Polynesian ethnopharmacology should also include positive evidence for its practice. These two requirements make it difficult to argue for precontact Polynesian herbalism, yet I suggest that a careful consideration of the evidence indicates that Polynesian herbal medicine existed long before any European first set foot in Polynesia.

The question of antecedents to Polynesian ethnopharmacology is not merely of anthropological interest. The indigenous pharmacopoeia of Polynesia would be of much greater interest to Western medicine if Polynesian ethnopharmacology proved to be of prehistoric invention and if this tradition proved to be conservative, in the sense that the same plant taxa had been used for generations.

Why then did early missionaries discount the existence of Polynesian herbal medicine? For example, John Stair, a missionary in Samoa from 1838 to 1845, dismissed the possibility of an indigenous ethnopharmacological tradition while emphasizing native beliefs in sorcery and witchcraft:

> Although they had much sickness, their remedies were few, and for the most part unreliable, notwithstanding the fact that the flora of the group included many medicinal plants and herbs of much value. In case of sickness, where the family could afford it, recourse was had to sorcery. The *Taulāaitu*, or anchor of the god, was summoned that he might intercede with the particular deity he represented to help them in their calamity . . . Of native doctors, strictly speaking, the best obtainable were the Tongan doctors, many of whom were found on Samoa. These men had a much better knowledge of the native herbs and plants than the Samoans themselves. Still there were many Samoans who followed this particular employment (Stair 1897, 164–165).

Missing from Stair's account is a description of "the many Samoans who followed this particular employment." Who were they, what plants did they use, and how did they use them? Stair is silent on these points of quintessential interest to an ethnobotanist. Yet, conversely, Stair's subsequent account of Samoan spiritualism is replete with detail. Why would Stair and other missionaries gloss over the existence of Polynesian herbalists yet detail the practices of "sorcery"? I suggest his and other missionary accounts are lacking in details on Polynesian herbalism because (1) spirit possessions and religious healings were of high saliency to the early missionaries, and (2) the missionaries usually lacked the botanical experience and linguistic ability to deal with a difficult topic such as indigenous herbal traditions.

The early missionaries viewed their proselytizing efforts as direct warfare against Satan and were looking for evidences of Satanic power and mischief. Certain Polynesian cultural practices, such as propitiation to pagan deities on behalf of sick persons or possession by evil spirits, were of high saliency to the Christian missionaries since these events had direct bearing on the evangelical vocation. It should be of no surprise, then, that the missionaries paid a good deal of attention to any healing practices involving the supernatural and ignored the indigenous pharmacopoeia. The use of medicinal plants had little bearing on the Christian profession, and thus was of low saliency to the missionaries.

When early European visitors did find evidence of herbalism, they discounted it and suggested that it had been learned from other quarters. Stair (1897) and Turner (1861) both suggested that Samoan knowledge of medicinal plants came from Tongans or Hawaiians resident in Samoa. However, Ellis (1826) in Hawaii discounted the existence of Hawaiian herbalism and William Mariner (1817) in Tonga asserted that all Tongan herbalism came from Fiji. It seems that each missionary sincerely believed that his own group of Polynesians was too savage to have invented its own ethnomedicinal tradition.

For example, Stair's view of Samoan medicine relying on the supernatural while lacking a significant ethnopharmacological tradition was perhaps influenced by his own personal experience with *aitu* or evil spirits. He discussed at length (Stair 1897, 260–270) the actions of evil spirits in his Samoan residence, as evidenced by noises in the hallway, unexplained crashes at the front door, bells mysteriously ringing, stones bombarding the roof in the middle of the night, and so forth, quoting Ephesians 6:12:

> For we wrestle not against flesh and blood, but against principalities, against powers, against the rulers of the darkness of this world, against spiritual wickedness in high places.

The possession of a heathen nation by evil spirits was precisely what the missionaries had expected to encounter. They did not expect to encounter a highly sophisticated society with a complex and intricate system of herbal medicine, nor did they look for one.

Some missionaries may have had an additional reason for ignoring or denigrating indigenous herbal medicine. To increase interest in his missionary labors, and as a humanitarian gesture, Turner began to manufacture and dispense to Samoans his own medicinal powders and preparations:

Whether I would or not, I was obliged to turn out "Graham's Domestic Medicine" and become *head doctor* of the district. Day after day I had twenty, thirty, or fifty calls for advice and medicine. I appointed an hour, morning and afternoon, for the purpose, and, by making a small charge of something useful to the servants, such as a hank of cinet [*sic*], or a few taro roots, for a dose of medicine, I was able to keep the rush and inconvenience within bounds (Turner 1861, 113).

The practice of dispensing medicines spread among the missionaries and was widespread in 1866, as documented by Thomas Trood, whose father was British Consul in Apia:

In those days the missionaries, as far as they knew, supplied the public with medical comforts and medical advice... The missionaries gave out liberally many other medicines besides salts, properly insisting on the natives making a fit return in fowls and vegetables, &c., but not cash (Trood 1912, 65).

Eventually this practice met with disfavor among visiting Europeans. For example, A. B. Steinberger, who visited Samoa a decade later wrote:

The missionaries dispense medicine to their people. This is a grave error. Excepting Dr. Turner, of Apia, none are regularly-trained physicians. They adhere to the old school of practice, and ignorantly dispense blue-mass, gray powders, calomel, and other preparations of mercury, while Dover's powders, podophyllum, preparations of arsenic, &c. are freely given. I foresee in this reckless issuance of drugs no little mischief in the future, as mercurial diseases must certainly develop themselves unless it is abandoned (Steinberger 1876, 33).

If, as I argue, the Polynesians did have consistent systems of ethnopharmacology, why did they embrace the medicines introduced by the missionaries? Simply because European contact introduced far more than religious changes into Polynesian culture; it also introduced highly virulent diseases. Polynesians died by the thousands from introduced diseases. In New Zealand the Maoris told stories of a *pakeha* disease, *rewa-rewa*, that spread through the North Island, killing many thousands (Crosby 1987). In Hawaii, thousands died from a disease they called *okuu*. Sadly, the introduced diseases demonstrated not the deficiency of Polynesian herbalism, but rather the deficiency of Polynesian immune systems, long-isolated from the diseases and plagues of Europe.

The early missionaries did not have the botanical training or linguistic ability to investigate indigenous medicinal plant uses. It is interesting that very few Polynesian names for forest plants are found in missionary accounts. Is this evidence that Polynesian plant names and ethnotaxonomies were also a post-European development? It is interesting that as soon as botanically trained observers arrived in Polynesia, accounts began to appear of Polynesian herbal medicine. Thomas Powell, a Fellow of the Linnean Society of London, published a list of Samoan plants in 1868. Seventeen of these he noted as having pharmacological value (Powell 1868). Franz Reinecke, together with Augustin Kramer (1903), published extensive lists of Samoan medicinal plants. I therefore suggest that the relative paucity of accounts of Polynesian herbalism by early missionaries should be viewed as an artifact of their training as well as their expectations and should not be seen as evidence that Polynesian ethnopharmacology did not exist at all.

Is there any positive evidence for the existence of Polynesian herbal medicine in precontact times? Unfortunately, since Polynesian pharmaceuticals are generally formulated from soft plant tissues, its practice leaves few material remains that could be used in an archeological sense to verify its existence. Perhaps the only durable goods its practice requires are the pounding stones and blocks used to macerate the plants, yet even their presence yields few clues since they are also used to pound *kava* or taro.

However, I suggest that the practice of Polynesian herbal medicine in precontact times can be adduced from ethnohistorical evidence. First, the large similarities between methods of medicinal plant preparation, usage, and delivery systems between different Polynesian groups are striking. Why should healers in Tonga, Samoa, and Tahiti use similar words for plant remedies and have similar concepts of plant ownership protecting not proprietary rights (as in Europe) but the efficacy of the remedy? Second, why would remedies differ from family to family, with some families being known as always producing gifted healers? Would not a European-introduced tradition have been diffuse throughout the society? Third, why do Polynesians themselves believe their herbal traditions to be indigenous? I have yet to meet a healer anywhere in Polynesia who believes that Polynesian herbalism is an introduced tradition. Ethnohistorical accounts are quite detailed as to introductions of plants and plant technologies from other areas (e.g., the fine mats came from this island, *kava* came from that). More recent events, such as the introduction of new icthyotoxic plants by Polynesian missionaries to Melanesia (Cox 1979), are recounted in Polynesian oral traditions. Why would herbal medicine be universally claimed as an indigenous tradition if it was not? Fourth, the number of plant species in the Polynesian ethnopharmacopoeia that are indigenous to Polynesia is striking. Zepernick's data (Fig. 1) indicate that 66 percent of the medicinal plants used in Polynesia were not used for medicine anywhere else. How could the early European missionaries and explorers have taught the Polynesians how to use such plants?

We know from ethnobotanical studies in other parts of the world that nearly every culture known has developed an ethnopharmacological tradition and a repertoire of medicinal plants. Why should the Polynesians be any different?

I argue that Polynesian herbalism was an important component of early Polynesian cultures and that there is some evidence that it perhaps descended from an earlier tradition brought by the first Polynesians to their new homelands. Surely people bright enough to discover plant fish poisons (Cox 1979), selectively choose *kava* cultivars for their specific pharmacological activity (see Lebot, this volume), and develop anaerobic pit fermentation into a major scheme for food preservation during times of warfare and famine (Cox 1980a, 1980b) were also clever enough to discover the plants in their local floras that could be used in medicine. The wealth of ethnopharmacological information that the Polynesians have to bequeath us may not only eventually alter opinions about their ability to discover and use the indigenous plants of their island environments, but may also ultimately enrich the pharmacopoeias of Western medicine.

Literature Cited

Bloomfield, S. F. 1986. *"It Is Health We Want": A Conceptual View of Traditional and Non-Traditional Health Practices in Tonga With Special Emphasis on Maternal Child Health and Family Planning.* M.A. Thesis, Univ. of the South Pacific School of Social Economic Development, Suva, Fiji.

Burkill, I. H., and M. Haniff. 1930. Malay village medicine. *Garden Bul. Straits Settl.* 6:165–321.

Chambers, A., and K. S. Chambers. 1985. Illness and healing in Nanumea, Tuvalu. In *Healing Practices in the South Pacific.* Ed. C. D. F. Parsons. Laie, Hawaii: Institute of Polynesian Studies. 16–50.

Chun, M. N. 1986. *Hawaiian Medicine Book: He Buke Laau Lapaau.* Honolulu: Bess Press.

Cox, P. A. 1979. Use of indigenous plants as fish poisons in Samoa. *Econ. Bot.* 33:397–399.

———. 1980a. Masi and tanu 'eli: two Polynesian technologies for breadfruit and banana preservation. *Pac. Trop. Bot. Garden Bul.* 4:81–93.

———. 1980b. Two Samoan technologies for breadfruit and banana preservation. *Econ. Bot.* 34(2):181–185.

———. 1990. Samoan ethnopharmacology. In *Economic and Medicinal Plant Research.* Vol. 4, *Plants and Traditional Medicine.* Eds. H. Wagner and N. R. Farnsworth. London: Academic Press.

Cox, P. A., L. R. Sperry, M. Tuominen, and L. Bohlin. 1989. Pharmacological activity of the Samoan ethnopharmacopoeia. *Econ. Bot.* 43:487–497.

Crosby, A. 1987. *Ecological Imperialism and the Biological Expansion of Europe.* Austin: Univ. of Texas Press.

De Clercq, F. S. A. 1927. *Nieuw plantkundig woordenboek voor Neder,landsch-Indie.* Amsterdam: Tweede, hierzene en vermeerderede druk bewerkt door A. Pulle.

Duke, J. A. 1985. *A Handbook of Medicinal Herbs.* Boca Raton, Florida: CRC Press.

Ellis, W. 1826. *Narrative of a Tour Through Hawaii, or Owhyhee; with Remarks on the History, Traditions, Manners, Customs, and Language of the Inhabitants of the Sandwich Islands.* London: H. Fisher, Son, and P. Jackson.

Feinberg, R. 1979. Anutan concepts of disease: a Polynesian study. Publication Institute of Polynesian Studies 3:1–51.

Ferrigni, N. R., J. E. Putnam, L. B. Jacobsen, D. E. Nichols, D. S. Moore, J. L. McLaughlin, R. G. Powell, and J. R. Smith. 1982. Modification and evaluation of the potato disc assay and antitumor screening of Euphorbiaceae seeds. *J. Nat. Prod.* 45:679–686.

Feyerabend, P. 1978. *Science in a Free Society.* London: NLB.

George, L. M. 1989. *Tongan Herbal Medicine.* M.S. Thesis, Brigham Young Univ., Provo, Utah.

Grepin, F., and M. Grepin. 1984. *La Médecine Tahitienne Traditionnelle.* Papeete, Tahiti: Les Editions du Pacifique.

Guerrero, L. Ma. 1921. Medicinal uses of Philippine plants. In *Minor Products of Philippine Forests.* Ed. W. H. Brown. Philippine Bur. For. Bul. 22(3): 149–246.

Gustaffson, K., J. Cardellina, O. Weislow, J. Beutler, J. McMahon, J. Ishitoya, N. Sharkey, P. Blumberg, P. Cox, G. Cragg, and M. Boyd. 1990. Prostratin, an AIDS-antiviral agent from the Samoan medicinal plant *Homalanthus acuminatus. J. Biol. Chemistry.*

Handy, E. S. C., M. K. Pukui, and K. Livermore, eds. 1934. Outline of Hawaiian physical therapeutics. Bernice P. Bishop Mus. Bul. 126.

Holdsworth, D. K. 1977. Medicinal plants of Papua New Guinea. S. Pac. Comm. Tech. Paper 175.

Hooper, A. 1978. Tahitian Folk Medicine. In *Rank and Status in Polynesia and Melanesia.* Publication Société Océanistes 39:61–80.

———. 1985. Tahitian healing. In *Healing Practices in the South Pacific.* Ed. C. D. F. Parsons. Laie, Hawaii: Institute of Polynesian Studies. 158–198.

How, F. C., chief ed. (and 15 others). 1956. *Flora of Canton.* Trans. T. S. Wei. South China Branch, Bot. Inst. Acad. Sinica, Canton.

Kinloch, P. 1985a. Midwives and midwifery in Western Samoa. In *Healing Practices in the South Pacific*. Ed. C. D. F. Parsons. Laie, Hawaii: Institute of Polynesian Studies. 199–212.

———. 1985b. *Talking Health But Doing Sickness. Studies in Samoan Health*. Wellington: Victoria Univ. Press.

Kirch, P. V. 1991. Polynesian agricultural systems. In *Islands, Plants, and Polynesians*. Eds. P. A. Cox and S. A. Banack. Portland, Oregon: Timber Press, Dioscorides Press.

Kramer, A. 1903. *Die Samoa-Inseln*. II Band. *Ethnographie*. Stuttgart: E. Nagele.

Kuhn, T. S. 1962. *The Structure of Scientific Revolutions*. Chicago: Univ. of Chicago Press.

Lebot, V. 1991. Kava (*Piper methysticum* Forst. f.): the Polynesian dispersal of an Oceanian plant. In *Islands, Plants, and Polynesians*. Eds. P. A. Cox and S. A. Banack. Portland, Oregon: Timber Press, Dioscorides Press.

Mariner, W. 1817. *An Account of the Natives of the Tongan Islands Compiled by John Martin*. 2 vols. London: Constable and Company.

Matthes, H. W. D., B. Luu, and G. Durisson. 1980. Chemistry and biochemistry of Chinese drugs. Part 6, Cytotoxic components of *Zingiber zerumbet* and *Curcuma zedoaria*. *Phytochemistry* 19:2643–2650.

Menaut, B. 1929. Matière medicale cambodgienne. 1, Les drogues usuelles. Bul. Econ. Indochine 32:197–276.

Moyle, R. M. 1974. Samoan medicinal incantations. *J. Polynesian Society* 83:155–179.

Neal, M. C. 1934. Plants used medicinally. In *Outline of Hawaiian Physical Therapeutics*. Eds. E. S. C. Handy, M. K. Pukui, and K. Livermore. Bernice P. Bishop Mus. Bul. 126:39–49.

———. 1965. In Gardens of Hawaii. Bernice P. Bishop Mus. Special Publication 50:1–924.

Norton, T. R., M. L. Bristol, G. W. Read, O. A. Bushnell, M. Kashiwagi, C. M. Okinaga, and C. S. Oda. 1973. Pharmacological evaluation of medicinal plants from Western Samoa. *J. Pharm. Sci.* 62:1077–1082.

Oliveros, M. B., and M. C. Cantoria. 1982. Pharmacognostic studies on *Zingiber zerumbet* (Linne) Smith and its proposed variety (Zingiberaceae). *J. Crude Drug Research* 20:99–123.

Parsons, C. D. F. 1985. Tongan healing practices. In *Healing Practices in the South Pacific*. Ed. C. D. F. Parsons. Laie, Hawaii: Institute of Polynesian Studies. 213–234.

Powell, T. 1868. On various Samoan plants and their venacular names. *J. Bot.* 6:278–285, 342–347, 355–370.

Quisumbing, M. 1951. Medicinal plants of the Philippines. Dept. Agr. Nat. Resources, Tech. Bul. Manila. 16:1–1234.

Reid, J. 1983. *Sorcerers and Healing Spirits*. Canberra: Australian National Univ. Press.

Roggeveen, J. 1771–1772. *Journal*. Ed. A. Sharp. Oxford: Clarendon Press.

Singh, Y. N., T. Ikahihifo, M. Panuve, and C. Slatter. 1984. Folk medicine in Tonga. A study on the use of herbal medicines for obstetric and gynecological conditions and disorders. *J. Ethnopharmacology* 12:305–329.

Soriano, A. L. 1940. Herbolario practices. *Revista Filip. Med. Farm.* 31:229–235.

Spencer, D. M. 1941. *Disease, Religion, and Society in the Fiji Islands*. Seattle: Univ. of Washington Press.

Stair, J. B. 1897. *Old Samoa*. London: Religious Tract Society.

Steinberger, A. B. 1876. Message from the President of the United States. 44th Congress, House of Representatives, Executive Document 161:1–125.

Stopp, K. 1962. The medicinal plants used by the Mt. Hagen people (Mbowamb) in New Guinea. *Econ. Bot.* 17:16–22.

Trood, T. 1912. *Island Reminisces*. Sydney: McCarron, Stewart, and Co.

Turner, G. 1861. *Nineteen Years in Polynesia*. London: John Snow.

Ungsurungsie, M., O. Suthienkul, and C. Paovalo. 1982. Mutagenicity screening of popular Thai spices. *Food Cosmet. Toxicol.* 20:527–530.

Van Steenis, M. J. 1953. Select Indonesian medicinal plants. Organiz. Sci. Res. Indonesia, Bul. no. 18:1–90.

Vidal, J. 1959. Les plantes utiles du Laos. *J. Agr. Trop. Bot. Appl.* 7:417–440.

Weiner, M. A. 1971. Ethnomedicine in Tonga. *Econ. Bot.* 25:423–450.

Whistler, W. A. 1985. Traditional and herbal medicine in the Cook Islands. *J. Ethnopharmacology* 13:239–280.

———. 1988. Ethnobotany of Tokelau: the plants, their Tokelau names, and their uses. *Econ. Bot.* 42(2):155–176.

———. 1991. Polynesian plant introductions. In *Islands, Plants, and Polynesians.* Eds. P. A. Cox and S. A. Banack. Portland, Oregon: Timber Press, Dioscorides Press.

Yuncker, T. G. 1943. The flora of Niue island. Bernice P. Bishop Mus. Bul. 178.

Zepernick, B. 1972. *Arzneipflanzen der Polynesier.* Berlin: Verlag von Deitrich Reimer.

CHAPTER 9

Kava
(Piper methysticum *Forst. f.*):
The Polynesian Dispersal
of an Oceanian Plant

VINCENT LEBOT

Laboratoire de Botanique Tropicale
Université des Sciences
163 rue A. Broussonnet
34000 Montpellier, France

Starting with their very first observations, scientists have tried to understand how indigenous Polynesian populations found the key to "artificial paradises" as the plant species usually cultivated as recreational drugs were not present in the Pacific (i.e., *Cannabis indica, Erythroxylon coca, Datura* spp., *Papaver somniferum*). However, early European explorers observed the use of a species unknown to them: *kava* (*Piper methysticum* Forst. f., Piperaceae) (see Fig. 1). Melanesians, Micronesians, and Polynesians alike grind the fresh or dry roots of this shrub to prepare their traditional beverage. In terms of the cultural role it performs, *kava* is to a large part of the Pacific what wine is to southern Europe. *Kava* has always played a special part in the history of Pacific societies and is today enjoying a resurgence of popularity with the Oceanic peoples, who are anxious to assert their cultural identity. By pharmacological standards, *kava* is not classified as a drug, as its consumption never leads to addiction or dependency. It has psychoactive properties but is neither an hallucinogenic nor a stupefacient. Experimental studies have shown that *P. methysticum* contains active ingredients called kavalactones, with diuretic, soporific, anticonvulsant, spasmolytic, local anesthetic, and antimycotic properties. *Kava* has been classified as a narcotic and a hypnotic (Schultes and Hofmann 1979), and this helps to understand the atmosphere of sociability felt when drinking it.

Dr. Lebot's present address: Department of Horticulture, University of Hawaii, 3190 Maile Way, Honolulu, Hawaii 92822

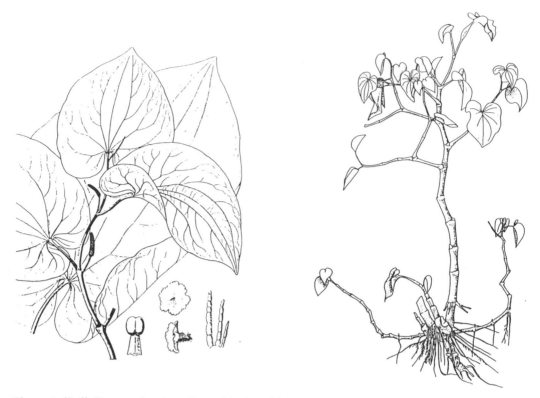

Figure 1. (*Left*) *Piper methysticum* Forst. f (original from Benjamin De Lessert, 1837); (*Right*) plant appearance (original from Lebot and Cabalion, 1986)

In this paper, I intend to review the ethnobotanical data about *kava* and to discuss the problem of its surprising distribution. As *P. methysticum* is always propagated vegetatively, the identification of its area of origin should help clarify the question of cultivars' diversity and sources. Kava might then serve as an indicator of Pacific populations' migrations.

Botanical Aspects

Parkinson sailed with Cook on his first voyage aboard the *Endeavour* (1768–1771). He was certainly the first scientist to take an interest in *kava*, which he observed for the first time in Tahiti (Parkinson 1773). During his second voyage from 1771 to 1775, Cook was accompanied on the *Resolution* by two German botanists employed by the British Admiralty: J. R. Forster and his son, Johann Georg Adam Forster. The first description of *kava* is credited to J. G. A. Forster, who named it *Piper methysticum* (1786) or "intoxicating pepper," *methysticum* being the Latin transcription of the Greek *methustikos*, which is derived from *methu*, meaning "intoxicating drink" (Barrau 1957; Steinmetz 1960).

Piper methysticum is an elegant shrub measuring from one meter to over four meters in height, depending upon the cultivar. It is a hardy, slow-growing perennial. When it reaches maturity, the plant looks like a bouquet of ligneous stems clustered together at the base. The leaves are thin, single, heart-shaped, alternate, and petiolate. The inflorescence, opposite the leaves, is a spadix typical of the Piperaceae. The flowers are sessile and have neither calyx nor corolla. The species is dioecious; the male flowers with their stamens are therefore found on one plant and the female flowers with their pistils on another (Lebot and Cabalion 1986).

None of the collected specimens of *P. methysticum* existing in the largest herbaria has seeds. Female plants are uncommon. Botanists agree that the sex ratio is unbalanced and several authors have stated that they have never seen any female flowers (De Lessert 1837; Degener 1940; Hänsel 1968). Among publications dealing with *kava*, only two give descriptions of seeds (Baker and Baker 1936; Guillaumin 1938). Close inspection of the specimens described, however, has confirmed that the fruits are from *Macropiper latifolium* Forst. f. (Lebot et al. 1986). When hand-pollinated, female inflorescences fall off before producing fruits. Growers in the Pacific islands are unanimous in stating that no seeds have ever been seen on a cultivar.

There is a wealth of variation in chromosome numbers in the genus *Piper*, both between and within species. Ploidy levels are based predominantly on $x = 13$. Recent work conducted on *Piper methysticum* (Lebot 1988, unpublished data) has shown that this species has a somatic complement of $2n = 130$. This is the first time that a decaploid has been recorded in this genus. Such a high ploidy level could explain the sterility phenomenon in *P. methysticum*.

Origin of Kava

Several botanists have discussed the origin of *kava* (Degener 1940; Yuncker 1959; Smith 1981; Lebot and Cabalion 1986; Lebot and Lévesque 1989). Among the related species are three endemic to Papua New Guinea, the Solomon Islands, and Vanuatu: *Piper wichmannii* C. DC., *P. gibbilimbum* C. DC., and *P. plagiophyllum* K. Schum. & Lauterb. The wild source is almost certainly *P. wichmanni* C. DC. (Lebot et al. 1986). This species is endemic to New Guinea, the Solomon Islands, and the northern part of Vanuatu. No significant difference has been found between *P. methysticum* and *P. wichmannii* in either male or female flowers. These two species have similar growth patterns and morphological features. The major morphological difference is the inflorescence length, which is always longer for *P. wichmannii*. However, variability in inflorescence length for cultivars of *P. methysticum* is also observed. On the other hand, anatomically, the roots of *P. wichmannii* are more ligneous, and chemically the composition is rather different, although the active ingredients are identical. *Piper wichmannii* and *P. methysticum* are the only *Piper* species from which kavalactones have been isolated (Saüer and Hänsel 1967; Sengupta and Ray 1987; Lebot and Lévesque 1989). Based on personal field observations, I believe *P. methysticum* should not be considered as a different species but rather as a group of sterile cultivars selected from wild forms of *P. wichmannii* (Chew Wee-Lek, per. com. 1986; Lebot and Lévesque 1989).

In Vanuatu, oral tradition on the myth of *kava*'s origin seems to indicate that the ancestors of the present inhabitants used *P. wichmannii* to prepare the beverage. On the island of Pentecost, roots of both *P. wichmannii* and *P.*

methysticum are mixed, the former being used as a "stretcher," when there is not enough of the best cultivars for a feast. In local tradition, *P. wichmannii* is believed to be the *kava* used by the forefathers (Lebot et al. 1986).

When farmers select a cultivated species from a wild source, they select for characteristics which are important to them. The new plant often bears little likeness to the original one as the domestication purpose is to adapt the wild form to meet with the needs of people. For *kava,* morphological characters are less important than chemical characters. Therefore, it is not surprising that the cultivated species has a phenotype similar to that of the wild.

Area of Distribution

A review of more than 240 specimens scattered in 19 of the largest herbaria in the world (Lebot and Lévesque 1989) indicated that *P. methysticum* has been collected: in Micronesia Pohnpei (Ponape), and Kosrae; in Polynesia Oahu, Molokai, Kauai, Maui, Hawaii, Nuku Hiva, Fatu Hiva, Uapou, Raiatea, Tahiti, Mangaia, Rarotonga, Aitutaki, Niue, Upolu, Savaii, Tau, Tutuila, Tongatapu, Vava'u, Eua, Wallis, Futuna, and Alofi; and in Melanesia—Vanua Levu, Viti Levu, Vanua Balavu, Lakeba, Rewa, Tanna, Anatom, and Pentecost. Only 13 specimens of *P. methysticum* have come from Papua New Guinea, and 3 from Irian Jaya (on the southern border with New Guinea). One hundred and eleven specimens of *P. wichmannii* have been collected, all from Papua New Guinea, the Solomons, and Vanuatu.

The information gained from the collected specimens, coupled with the bibliography and my own field trips in more than 49 islands of the Pacific, resulted in the identification of the past and present areas of distribution (Fig. 2). This area was much wider before the arrival of Europeans. During the colonial period, the religious and secular authorities tried to stamp out *kava* drinking on hygienic grounds or because of its association with paganism. These taboos were responsible for its disappearance from several islands, especially from the Marquesas, the Society Islands, the Cooks, and Niue. Its western limit is Irian Jaya while the eastern boundary is Hawaii and the Marquesas. It has never been collected in Indonesia, the Philippines, or South America.

Kava was drunk throughout Polynesia before the European arrival, except on the flat coral atolls where the plant could not grow due to ecological reasons. Most certainly, *kava* has been introduced to all the islands reached by the Polynesians during their migrations. In New Zealand, the climate was, of course, too cold, but it is suspected that the Maoris gave the name *kawa-kawa* to *Macropiper excelsum* in memory of the plants they most certainly introduced and attempted to cultivate. In the Austral islands, the people of Tubuai drank *kava* but its consumption was abolished by missionaries after their arrival. There are no accounts of *kava* consumption on Rapa, Easter Island, the Chatham Islands, Kiribati, and the Tuvalu Islands.

Bougainville did not record *kava* in Tahiti, but provided a list of other cultivars (1772). Ferdon (1981) stated that *kava* was "certainly the last introduced plant into Tahiti. . . . The active diffusion east towards Tahiti was still going on as

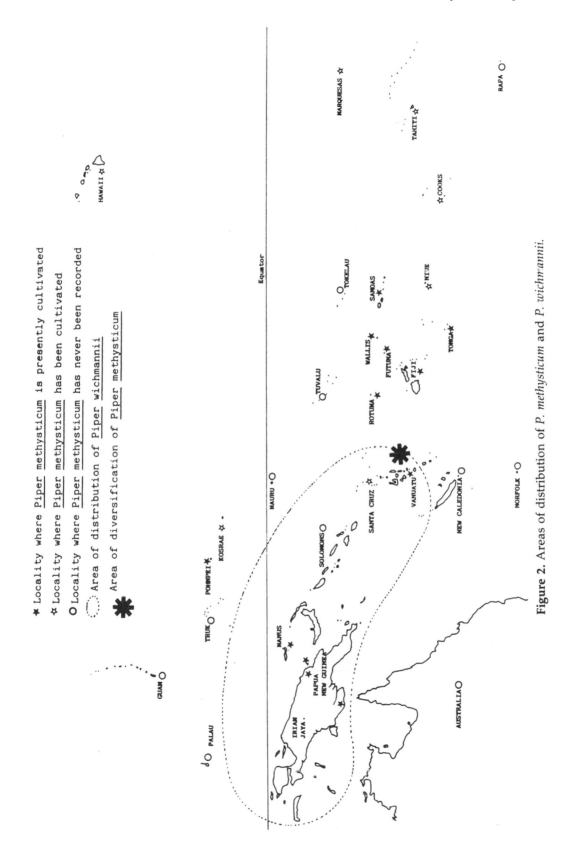

★ Locality where <u>Piper methysticum</u> is presently cultivated

☆ Locality where <u>Piper methysticum</u> has been cultivated

○ Locality where <u>Piper methysticum</u> has never been recorded

⬭ Area of distribution of <u>Piper wichmannii</u>

✳ Area of diversification of <u>Piper methysticum</u>

Figure 2. Areas of distribution of *P. methysticum* and *P. wichmannii.*

late as 1774–1775." Ferdon referred to a chief of one Tahiti district as not having a single plant, whereas two years later large *kava* fields were planted. This statement is surprising, because *kava* was most certainly one of the first plants that aboriginal voyagers would have taken with them (Smith 1981), and it would indicate that at one stage *kava* may have been abandoned in one Tahitian area, and that *kava* drinking had had a much wider distribution, but that a number of people had subsequently given it up. Either *kava* was abandoned at one stage, and later reintroduced just before the European era, or else there was a time in Tahiti when drastic steps were taken to restrict access to *kava,* possibly even to the extent of preventing it from being planted in some areas.

The same can be said for Hawaii, where *kava* consumption was at one stage restricted to certain people. This situation can be partly explained by a shortage of planting material, which occurs quite often today in Tonga, for example. When supply can easily meet demand, there is no need to excessively ritualize consumption. If, upon the arrival of the Polynesians to their islands, *kava* production was low, consumption may have been restricted to important occasions, but as the stock of planting material increased, consumption spread to everybody. According to Titcomb (1948), in very early Hawaiian history *awa* was drunk by chiefs or people of high social rank and never by commoners, probably because the plant was rare. However, by the beginning of the nineteenth century, there was enough for everyone and *awa* was drunk by all social classes.

The distribution of *kava* consumption outside Polynesia is very scattered and puzzling (Fig. 2). In Micronesia, the consumption of *kava* was restricted to the eastern Carolines, Kosrae, and Pohnpei, where *kava* is known as *Sakau. Kava* was unknown to the people of Guam, Palau, and Truk. Although one specimen was gathered on Palau in 1929 (Kanehira no. 453), and on Guam in 1818, Stafford (1905) observed that *kava* was unknown to the local people. The reported sighting could have been an early misidentification of *Macropiper guahamense* C. DC. (Smith 1975). According to Glassman (1952), there is no definite information concerning when and how *kava* was introduced in Pohnpei, but it is obvious that it came from either Polynesia or Melanesia. When considering possible transmission routes, it is interesting to notice similarities between preparation techniques, and ceremonial as well as linguistic affinities of the materials used for it. In Pohnpei and Baluan, Admiralty Islands, the cultural elements associated with *kava* drinking indicate a relationship with Vanuatu rather than with Polynesia (Brunton 1987). As Pohnpei and Baluan are the only islands in the Pacific where *kava* is prepared by pounding the fresh roots on a large, flat basalt slab, and because in Pohnpei the word *sakau* sounds like the word *kau* used by the people of Baluan for *kava,* there is strong evidence that *kava* was introduced to Micronesia from Melanesia.

In Kosrae, before the drink was banned by the missionaries in 1828, *kava* was called *seka* (Glassman 1952). This name also seems to be of Melanesian origin as *kava* is called *sika* and *saka* in parts of the Western Province of Papua New Guinea (Brunton 1987). Importation from New Guinea seems more feasible. This theory's plausibility is confirmed by the great distances the central and eastern Pacific navigators would have had to sail with cuttings on board between Polynesia and Kosrae or Pohnpei in Micronesia. Furthermore, most of the islands located on the route between the *kava*-cultivating areas of Polynesia and Micronesia are atolls unsuitable for *kava* cultivation. The Admiralty Islands were probably the area of greatest consumption in Papua New Guinea. *Kava* was used on Lou, Baluan, Pam, the Fedarb Islands and Rambutyo. All were said, or known, to have had large flat stones used to pound the *kava*. On Lou, the last remaining plants were killed because the population was converted to the Seventh Day Adventist church (H. MacEldowney, per. com.1986, Anthropology Dept., A.N.U., Canberra). Baluan is the only part of Manus province where *kava* is still used, although not very often. In the Admiralties, the cultural aspects of *kava* drinking suggest a closer relationship with Pohnpei than with the northern coast of New Guinea. *Kava* is pounded on a flat stone in Baluan and Pohnpei but chewed in New Guinea, the process of preparing the drink is also very similar.

The people of Karkar and Bagabag islands used *kava* traditionally but those from the latter no longer drink it. People in a few villages of Maclay coast and around Madang do still drink it. Mickloucho-Maclay saw *kava* being prepared in Astrolabe Bay in 1872; thus, it was present before European contact. But maybe on that occasion the *kava* referred to was *Piper wichmannii*. Mickloucho-Maclay (1886) himself stated that he was not sure whether the plant named *keu* used to prepare an intoxicating drink was really *P. methysticum*. When he sent samples for identification he received ". . . a note from Dr. Scheffer with the statement that the *keu* bundles contained two different species of *Piper*, both of which were different from the *Piper methysticum*" (Mickloucho-Maclay 1886). This is not surprising as today, in the small island of Baluan, farmers are cultivating several plants of *P. wichmannii* for their personal consumption and consider it as *kava* on the same basis as their two cultivars of *P. methysticum*.

In New Guinea, the major *kava*-drinking region covers a large part of the Western Province with an extension into Irian Jaya. Williams (1940) observed that, in the Lake Kutubu area, only two plants of *P. methysticum* were known before World War II. Crawford (1981) explained that a *sika* cult existed in the village of Isago, not far from Balimo, in defiance of the mission there. Brunton (unpublished data 1987) has compiled the vernacular names used for *kava* in Papua New Guinea and observed several affinities within this geographical area, suggesting internal exchanges of planting material. A linguistic approach to the question of the origin of *kava* in the Western Province would indicate that the plant is indigenous, since the languages of this region are Papuan (or non-Austronesian) languages (Terrell 1986), which, in spite of their proximity, do not show any evidence of having borrowed from each other with respect to the plant name, each identifying it with a different lexeme. Such an approach is, however, not conclusive. It is also important to mention that most of these names simply mean "roots," implying that the plant and its use were introduced, because it is referred to by the name of its useful part rather than by any vernacular name of its own (Anthropology Dept., Unitech, Lae, per. com. 1987).

E. E. Henty, who spent nearly 20 years as the curator of the Lae Herbarium believes

> it arrived in the Maclay area by direct introduction rather than diffusion . . . There are no early records of *P. methysticum* in the western district. This was a very isolated area and was made so by the Asmats, the dangers

of navigation in Torres Straight and the hostility of the local people. When missionary work began, earlier this century, "catechists" or "lay readers," were recruited, trained in Tonga and Fiji, and were employed. It is possible that one of them took a root to Daru or one of the other stations (Henty, per. com. 1988).

Serpenti (1965) felt *kava* was introduced into the western area after the Dutch government had established its presence on the island. In Papua New Guinea, *P. methysticum* is always very localized and situated on the coastal area. Therefore, there is very strong evidence, based on field observations, that *P. methysticum* has been recently introduced in few places through human's interference (Lebot and Lévesque 1989).

According to Whitmore (1966) no sample of *P. methysticum* has been collected in the Solomon Islands. However, the presence of *kava* has been reported a number of times in the Polynesian outliers of the Santa Cruz Islands: Vanikoro, Tikopia, and Utupua (Rivers 1914; Firth 1954). When Kirch and Yen (1982) visited Tikopia, they observed:

> *Kava* has now become extinct, with only a wild form *kavakava atua*, (kava-diminutive-spirit), remaining that cannot, according to informants, be used for preparation (although it has been identified as *P. methysticum* by Solomon Islands and Bishop Museum botanists . . .).

Brown (1935) mentioned that the word for *Macropiper latifolium* in the Marquesas is *kavakava atua*. According to a dictionary of the *Are are* language of Malaita, the word *kakawa* concerns a tree whose roots are sucked to produce intoxication, and D. Brass recorded that the local name for *Piper wichmannii* in the southeast part of Santa Isabel was *kava qwua* (R. Brunton, per. com. 1987), but in Guadalcanal it is called *kwakwako* (Lebot, field obs. 1987).

In Vanuatu, although there were significant differences in the traditional *kava* ritual, it was of great importance everywhere except for Ambrym and parts of Malekula and Santo. All the inhabitants of this archipelago claim to have drunk *kava* and continue this usage today. There is no controversy about the traditional use of *kava* throughout Fiji where it is known as *yaqona*. *Kava* was never cultivated in New Caledonia as it does not seem to flourish there.

As the presence of *kava* always seems to result from human's involvement, a linguistic approach makes it possible to define two main zones, one in Polynesia and southern Vanuatu where the plant is called *kava,* and the other in northern Vanuatu, Fiji, New Guinea, and Pohnpei where it has Melanesian generic names. The most common name, *kava,* most certainly derives from the Polynesian word *ava,* meaning "bitter" and "inebriating drink" (Steinmetz 1960). In the southern islands of Vanuatu, especially on the islands of Tanna, Anatom, and Futuna, *kava* could have been introduced, along with its generic name and rituals. Bonnemaison (1985) stated that Tongan navigators' visits were not uncommon as they came to take women in southern Vanuatu. This may be why the local name for *kava* in the vernacular languages of Tanna is *kava,* the same word as used in Tonga.

Myths and Legends

In Vanuatu, a northern legend from the island of Maewo has it that

A very long time ago, orphan twins, a brother and sister, lived happily on Maewo. One night, the boy, who loved his sister very much, had to protect her from a stranger who had asked to marry her but whom she had refused. In the struggle the frustrated suitor loosed an arrow which struck the boy's sister and killed her. In despair, the brother brought his sister's body home, dug her a grave and buried her. After a week, before any weeds had grown over her tomb, there appeared a plant of unusual appearance which he had never seen. It had risen alone on the grave. He decided not to pull it up. A year passed and the sorrowful boy had still not been able to quell the suffering he felt at his sister's death. Often he went to mourn by her grave. One day, he saw a rat gnaw at the plant's roots and die. His immediate impulse was to end his own life by eating large amounts of these roots, but instead of dying he forgot all his unhappiness. So he came back often to eat the magic root and taught its use to others. (Recorded by Lebot, February 1984, at Loltong, Pentecost Island, cited in Lebot and Cabalion 1986).

Another legend, this time from the south, explains the origin of *kava* differently:

Long ago the islanders drank only one sort of *kava*, the wild *kava*. Then, one day, a Futunese woman was peeling yams alone by the seaside. As she crouched in the water, an evil spirit took advantage of her posture to slip a magic pebble into her vagina. When she realized it was there, she pulled it out and looked at it. She was intrigued to find that it was slender and covered with knots and buds and decided to take it back to the village. (According to Chief Siaka of Henamanu Village, Tanna, May 1982, recorded by Lebot, and cited in Lebot and Cabalion 1986).

Bonnemaison (1985) reports another interesting local myth. The first canoes arrived from the north carrying with them yam, taro, breadfruit, and banana. These plants were sent by the god of the gardens, Mwatiktiki. Later, another canoe arrived from the southeast, sent by the god Karapanemum, and brought the pig, *kava*, and the magic stones. According to legends, *kava* is of local origin in the northern part of Vanuatu, but has been introduced in the southern part of this archipelago.

In Fiji, on the island of Vanua Levu, legend has it that *kava* appeared on the grave of Prince Ranggona who had died a short time previously, perpetuating his memory with the name *Yanggona* (*Yaqona*) (Hocart 1952, cited in Sterly 1970).

In Western Samoa, a local legend from Fagaloa Bay on Upolu Island reports that

kava first came to Samoans through Tagaloa, the first *Matai* or chief. Tagaloa had two sons, Ava and Sa'a. As Ava lay dying, he murmured to Sa'a that from his grave would come a plant of great value to the Samoan people. Ava died and was buried. Sa'a and his children watched the grave and on the third day after Ava's burial, two plants were seen growing from the head of his grave. As Sa'a and the children watched, a rat came and ate the first plant. It then moved to the second one and began to eat, but quickly became intoxicated. The rat went staggering home as the people watched in astonishment. They named the first plant *Tolo* or sugarcane, and the second *Ava* in honor of the man from whom it sprung. (Recorded by Lebot, in Fagaloa Bay, May 1987).

In Tonga, Gatty (1956) reports a legend very similar to those of Vanuatu, Fiji and Samoa:

[O]n the Island of Euaiki, the chief Loau recognized human flesh at a meal and told the people not to eat it—it should be planted in the ground and brought to him when it matured into a plant . . . the body grew up into a *kava* plant arising from different parts of the body. And when it matured he noticed that a rat chewed on the *kava* and became paralysed.

French navy pharmacist Cuzent (1856) did not mention any legend or myth relating to *kava* origin in Tahiti and the Marquesas. In Hawaii, Titcomb (1948) recorded a legend giving credit to Oilikukaheana for first bringing forth *kava*. This author refers to a statement by Fornander (1919) to the effect that on Oahu

Ewa had the courage to test its effect . . . Ewa said: "Let me first eat of this plant, and should I die, do not plant it, for it would be valueless; but should I not die, then we will be rich" . . . When Ewa ate it, she became drunk and was intoxicated all day, then she awoke she called this plant Awa; from thence forward this plant was called Awa, the Awa from Kaumakahea, the chief.

According to Gatty (1956), oral tradition in Hawaii has it that *kava* was introduced from Tahiti and first planted on Oahu, but Titcomb (1948) suggests many points of introduction in the archipelago.

In Pohnpei, local tradition has it that *kava* was first introduced from the island of Kosrae by a woman who brought it secretly (Lebot's record, August 1987). According to Ashby (1987)

[I]n one legend, the discovery of *sakau* is attributed to a rat seen nibbling a root and acting quite intoxicated. In another legend, more detailed, the original is traced to Pohnpeian god Luk. The skin of a heel of a mortal man, Uitannar, was given by Luk to a woman in payment for her kindness. She was told to bury the skin and a plant would grow in its place. The juice of the plant would make people intoxicated and change their lives. This was done and the *sakau* plant was later spread throughout Pohnpei.

According to the Marind-Amin of the Western Province of Papua New Guinea, *kava* came from a devil-stork whose spindly legs were thought to resemble the knotty stems of the plant (Nevermann 1938, cited in Sterly 1970). In the center of Papua New Guinea, near Lake Kutubu, *kava* is said to have come out of the ground, where Waki, the "underground-man," lived. Other versions have the "big-man Sagainya" or Tokorabu reappearing from beneath the ground in the form of *kava* (Williams 1940, cited in Sterly 1970).

In the places where the origin of *kava* has a mythical explanation, it is likely that the plant was introduced or its use developed at some stage. Explanations abound in these legends, attributing *kava* origin to gods, to spirits of the dead, or even to animals, such as the pig in New Guinea and the rat in Fiji, Samoa, and Tonga (Risenfeld 1950; Gatty 1956; Sterly 1970) and Vanuatu (Lebot and Cabalion 1986). There is a factual basis for these myths, because rats and pigs have often been seen chewing *kava* roots and are not repelled by the smell (Lebot, field obs.). It is also interesting to observe that in these remote islands, separated by thousand of miles of ocean and inhabited by three ethnic groups with different customs and cultures, a similar theme recurs in nearly all these myths and legends: *kava* comes from a body buried in the ground, a rat is first observed chewing the root, and a woman is often associated with the discovery. According to Wodzicki (1979), rats often play an important role in Polynesian mythology. The Polynesian rat, *Rattus exulans* Peale, was introduced in the Pacific from southeast Asia during the first migrations (Wodzicki 1979). It is, however, doubtful that this myth can have a factual basis in Polynesia; a rat could not be seen chewing the roots of a cultivated plant that could not be known to the Polynesian, as *kava* dispersal is due to human intervention. The hypothesis of a rat being observed chewing the roots of a wild species seems more likely in Melanesia where *Piper wichmannii* occurs. Whatever the case may be, even if these legends do not provide a reliable explanation, they all seem to share a common origin. It is likely that the myths and legends were introduced with the plant by Polynesian migrants and they fall in line with the idea of a Melanesian origin of *kava*.

Methods of Preparation

Kava receives the tender care growers lavish on their traditional crops. Most authors describe *kava* as a traditional crop suited to existing agricultural systems and highly flexible in cultivation. Local techniques have been developed which aimed at improving the yield or appearance of the root system. On the island of Tanna, *kava* is planted in the hollowed-out trunk of a tree fern that is placed vertically and filled up with organic matter (Fig. 3A). The roots obtained from such a technique are protected from nematodes and the surface is whiter and smoother than that of ordinary *kava*. In Maewo, several cultivars are known to have high water requirements and are therefore planted on the ridges of the irrigated taro terraces. Once planted this way, they contribute to the terraces' maintenance (Fig. 3B). In Savaii, Western Samoa, where lava takes time to disintegrate into fine soil, *kava* is often cultivated in pits filled up with organic matter (Fig. 3C). In the Western Province of Papua New Guinea, farmers claim that their plants never reach two years, and have to be tended; if not, they die. *Kava* is therefore planted in beds under sago palm leaves (*Metroxylon sago*) (Fig. 3D).

Generally, a plant is rarely uprooted before it is 2 or 3 years old. In some countries it is consumed fresh, as in Pohnpei, Papua New Guinea, Vanuatu, Wallis, and Futuna; in others it is consumed after drying, as in Fiji, Samoa, and Tonga. The basal stems, stumps, and roots comprise a multitude of ligneous fibers as well as over 50 percent starch. Around the center of the pith, which consists of starch cells, are layers of vascular and ligneous tissue which alternate with small cells also filled

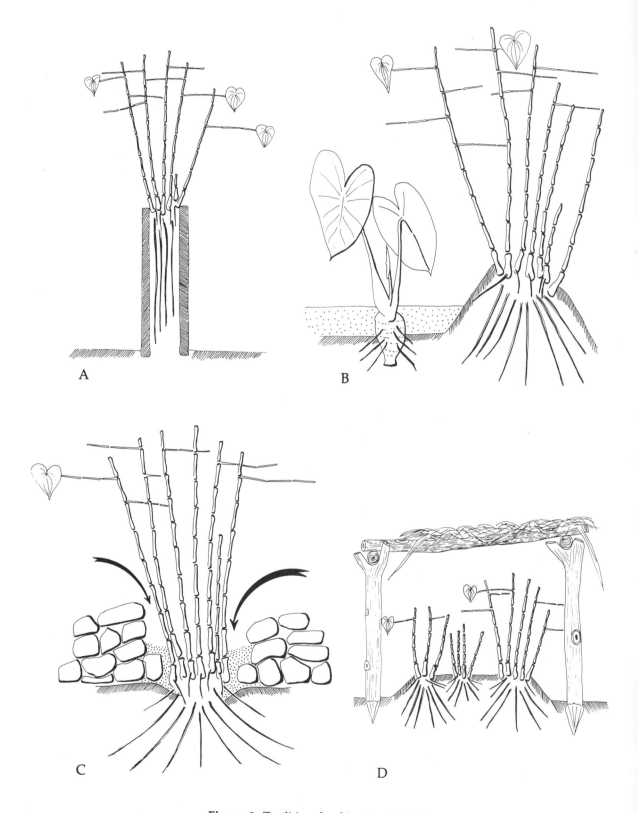

Figure 3. Traditional cultivation techniques.

up with starch. Such a substance, of course, cannot be consumed without further preparation. There are two methods of preparation, depending on whether fresh or dried roots are used. The principle applied is very simple and remarkably efficient in allowing easy extraction of the chemical constituents by either chewing or grinding, followed by maceration. Today, mastication of the fresh roots is practiced only in the southern and central parts of Vanuatu and in the Western Province of New Guinea. This method was very widespread in Polynesia and Fiji at the beginning of the pre-European era, but was abandoned under the influence of the missionaries, who considered the practice unhygienic. Nowadays, *kava* is prepared in these countries by maceration of the fresh or dry root.

In Pohnpei, *sakau* was traditionally a drink reserved for the elite, but its use is now widespread among all levels of people. It is the focal point of almost all ceremonies, and is also consumed nightly in private gatherings. It is prepared by pounding roots and then squeezing the material through a filter made of the inner layers of *Hibiscus tiliaceus* bark into half a coconut shell. This is a procedure also reported in various Polynesian islands, but no longer practiced. When prepared this way, *kava* takes on a very slimy consistency due to the mucilage existing in the bark of *H. tiliaceus*. The coconut shell is passed round in order of rank, both men and women drinking from the same shell (such a mixing of the sexes being unique in the Pacific).

In the Western Province of Papua New Guinea, the Gogodola prepare the drink by masticating the roots, and spitting the contents of the mouth into a coconut shell. When all shells are full, their contents are strained through a coconut stipule into a common bowl from which each person's shell is refilled. The drinkers quickly swallow the *kava* before having a meal of sago and fish. Shaw (1985) reported the use of *kava* among the Samo of the Nomad River area, where it is called *oyo*. He made a very interesting statement on the preparation:

> [T]he brew is made by mixing palm leaf ash with the masticated *Piper methysticum*. Nowhere else has the mixing of ash been reported in conjunction with the preparation of *kava*. But throughout the Nomad area this practice is necessary as people maintain that by itself the root is too strong, bitter and unpalatable.

According to Lawrence (1984), the Garia who live in the mountains just north of Usino, in Madang province, refer to *kava* in pidgin English as *koniak* and in their own language as *isa*. The Garia prepare *kava* for funerals and the dead person's relatives consume about half a coconut shell before bearing the body to the grave. Informants claimed that it had a toxic effect, and this seems to be borne out by the fact that, after the funeral, those who drank it immediately fell asleep (Lawrence 1984).

In Tonga, at the beginning of the last century, the old and young roots, once pared, were cut into pieces which could be held in the mouth (Beaglehole 1941). In Fiji, they were ground on a stone and were then masticated by men or women, but especially by young boys and girls with strong jaws. They chewed until they were exhausted, and the drinkers were vigilant that none was swallowed. Water was added and the mixture was then strained through the fiber of the stipule of coconut leaves which acted as a filter and was called *fau* in Samoa (Kramer 1903).

This task was performed by a young girl, preferably the village virgin or *taupou*, who had been "purified" for the ceremony by washing her hands and wrists (Steinmetz 1960). According to Kramer (1903), the ceremony, which was very strict in Samoa, required that the girl should sit cross-legged on a mat, bare-breasted, with flowers carefully arranged in her hair and her hips swathed in a grass skirt, thus representing an image of beauty which was supposed to attenuate the impression left by the beverage preparation. However, in most Pacific islands the ceremony in which young boys and girls were obliged to chew *kava* has been outlawed. In Hawaii a law was passed in the 1850s forbidding *kava* consumption without medical control or advice, but it was not strictly enforced.

In Wallis and Futuna, Samoa, and Tonga, *kava* is prepared mainly by scraping the stump and then grinding it between two stones, one of which is a small stone with a concave top. The ceremony begins as soon as water is poured on the ground *kava,* but this differs greatly from island to island. When the water has been left long enough to permeate the *kava,* the plant residue is extracted from the mixture. Each guest attending the ceremony drinks from a common cup formed from half a coconut shell.

In Futunese society (Gaillot 1962), as in Samoa, *kava* is a symbol of forgiveness. Custom requires that the person offended or injured be offered a *kava* root, the offender thereby obtaining pardon.

The method of preparation by mastication has also disappeared on Futuna, after a missionary in 1930 introduced the grinding technique. The Futunese ceremony was always performed in the presence of a master of ceremonies who directed the stages of preparation and decided whether the *kava* was as it should be or too strong.

As in Fiji, Samoa, and Tonga, the beverage, which in the past was prepared by mastication, was drunk only by adult men and formed a rite which was an integral part of religious and social life. Drinking *kava* is important during feasts; it is a sign of hospitality whose ritual varies enormously from one culture to another. To drink *kava* is therefore more a rite than an act of "debauchery." In Hawaii, every social class drank *kava* to relax. Royalty drank it as a mark of hospitality and for pleasure, the *kahuna* (priests) for ritual and esoteric purposes, and the under-privileged class for well-deserved relaxation after work (Handy 1940). *Kava* was used in central Polynesia to produce a "serene state of mind." On the island of Uea, Fiji, whose culture is similar to that of Samoa, *kava* was deliberately drunk to stimulate inspiration (Handy 1927). The Tongans considered this drink as beneficial for healthy people but not advisable for the sick. They usually drank it in moderation, claiming that a man addicted to *kava* became weak and lazy, and encountered family problems through "neglect of his responsibilities" (Beaglehole 1941).

Effects Felt by Kava *Drinkers*

Different attitudes towards *kava* drinking may affect the responses to ingestion of the beverage. Those who expect or desire an intoxicating effect are more likely to experience it. When the beverage is not too concentrated drinkers attain a state of happy unconcern, well-being, and contentment. They feel relaxed and free of any physical or psychological excitement. At the beginning, conversation flows gently and easily; hearing and vision are also improved, allowing subtle sounds and shades to be perceived. Drinkers remain masters of their conscience and reason because *kava* is not a central nervous system depressant but acts on the spinal system. The beverage soothes temperaments and drinkers never become angry, unpleasant, noisy, or quarrelsome. *Kava* is considered as a means of easing moral discomfort and killing anxiety. In many cases, it helps thought processes and solves the problems of everyday life as drinkers can talk to each other without any nervous tension. The following day, drinkers awaken in excellent shape, having fully recovered their physical and mental capacities, except with some cultivars known as "two-day *kava*" that have a more lasting effect (Lebot and Cabalion 1986).

However, when consumption is excessive, drinkers suffer from photophobia and diplopia. In some cases, temporary oculomotor paralysis occurs. Muscles no longer respond to the control of the mind, walking becomes unsteady, and drinkers look inebriated. They feel the need to sleep and in some cases they can be found prostrate at the place where they have drunk. Of course, these effects are highly correlated with the chemical composition of the cultivar used to prepare the drink; as different "vintages" occur, their effects differ.

Nevertheless, one deleterious side effect brought on by the heavy consumption of *kava* is skin lesions and drying up of the epidermis, producing an advanced exanthema whose urticarial patches produce intense itching. Such reactions are only found in heavy drinkers and can be attributed to *kava*'s active ingredients, the kavalactones. These are related to sesquiterpenical lactones which are severe allergens that can attach themselves to the skin proteins. These skin lesions, called *kani kani* in Fiji, disappear as soon as the amounts of *kava* consumed are reduced. Their occurrence is, in fact, very uncommon. They afflict drinkers who are prone to allergies, and are due to the chemical composition of a few well-identified and undesirable cultivars.

The situation is sad in Australia where some Aborigines are consuming abusive amounts of *kava*. Mathews et al. (1988) have studied the effects of heavy usage of *kava* in Arnhem Land. It is obvious that there is a clear preference for *kava* over alcohol as it does not produce violent behavior. But Mathews et al. have shown that heavy users present general ill-health, are often underweight, and have puffy faces and scaly rashes. The heavy consumption of *kava* in Arnhem Land leads, according to these authors, to effects far different than those of socially regulated, moderate consumption. However, these authors did not specify accurate percentages of active ingredients.

Whichever island, ceremony, or method of preparation is referred to, *kava* was always drunk at dusk and before the meal, never after, probably because of its properties. Lewin (1886) reported that Captain Cook often saw Samoans take several bowls of *kava* during the morning. This report is unusual since Captain Cook never visited Samoa, and today such a habit, except on feast days, would seem illogical. Yet consumption of *kava* in the morning in modern Samoa does occur, particularly during *kava* ceremonies which are usually held in the morning (P. Cox, per. com.).

Kava *as a Ritual Offering*

The Oceanic peoples who are familiar with *kava* hold it in esteem primarily as a ritual offering or a ritualized form of payment. *Kava's* medicinal reputation would appear, at least originally, to be a corollary of its narcotic action and its role in the exchange system between individual and especially between human beings and the gods. Other plants also play the part of a customary gift, but *kava* has acquired a special favor. Such a pre-eminent role over many different plants is believed to be due to its pharmacological properties.

The most frequent use of *kava* is in the form of an essentially ritual and social drink because of its soporific and anxiety-relieving properties. By offering *kava* to the gods and spirits, humans were gaining their goodwill, and by drinking it they could move closer towards the supernatural world. As a present or offering to the gods, ancestors or spirits, *kava* was used as a sign of respect towards them, to obtain their favor, to appease their resentment or anger if due respect had not been shown to them, and, through divination, to communicate with them and to accede to the supernatural world and therefore to the secrets hidden from the mere mortal.

In Hawaii, as a ritual oblation on the family altar, *kava* was offered to the spirits of the ancestors or the gods, such as the "protecting shark" (Handy 1940). In some cases, the gift was made through a medium who imbibed in the name of the called-upon spirit. *Kava* was occasionally given to "clairvoyants" who contemplated it and drank it "in order to produce a desired passiveness or trance" (Handy 1940). For such events it was used as a hypnotic, which is still the case on Tanna, south Vanuatu, with the healers. In this archipelago, people believed that *kava* was a vehicle for communication with ancestral spirits and deities.

As a gift to people, *kava* is still used to seal or to publicly bind an agreement made between two partners. More often, it is simply used as a sign of sociability and as a ritual sign of the sacred character of a place or occasion. In Samoa, *kava* is used as a token of respect, and the arrival of a travelling party is greeted with *lupesina* or very large stumps with attached stems which are not intended for consumption (Cox and O'Rourke 1987). In Fiji, the ceremony called *sevusevu* is an offering from the travelling party and much solemn ritual is included.

Kava *in Traditional Pharmacopoeia and Medicine*

If *kava* was still an unknown plant, all its traditional therapeutic indications would have to be sifted through. Modern medical science tries to find a logical relation between cause and effect in order to apply an etiological or symptomatic remedy, whereas traditional medicine seeks the cause of the illness, primarily in the breaching of taboos, and then treats it with medicines tested empirically. Both often seem to neglect the placebo effect by favoring a supernatural or a rational explanation only. *Kava* is a panacea; Zepernick (1972) noted about 30 syndromes treated with *kava*-based preparations. Several syndromes are enumerated in Table 1. The use of *kava* as an anaesthetic and a galactagogue is reported by Steinmetz (1960). In Fiji, *yaqona* is considered as a powerful diaphoretic (Parham 1939). It is

Table 1. Syndromes Treated With *Kava*

Place	Syndrome	Medication	Source
Pacific Islands	Gonorrhoea and chronic cystitis	The beverage, orally	Steinmetz 1960
Tubuai	Inflammation of the urogenital system	Maceration of young *kava* shoots, orally	Aitken 1930
Hawaii	Difficulties in urinating	Stump	Handy et al. 1934
	Irritation of the urogenital system	Stump	Handy 1940
	Feminine puberty syndromes, weakness	Drinking masticated *kava*	Titcomb 1948
	Menstrual problems, dysmenorrhea	Kava-based medication	Handy 1934
	Painful migraine headache	Drinking masticated *kava*	Titcomb 1948
	Vaginal prolapsus	Maceration of *kava*	Titcomb 1948
	To provoke abortion	*Kava* leaves *in situ*	Handy 1934
	Headaches	Masticated *kava* as a drink or masticated *kava* as such	Handy 1940
	General weakness and sleeping problems	Maceration of masticated *kava* diluted with water and boiled, orally	Titcomb 1948
	Chills and general treatment of diseases	Maceration of *kava*, fumigation with leaves	Titcomb 1948
	To prevent the risk of infection	Drinking masticated *kava*	Handy 1934
	Irritation of the respiratory tracts, asthma and pulmonary pains	Preparation containing the juice	Handy 1940
	Tuberculosis	Medication containing the juice extracted from the stump	Degener 1945
	Leprosy	External application of the juice extracted	Degener 1945
	Skin diseases	Masticated stump in a poultice	Hänsel, et al. 1966
Vanuatu	Intestinal problems	Fresh leaves applied on the skin	Walter per. com. 1988
	Otitis	Juice obtained from fresh leaves, *in situ*	Walter per. com. 1988
	Abscess	Juice obatined from fresh leaves, orally	Walter per. com. 1988
	Urinogenital system infection	Juice obtained from fresh leaves, orally	Walter per. com. 1988
	Cough	Maceration of bark	Walter per. com. 1988

(According to Lebot and Cabalion 1986.)

also consumed by women as a fortifying drink, a laxative, and a diuretic. In pregnancy, the absorption of small quantities of *kava* is said to facilitate delivery. During breast feeding, the absorption of *kava* is thought to favor the production of milk. The absorption of many mouthfuls of *kava* can help clear up the first stage of diarrhea (Thompson 1908; Steinmetz 1960).

The soporific properties of *kava* have been known in Vanuatu for centuries. Garanger (1972) states that during the excavation of the funeral site of Roimata (who reigned over the Shepherd Islands and Efate in the thirteenth century), the position of the servants' and main dignitaries' skeletons reveals that they were probably buried alive in a peaceful attitude. The position of the women, on the contrary, shows a sensation of horror. According to oral tradition, this is explained by the fact that the men buried alive were under the influence of *kava*. The wives, on the other hand, were not allowed this potion and were not under any narcotic effect when buried.

An awareness of *kava*'s traditional reputation and the properties of kavalactones makes it possible to explain most of the above-mentioned indications. This does not apply to women's complaints however. How could *kava*, according to what is known, play a role in hormonally regulated physiological mechanisms? The bactericidal or bacteriostatic activity of kavalactones helps us to understand *kava*'s reputation as a remedy for urogenital infections, but does not leave room for an hormonal explanation. The plant's indications as a contraceptive, abortifacient, or galactagogue, therefore, remain to be verified and explained, maybe by research to identify compounds other than kavalactones.

Active Substances of Kava

Chemical and pharmacological studies have produced a wealth of documentation and many publications. Such research has a dual aim: to identify the active principles responsible for the properties listed above, and to analyze the physiological activities of those ingredients. A number of scientists thought they had found alkaloids among the substances extracted from the roots without succeeding in isolating them. The effect felt on consuming *kava* is so close to the one produced by an extract of coca leaves that the temptation to seek alkaloid structures is easily understandable. However, nitrogen, a component of alkaloids, was absent from the products obtained from the plant. Nonetheless, in 1979 R. M. Smith isolated and identified an alkaloid specific to *kava* which he named pipermethystin; this substance was found only in the plant's leaves. At least in this case, alkaloids are not responsible for the physiological effects of the beverage obtained by grinding the roots.

The skeleton of the lactonic molecules isolated from *kava* consists of 13 carbon atoms, 6 of which form a benzene ring attached by a double bond to a saturated lactone (Fig. 4). A total of 15 compounds has been isolated and fully identified (Hänsel 1968; Lebot and Cabalion 1986; Lebot and Lévesque 1989). Six of these compounds are of major importance: demethoxyyangonin, dihydrokavain, yangonin, kavain, dihydromethysticin, and methysticin. Nine others are of

Figure 4. Elementary structure of kavalactones.

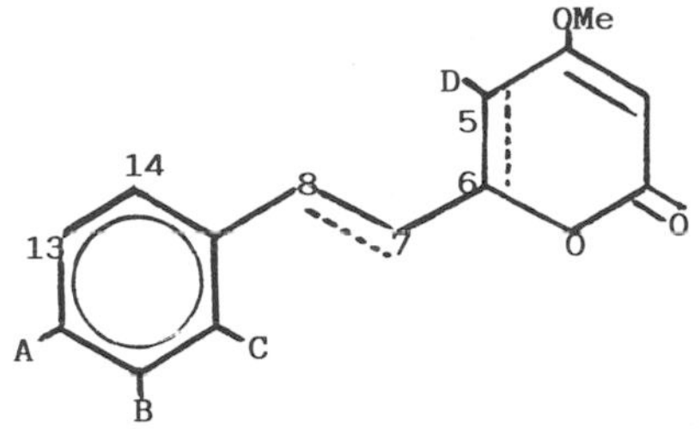

	A	B	C	D	C5–C6	C7–C8
1) Kavain					–	=
2) 7,8-Dihydrokavain					–	–
3) 5,6-Dehydrokavain					=	=
4) Yangonin	OMe				–	=
5) 5,6,7,8-Tetrahydroyangonin	OMe				–	–
6) Methysticin	O–CH2–O				–	=
7) Dihydromethysticin	O–CH2–O				–	–
8) 5,6-Dehydromethysticin	O–CH2–O				=	=
9) 5,6-Dihydroyangonin	OMe				–	=
10) 7,8-Dihydroyangonin	OMe				=	–
11) 10-Methoxyyangonin	OMe		OMe		=	=
12) 11-Methoxyyangonin	OMe	OMe			=	=
13) 11-Hydroxyyangonin	OMe	HO			=	=
14) Hydroxykavain				OH	–	=
15) 11-Methoxy-12-hydroxy-dehydrokavain	OH	OMe			=	=

minor importance (Duve 1981). After Hänsel, Jössang and Molho (1967) tried to explain the formation of kavalactones by two biosynthetic processes, one starting from cinnamic acid and ending up with styrilpyrones like demethoxyyangonin, and the other from the corresponding alcohol to arrive at styrildihydropyrones like kavain. The absence of the latter in the leaves was explained by the immediate reduction of their double bond, 7,8, by ascorbic acid. The most that is known, thanks to R. M. Smith (1983), is that the biogenetic activity is essentially the same in the various parts of the vegetative system and that it leads to different compositions in the stump and the roots.

Kava, like most medicinal plants, contains more than a single active principle. These active substances, often very similar in structure, form in the extract a very complex mixture of elements with often very different activities. Although the synthesis of kavain and methysticin held no more secrets, these substances did not in any way induce the same physiological effect as the natural extract. The latter's activity did not stem from a single substance, but from a mixture, a natural blending of several compounds bringing about a resulting activity. Several constituents are of secondary importance, but most certainly play a role. In fact, each element is so dependent on the presence of the others that the extract used without the slightest alteration gives much better results than any single one of these substances isolated (Steinmetz 1960; Lebot and Caballon 1986; Lebot and Lévesque 1989). The problem is that the composition of these extracts is very variable.

When Hänsel (1968) concluded his studies on *Piper methysticum,* he wondered why *kava* was so little used in modern pharmacopoeia despite its potential, and had to admit that the answer was not clear. The industry has not totally rejected the use of natural extracts of *kava* but has never been able to realize their full potential, no doubt because the production of raw materials has always been inadequate in quantity and quality. In 1975 five allopathic and one homeopathic medicines containing *kava* natural extract were distributed on the French market. Today, the medicines which remain are indicated for a decongestive action in the pelvic area coupled with an antiseptic and sedative effect. In France, for example, Kaviase is produced with a natural extract and is commonly sold in drugstores. In Switzerland Kavaform, containing synthetic kavain, is on the market.

Although *kava*'s physiological properties are very interesting, many laboratories refuse to develop new products due to the variability of composition. This problem was first observed by Keller and Klohs (1963) when they published their review of *kava* chemistry

> No systematic scientific survey appears to have been made as to the relative potency of extracts from various forms of *P. methysticum*. and, since all of the growth forms would most likely not be thought worthy of recognition as separate taxa by plant taxonomists, this area remains one for possible future study and clarification.

Young et al. (1966) stated that the taxonomic value of morphological and chemical relationships in *kava* needed to be shown through subsequent work in this area. Jössang and Molho (1967) confirmed that the variation in composition of the extracts from Fiji was an important point needing clarification. More recently, Duve and Prasad (1981) concluded their quality evaluation by saying that variation in the active constituents of *P. methysticum* with age, cultivars, and environmental factors needed to be studied before chemical standards of *kava* could be formulated.

Cultivars of Kava and Traditional Classifications

Results gained from ethnobotanical studies conducted in 49 Pacific islands have shown a considerable degree of specialization in the use of particular cultivars (Lebot and Lévesque 1989). These are classified according to principles and criteria that vary from island to island but are essentially based on physiological effect, morphology, and order of importance in the exchange system (i.e., according to their social and ritual uses).

Kava always results from cloning. The clone, a community derived from the same individual by vegetative propagation, is genetically homogenous because it corresponds to a single genotype. A single clone may occur as different morphotypes, according to circumstances. (A morphotype is a coded transcription, using morphological descriptors, of a particular phenotype.) The traditional classification of clones amounts to a study of the uniformity of a population produced by vegetative propagation from a single selected individual. Its purpose is to observe interclonal variability and also, where it occurs, intraclonal variability, because that is the point of the departure of a new cultivar. The problem faced by the growers is the judicious choice of the initial individuals, by eliminating unsuitable mutations, if necessary, or by using the favorable mutations (morphological or chemical) as the starting point for new clones.

Figure 5 shows the procedure currently followed by farmers: the plant is first uprooted and the stems left in the hole produced by the harvest of the stump. The beverage is then prepared and farmers judge its physiological effect. If it is pleasant, they go back to this traditional nursery and collect the cuttings, which are then used for propagation. If it is not interesting, they leave the cuttings at their place where they will soon collapse. Therefore, the selection pressure acts each time an individual plant is harvested, following a genealogical procedure based on appraised chemical characteristics. Evolutionary changes in plants involve morphological or chemical changes according to the selection pressures applied. These clones have remained in the same place for a long time and are known by a precise name in the vernacular language. They are most likely the result of local selection carried out by the farmers themselves. The various cultivars possess a set of morphological features which are significant for one island's or one region's farmers and are therefore valid for identification of local cultivars but do not lend themselves to the identification of these same forms in other islands. These features relate principally to the aerial part of the plant and vary greatly according to the environment. The efficiency of local methods of differentiation is reduced when applied outside the original environment; they are significant only for the concerned cultivation area. Similarly, the same cultivar may be classified differently in the ranking order of two islands.

Local cultivars possess a vernacular name in most Pacific island languages. In Vanuatu, cultivar names consist of a "big name" (in Bichelamar, pidgin English), the equivalent of a generic name, followed by a "small name," or the name of the particular cultivar, together forming a binomial, as in the Linnean system. Generally, when speaking of a well-known cultivar or one to which reference has

Figure 5. Traditional nursery.

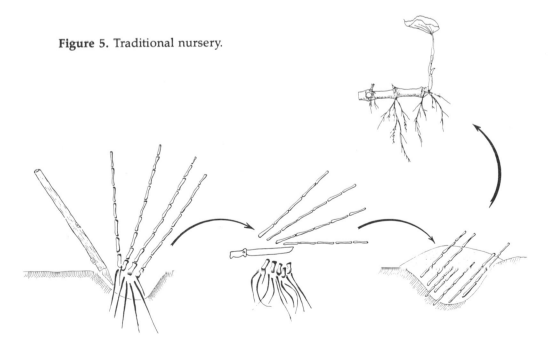

been made in the conversation, and if the "small name" is a long one, the "big name" is not repeated, whereas both names will be used if the "small name" is short. This rule exists in other Pacific countries and is not specific to *kava* or Vanuatu. The vernacular name marks the cultivar's main feature, a legend, or, quite simply, the name of the first person to select that clone. The often brief description given by the grower and the meanings of the vernacular names are a guide in forming theories about name relationships.

In Fiji, Samoa, Tonga, Wallis, and Futuna the cultivar name refers, in most cases, to the plant's morphology. A very simple dichotomous key allows the farmers to describe the cultivar to which they are referring by saying its name. For example, in Fiji, the first character is the stem color which is light (*vula*) or dark (*loa*). The second character used is the shape of the internode which is either long (*balavu*), short (*leka*), or "as thick as a planting stick" (*dokobana*). The cultivar with dark internodes is well known throughout Fiji as *loa kasa leka* (*kasa* meaning "internode"). The one which is light green with long internodes is known as *vula kasa balavu*.

The procedure is similar in Polynesia, but cultivar names referring to myths are more often used, for example, *ava lea* or *ava la'au* in Samoa. In 1860 French navy pharmacist G. Cuzent listed 14 cultivars of *ava* used traditionally by Tahitians. The names and the traditional classification essentially referred to the physiological effect felt by the drinker and the characteristics of the root: color, flavor, hardness, and taste when chewing. This classification is very similar to the one reported by Brown in 1935 and used by the Marquesans to identify their 19 cultivars at that time. However, today this traditional knowledge has disappeared as have most of the cultivars from the Society Islands, the Marquesas, and Hawaii.

Morphotypes

A taxonomy of *kava* cultivars is in itself highly worthwhile, not only because it will help us to clarify some ambiguous ethnographic and historical problems related to synonymy, but especially because it will provide a baseline from which relevant decisions can be formulated towards germplasm conservation. In Vanuatu, for example, 222 vernacular names of cultivars have been recorded (Lebot and Cabalion 1986). However, this figure does not represent 222 morphotypes, because mixing of genetic stock has taken place along the traditional exchange routes. The same is true of other Pacific islands.

In 1986 and 1987 I conducted a survey of the genetic resources of *Piper wichmannii* and *P. methysticum* over the total area of distribution of these two species, collected the wild and cultivated forms, and planted them in germplasm collections (Lebot and Lévesque 1989). I then conducted morphological descriptions of all the accessions to identify accurately these cultivars as well as wild forms. The plants were described by using seven morphological descriptors: the general appearance of the plant (A), stem color (C), internode configuration (I), leaf color (L), lamina edges (E), leaf pubescence (P), and internode shape (S). After coded description was completed, it was possible to differentiate the local cultivars and wild forms in different morphotypes (Tables 2 and 3).

It is beyond doubt that *Piper methysticum* has reached its highest degree of diversification in Vanuatu. This country is probably an area of domestication for wild forms of *P. wichmannii*. In this country, for ecological and socio-cultural reasons, a substantial genetic endowment has evolved. It is a zone of widespread cultivation (23 islands surveyed), where a large part of the gene pool of the species and the cultivars is concentrated (Tables 2 and 3).

In the Cooks, Tahiti, the Marquesas, Hawaii, and Papua New Guinea, *kava* is an endangered species. Only a few plants survived in remote gardens on Mangaia, Cook Islands. My frequent field trips to the valleys of Tahiti ended with the discovery of only 11 scattered plants. In the Marquesas the situation is dramatic as only one cultivar has survived, on the island of Fatu Hiva. In Hawaii, the situation is quite different as it is possible to find groves in remote and lush valleys of Oahu and Maui, where the plant seems to survive with some maintenance from local people who apparently use it for their traditional pharmacopoeia. Even so *kava* is also an endangered species there. The situation is not better in Papua New Guinea. In Maclay Coast, Karkar Island as well as on the small island of Baluan, few plants remain and I took the opportunity during my collecting trips to advise farmers to save and propagate them.

Table 2. Origin of accessions of wild forms of *P. wichmannii* and cultivars of *P. methysticum*, by island group.

Country	Islands Surveyed	Forms Collected		
		Wild	Cultivated	Morphotypes
Vanuatu	23	6	241	82
Fiji	3	—	16	12
Tonga	2	—	7	7
Western Samoa	2	—	6	6
American Samoa	1	—	5	5
Wallis and Futuna	2	—	6	3
Cook	1	—	1	1
Tahiti	1	—	3	3
Marquesas	5	—	1	1
Hawaii	2	—	11	11
Pohnpei	1	—	2	2
New Guinea	5	2	9	7
Solomons	1	2	—	1
Totals	49	10	308	141

Table 3. Classification of the wild and cultivated forms gathered in the Pacific, based on their chemical composition. (Results of cluster analysis using hierarchical agglomerative clustering and Euclidean distance.)

Cultivar	Origin	Chemotype[1]						Morphotype[2]						
		1st	2nd	3rd	4th	5th	6th	A	C	I	L	E	P	S
A														
Vambu*	Vauna Lava	5	2	1	6	3	4	3	2	2	1	2	1	3
Buara*	Maewo	5	2	1	6	3	4	3	2	2	1	2	1	3
Bo*	Pentecost	5	2	1	6	3	4	3	2	2	1	2	1	3
Kau*	Tongoa	5	2	1	3	6	4	3	2	2	1	2	1	3
B														
Bundun*	Morobe	1	6	5	3	2	4	3	2	3	2	2	1	3
Kwakwako*	Gluadalcana	1	5	6	2	3	4	3	2	3	2	2	1	3
Kau Kupwe*	Baluan	1	6	5	3	2	4	3	2	3	2	2	0	3
C														
Waeld koniak*	Madang	2	5	6	1	3	4	(3)						
Borosak*	Karkar	2	1	5	6	3	4	3	2	3	2	2	0	3
E														
Tabal*	Pentecost	5	2	6	3	4	1	3	4	1	4	2	1	3
Tangurlava*	Maewo	5	2	6	4	3	1	3	2	2	1	2	1	3
Vila	Tanna	2	5	6	4	3	1	3	1	2	4	1	1	2
Marino	Santo	2	6	5	4	3	1	3	1	2	4	1	1	2
Palavoke	Santo	2	6	5	4	3	1	7	1	3	1	1	1	2
Hina kata loa	Wallis	2	5	6	4	3	1	3	1	1	5	1	1	2
Abogae	Pentecost	2	6	5	4	3	1	5	2	2.	4	2	1	2
Lalahk	Pentecost	2	6	5	4	3	1	5	2	2	2	2	1	2
Tudey	Santo	2	5	6	4	3	1	5	2	4	4	2	1	2
Hina leka	Wallis	2	5	6	4	3	1	7	1	1	5	1	1	1
Fock	Santo	2	6	5	4	3	1	7	1	1	4	1	0	2
Oahu 242	Oahu	2	5	6	1	3	4	5	3	4	4	1	0	2
Nimau	Tongoa	2	4	6	5	3	1	3	3	1	3	1	0	2
Akau	Tongatapu	2	4	6	5	3	1	3	3	3	1	1	0	2
Oahu 236	Oahu	2	6	5	4	3	1	3	1	1	1	1	0	2
Apin	Tanna	6	2	5	3	4	1	3	5	1	3	3	0	3
Apeg	Anatom	2	5	6	4	3	1	3	5	1	3	3	0	3
Palisi	Santo	2	6	5	4	3	1	5	1	2	4	2	0	2
Akau huli	Tongatapu	2	6	4	5	3	1	3	4	3	4	2	0	2
Huli kata loa	Wallis	2	5	4	6	3	1	3	4	3	4	2	0	2
Oahu 241	Oahu	2	5	6	1	4	3	3	3	1	1	2	0	2

1. Kavalactone concentrations ranked by order of decreasing importance in the composition of the roots extract.
2. coded phenotype:
A: 3 = Erect, 5 = Normal, 7 = Prostrate;
C: 1 = Pale green, 2 = Dark, 3 = Green with purple shading, 4 = Purple, 5 = Black;
I: 1 = Uniform, 2 = Mottled, 3 = Speckled, 4 = Striated and mottled;
L: 1 = Pale green, 2 = Dark green, 3 = Purple;
E: 1 = Undulate, 2 = Raised, 3 = Drooping, 4 = Regular;
P: 1 = Present, 0 = Absent;
S: 1 = Short and thick, 2 = Long and thin, 3 = Long and thick
3. Sample received from Unitech, Lae. Plant not described.
*Indicates that the form belongs to the species *Piper wichmannii*.
(According to Lebot and Lévesque, 1988)

Table 3, continued.

Cultivar	Origin	Chemotype[1]						Morphotype[2]						
		1st	2nd	3rd	4th	5th	6th	A	C	I	L	E	P	S
Omoa	Fatu hiva	2	6	5	4	3	1	3	4	3	1	2	0	2
Rahmwahnger	Pohnpei	2	4	5	6	1	3	3	2	1	2	2	0	2
Oahu 240	Oahu	2	1	4	6	5	3	5	3	3	4	2	0	1
Oahu 238	Oahu	2	5	6	1	4	3	3	4	1	3	2	0	3
Oahu 239	Oahu	2	6	5	4	3	1	3	2	3	3	2	0	3
F														
Nakasara	Emae	2	6	5	4	3	1	5	1	1	2	1	0	2
Kau pel	Baluan	2	5	4	6	1	3	3	4	1	2	1	0	2
Kau pwusi	Baluan	2	5	4	6	1	3	5	5	1	1	1	0	2
Ewo	Tongoa	2	4	5	6	3	1	5	3	1	3	1	0	2
Yevoet	Santo	2	6	4	5	3	1	5	2	4	2	2	0	2
Malogro	Santo	2	5	6	4	3	1	3	1	2	4	2	0	2
Aheyoke	Santo	2	5	6	4	3	1	5	3	2	3	2	1	1
Thyei	Santo	2	5	6	4	3	1	7	2	4	4	2	0	1
Merei	Santo	2	5	6	4	3	1	5	2	1	3	2	0	3
Malmabo	Pentecost	2	5	6	4	3	1	5	1	3	2	1	1	2
Ume	Fly	2	5	6	4	1	3	7	1	1	2	1	1	2
Isa	Usino	2	5	4	6	3	1	7	2	3	1	2	1	2
Sipaia	Morobe	2	5	6	3	4	1	7	2	3	1	2	1	2
Iwi	Madang	2	5	6	4	3	1	7	2	3	1	2	1	2
Ayou	Karkar	2	5	4	6	1	3	7	2	3	1	2	1	2
G														
Pirimerei	Santo	2	5	4	6	3	1	5	3	3	1	2	0	1
Tau	Tongoa	2	4	3	5	6	1	5	1	4	3	2	0	1
Asyaij	Anatom	2	4	6	5	3	1	5	1	1	3	1	0	1
Woko	Santo	2	6	4	5	3	1	3	1	2	2	2	0	2
Ahouia	Tanna	2	4	6	5	3	1	5	1	2	2	2	0	2
Pualiu	Tongoa	2	4	6	5	3	1	5	1	2	2	2	0	2
Amon	Tanna	2	4	6	5	3	1	5	2	3	1	2	0	2
Biya	Anatom	2	4	6	5	3	1	3	1	4	3	2	0	2
Aigen	Tanna	2	4	6	5	3	1	3	1	3	1	1	0	2
Ava ulu	Tutuila	2	4	6	5	3	1	3	1	3	1	1	0	2
Kiskisnian	Tanna	2	4	6	5	1	3	7	1	4	3	1	0	2
Metolei	Tongoa	2	3	4	6	5	1	3	2	1	3	1	0	2
Oleikaro	Tongoa	2	4	6	5	3	1	5	4	4	1	1	0	2
Borogu	Pentecost	2	4	6	5	3	1	3	2	2	3	2	0	3
Borogoru	Maewo	2	4	5	6	1	3	3	2	1	3	2	0	3
Poua	Malekula	2	4	5	3	6	1	3	4	1	3	2	0	3
Ava talo	Savaii	2	4	1	6	5	3	3	2	3	3	2	0	3
Ava talo	Tutuila	2	4	6	5	1	3	3	2	3	3	2	0	3
Riki	Anatom	2	4	5	6	3	1	5	1	3	1	2	0	3
Big hand	Efate	2	4	6	5	3	1	5	1	3	1	2	0	3
Puariki	Tongoa	2	4	6	5	3	1	5	1	3	1	2	0	3
Mita	Tanna	2	4	6	3	5	1	3	1	1	3	1	0	3
Bumalotu	Maewo	2	4	5	6	3	1	5	1	3	2	1	1	2
Akau hina	Vava'u	2	4	6	5	1	3	3	1	3	5	1	1	2
Leka hina	Vava'u	2	6	4	5	3	1	3	1	3	5	1	1	2
Small hand	Efate	2	6	5	4	3	1	5	2	2	3	2	1	2
Fulufulu	Tongatapu	2	4	6	5	3	1	5	1	1	5	1	1	1

Table 3, continued.

Cultivar	Origin	Chemotype[1]						Morphotype[2]						
		1st	2nd	3rd	4th	5th	6th	A	C	I	L	E	P	S
H														
Olitao	Emae	4	2	6	3	5	1	3	5	4	1	1	0	1
Yag	Aanatom	2	4	6	5	3	1	5	1	2	1	1	0	1
Tuan	Tanna	2	4	6	5	3	1	5	1	4	3	1	0	2
Visual	Santo	2	4	6	5	3	1	5	1	4	3	1	0	2
Palarasul	Santo	2	4	6	3	5	1	5	1	4	3	1	0	2
Leay	Tanna	2	4	6	3	5	1	7	1	2	3	1	0	2
Nidinolai	Anatom	2	4	6	5	3	1	3	1	3	1	1	0	2
Black hand	Efate	2	4	6	3	5	1	5	4	4	1	1	0	2
Kelai	Epi	4	2	6	1	3	5	5	3	4	1	1	0	2
Tikiskis	Tanna	2	4	6	5	3	1	7	1	2	3	2	0	2
Pia	Tanna	4	2	6	1	5	3	3	1	4	3	2	0	2
Small leaf	Efate	4	2	3	6	1	5	3	1	4	3	2	0	2
Rongrongwul	Pentecost	2	4	6	3	1	5	7	4	4	2	3	0	2
Malamala	Tanna	2	4	6	5	1	3	3	2	1	2	2	0	3
Kar	Santo	2	4	6	5	1	3	3	4	1	3	2	0	3
Tchap	Anatom	4	2	6	3	1	5	5	2	1	4	2	0	3
Paama	Tanna	2	4	6	1	5	3	3	2	2	3	2	0	3
Miela	Emae	4	2	6	3	5	1	3	3	4	1	1	0	3
Palimet	Emae	4	2	6	3	5	1	3	1	1	3	1	0	3
Urukara	Santo	4	2	6	3	5	1	3	1	2	4	1	1	2
Ava lea	Upolu	2	4	6	5	1	3	7	1	3	5	1	1	1
Ava lea	Tutuila	2	4	6	5	1	3	7	1	3	5	1	1	1
Ava lea 2	Upolu	6	4	2	5	3	1	7	1	1	5	1	1	1
Ava samoa	Tutuila	4	2	6	3	1	5	7	1	1	5	1	1	1
I														
Oahu 237	Oahu	6	4	2	3	5	1	5	1	1	1	1	0	1
Loa kasa leka	Vanua levu	6	4	3	2	5	1	7	4	3	4	2	0	1
Loa	Taveuni	6	4	3	2	5	1	7	4	3	4	2	0	1
Kabra	Taveuni	6	4	3	2	5	1	7	4	3	4	2	0	1
Leka huli	Tongatapu	6	2	4	5	3	1	7	4	3	4	2	0	1
Damu	Taveuni	2	4	6	5	1	3	5	3	1	5	2	0	1
Matakaro	Taveuni	6	2	4	5	3	1	3	3	3	1	1	0	2
Matakaro balavu	Vita levu	6	4	2	3	5	1	3	3	3	1	1	0	2
Honolulu	Vanua levu	6	4	2	3	5	1	5	1	1	5	1	0	2
Business	Taveuni	6	4	1	3	2	5	5	1	1	5	1	0	2
Loa kasa balavu	Vanua levu	6	4	2	3	1	5	3	4	3	4	2	0	2
Ava mumu	Savaii	4	6	3	2	5	1	3	4	3	4	2	0	2
Fataua	Tahiti	6	2	5	4	3	1	5	3	1	1	1	0	2
Paenoo	Tahiti	2	6	4	5	1	3	3	4	3	1	2	0	2
Rahdmel	Pohnpei	4	6	2	1	3	5	3	2	3	2	2	0	2
Gona vula	Viti levu	6	4	3	2	5	1	3	1	2	5	2	0	3
Dokobana vula	Vanua levu	6	4	2	3	5	1	3	1	2	5	2	0	3
Qila balavu	Taveuni	6	4	3	2	5	1	3	2	3	3	2	1	2
Vula kasa balavu	Vanua levu	4	6	2	3	1	5	3	1	3	5	1	1	2
Ava la'au	Upolu	4	6	2	3	5	1	3	1	3	5	1	1	2
Vula kasa leka	Vanua lelvu	6	4	3	2	5	1	7	1	3	5	1	1	2
Ava sa	Savaii	6	4	1	3	2	5	3	2	1	5	1	1	2

Chemotypes

For the drinker, the beverage can be weak or too strong, according to the method of preparation used, the concentration of active ingredients, and especially according to its composition. *Kava* can be soothing and induce a deep sleep without dreams, or on the contrary, it can fail to produce relaxation and in some cases, will cause nausea. Consumers are well informed of these variations and usually want to know which cultivar is being prepared. Farmers argue that the physiological effect varies according to the cultivar involved.

Kava presents different natural compositions of active ingredients having different properties. The physiological effect of the beverage prepared from a particular cultivar is governed by its dominant kavalactone concentration. Extraction of these substances from the roots and quantitative isolation by using high-performance liquid chromatography (Lebot and Lévesque 1989) showed that the six major kavalactones accounted for more than 96 percent of the whole extract. The six major kavalactones are: DMY = demethoxyyangonin (1), DHK = dihydrokavain (2), Y = yangonin (3), K = kavain (4), DHM = dihydromethysticin (5), and M = methysticin (6). These six active substances with different individual physiological properties therefore produce a natural "cocktail" which will itself produce a different effect according to the composition of the mixture.

In order to appreciate these differences, these compositions were coded in a decreasing order to the proportion of each lactone in the extract and this coded description is called the chemotype. For example, if the chemotype of a cultivar is *521364* this indicates that kavalactone number 5 (dihydromethysticin) is the most important, that kavalactone number 2 (dihydrokavain) is the second most important and so on (see Table 3). Of course; chemotype *521634* will produce an effect quite different from that of chemotype *625431*. In the code, the first three kavalactones often represent over 70 percent of the overall total; they are therefore the ones most important in characterizing the chemotype. In some cases the percentages of the major kavalactones, are very close (22, 25, and 23 percent, for example). What is then more important is the fact that they occupy the first three positions rather than their exact rank (*642* . . . instead of *426* . . . , for example).

When different cultivars are planted on the same day in the same plot they produce different chemotypes. This would indicate that the variability in chemical composition and total kavalactone content is related to genotype more than to environmental factors. In fact, the trials conducted in Vanuatu between 1984 and 1986 only confirmed the phenomen elucidated by ethnobotanical studies (Lebot and Cabalion 1986), where farmers reported that different cultivars uprooted from the same garden on the same day produced different effects. Several trials were conducted to evaluate the scope of variations of these preliminary results. When clones are planted the same day and harvested the same day, the results show that kavalactone content and chemotype are very homogenous among the clone. In other words, farmers have a high probability of preserving the same physiological effect by cloning the mother plant. Kavalactone content is not related to ontogeny. The cultivar's total kavalactone content is maximized after 18 months and its level remains unchanged during the growth of the plant while the yield in dry matter, of course, continues to increase year after year. Results of several trials conducted on two islands suggested that chemotypes were not related to ontogeny or environment (Lebot and Lévesque 1989).

This was an attempt to approach a major ethnobotanical problem using modern, high-efficiency, analytical techniques. When these results are compared to those obtained from ethnobotanical studies, a definite correlation is observed between a specific chemotype and the traditional uses of the cultivars. Correlations with ethnobotanical data show that drinkers do not appreciate a high percentage of DHM (5) and DHK (2). For example, chemotype 521634 is rarely consumed and farmers observe that its physiological effect is too severe to allow daily consumption because, when imbibed, an unpleasant nausea is felt. This is due to the very high proportion of the two most active kavalactones, DHK (2) and DHM (5), in the beverage (Hänsel 1968). On the other hand, the most appreciated chemotypes have a high percentage of K (4) and a low percentage of DHM (5). It is not surprising that these chemotypes yield a pleasant effect, considering the high percentage of kavain.

Kretzschmar (1970) described the "excellent psychopharmacological activity" of kavain: "emotional and muscular relaxation, stabilization of feelings and stimulation of the ability to think and act." On the other hand, the wild species, *P. wichmannii* C. DC., has very high concentrations of DHK (2) and DHM (5), in some cases representing more than 60 percent of the total extract (Lebot and Lévesque 1989). Because the selection is made each time an individual plant is uprooted, and after the farmer has experimented with the effect, it is thought that the domestication process could be portrayed as a process of clone selection. This genealogy of clones, from the wild species to the cultivars, is a lineage of chemotypes.

The aim was to demonstrate the importance of using the standard approach to characterizing chemotypes, and also to identify chemotaxonomic signatures assigned to all cultivars existing in the Pacific. This would help to identify cultivars within the Pacific islands and would help answer questions about human migrations throughout the area.

Dispersal of Cultivars

From the information yielded from our previous study (Lebot and Cabalion 1986; Lebot and Lévesque 1989), it is possible to assume that the origin and domestication area of *P. methysticum* is the northern part of Vanuatu. From this area, Polynesian travellers could have spread cultivars to other islands.

These cultivars are so polymorphic, however, that it is important to associate both chemotypes and morphotypes to accurately identify clones collected from different islands and known locally under different vernacular names. An attempt to classify 122 clones originating from 29 Pacific islands is presented in Table 3. The aim of such a classification is to produce convars, or groups of related cultivars, based on morphotypic and chemotypic affinities. The chemical data, coupled with the morphological descriptors, lead to the following conclusions:

Morphotypes of *P. wichmannii* scattered between the Admiralty Islands, in Papua New Guinea, and the Shepherd group in Vanuatu, are quite close to each other. However, their chemotypes vary greatly. Forms from Baluan, Morobe, and Guadalcanal are identical, although the one from Baluan is cultivated whereas the other two are wild. The wild form originating from Karkar Island presents a chemotype (*215634*) which is very similar to the one spread between the Banks and Shepherd groups in Vanuatu (*521634*). In Vanuatu, *P. wichmannii* presents chemotypes which are closer to those of *P. methysticum* than to the wild forms of *P. wichmannii* occurring in other Melanesian islands (*526431* for *Tabal* and *Tangurlava*). The numerous cultivars of *P. methysticum* existing may have arisen following mutations of seeded forms, hybridization of seeded variants of *P. wichmannii*, vegetative mutation with human selection of somatic mutants, or most certainly, by a combination of these ways. The creation of new cultivars by bud mutation (somatic cells) is a real possibility that occurs quite frequently in species exclusively asexually propagated. Selection must have taken place in order to preserve new cultivars as they appeared, and because individual uprooting of *kava* allows selection for the sole purpose of improving those chemical characteristics which are useful to human. Due to the occurrence and variability of seeded forms of *P. wichmannii* and, since dioecious species produce highly heterogenous progenies, it is likely that seeded forms showing valuable chemotypes were cloned by drinkers in order to preserve them. If these hypotheses are correct, this domestication process would have taken place in Melanesia because *P. wichmannii* does not exist in Polynesia.

Cultivars with chemotypes presenting high proportions of DHK (2) and DHM (5) are restricted to Melanesia. Cultivars with the most interesting chemotypes for the drinkers (e.g., *426* . . . or *642* . . .) are widespread in Polynesia. On the basis of these observations, it may be inferred that in Melanesia and in Vanuatu, especially, the whole *in situ* collections of the different clones produced from the domestication process of *P. wichmannii* are preserved. When Polynesian travellers came to collect their cultivars, they selected the most interesting clones and did not spread those with "wild characters" (e.g., *521634*) to Polynesia.

Piper methysticum is represented by only one cultivar in the northern part of New Guinea (Usino, Morobe, Madang, and Karkar), yet it is not possible to trace this cultivar elsewhere. On the other hand, the only cultivar existing in the Western Province (Fly River area) seems to be closely related to *Malmalbo*, a cultivar originating from Pentecost, in Vanuatu. The two cultivars of *P. methysticum* grown on Baluan (Admiralty Islands) are also closely related to cultivars originating from the Shepherd group in Vanuatu.

In Polynesia, it is easier to associate these cultivars, even if great distances separate them. For example, cultivar *Omoa* collected in the Marquesas seems to be related to *Oahu 241* from Hawaii. Similar observations can be made for other cultivars (e.g., *Aigen* from the island of Tanna, southern Vanuatu, is identical to *Ava ulu* from the island of Tutuila, American Samoa). Although a local myth suggests that *kava* came to Tanna from Tonga, the most likely agents of introduction are the Polynesians from the small islands of Aniwa and Futuna. They speak a language which, according to some linguists (Clark 1979), is related to Samoan. In central Polynesia, and between Fiji and Tonga, Wallis or Samoa, it is obvious that an exchange of planting material has taken place, based on the number of common characters shared by morphotypes and chemotypes of this area.

Revival of a Traditional Beverage

These observations confirm the hypothesis formulated previously and there is now very strong grounds for saying that *kava* drinking had a single point of origin. *Kava* is a sterile plant, the cultivars of which are the result of human selection and propagation. The linguistic affinities or the occurrence, in most of the areas of consumption, of words for *kava* that are cognates support this view. Its consumption throughout the Pacific is therefore the consequence of the diffusion by Polynesian travellers of the planting material and the knowledge of the preparation of the beverage. The sterility of cultivars of *P. methysticum* causes *kava* to die out if its cultivation is abandoned, as can be observed in most parts of Polynesia. Within its area of origin, Melanesia, are the Solomon Islands where *kava* does not exist. A very clear boundary running through the Santa Cruz Islands separates one area where the species does not occur and another where domestication and diversification have probably taken place. Very few species could have undergone such a surprising distribution within their area of origin.

The Pacific islanders have been cultivating *kava* for centuries. This plant enjoys great cultural standing and is held in high esteem. It is grown primarily to fulfil a social role, but is rapidly becoming a highly motivating cash crop. It is also the only species used in traditional Oceanic pharmacopoeia that has reached a stage of industrial development in Western laboratories. Its natural extract is now sold in Europe in tablet form and it has potential for wider use. In the Western world natural products are becoming increasingly fashionable. Both Europeans and Americans are using more and more tranquilizers to fight the permanent aggression surrounding their way of life. The odds are good that they would turn to *kava*, a natural product, instead of their daily synthetic soporifics, if they had the chance. As regards its export potential, *kava* rates as a drink and as a medicinal plant. Its potential is promising, especially now that the problem of the active ingredients' variability and composition is solved. Selection of suitable chemotypes for well-identified markets is realistic and feasible.

Kava opens up several research avenues. Few plants can attract such a wide range of interest. For linguists, *kava* helps trace the migrations of Oceanic peoples. For the sociologist, it is the catalyst for a convivial event at an impressive scale and of much potential. For the anthropologist, there are numerous rites, magic acts, stories, and legends. Botanists cannot fail to be intrigued by the definition of the species, by the plant's inability to reproduce sexually, and by its dependence on humans. For geneticists, interest lies in the variability of morphotypes and chemotypes and on their correlation. The agronomist will see in *kava* an under-exploited crop perfectly suited to the traditional agricultural system of Pacific islanders. For development officers, *kava* cultivation is a way of generating surpluses, difficult to find in countries which do not control the prices of their export commodities.

Literature Cited

Aitken, R. T. 1930. Ethnology of Tubuai. Bernice P. Bishop Mus. Bul. 70: 42.

Ashby, G. 1987. *A Guide to Pohnpei. An Island Argosy.* Oregon: Rainy Day Press.

Baker, J. R., and I. Baker. 1936. The seasons in tropical rain-forest, New Hebrides, Part 2. *J. Linn. Soc., Bot.* 39:507–519.

Barrau, J. 1957. A propos du *Piper methysticum. J. Agr. Trop. Bot. Appl.* 4:270–273.

Beaglehole, E. 1941. Pangaï village in Tonga. Memoirs Polynesian Society 18:112–123.

Bonnemaison, J. 1985. Les fondements d'une identité. Territoire, histoire et société dans L'archipel de Vanuatu (Mélanésie). Livre 1: L'arbre et la Pirogue. Collection Travaux et Documents de l'ORSTOM. 1–525.

Bougainville, L. 1772. *A Voyage Around the World.* Trans. J. R. Forster. London: J. Nourse.

Brown, F. B. H. 1935. Flora of southeastern Polynesia. Bernice P. Bishop Mus. Bul. 130:1–386.

Brunton, R. 1987. Kava drinking: the problem of its distribution. Manuscript.

Clark, R. 1979. Language. In *The Prehistory of Polynesia.* Ed. J. Jennings. Cambridge, Massachusetts: Harvard Univ. Press. 249–270.

Cox, P. A., and L. O'Rourke. 1987. Kava (*Piper methysticum,* Piperaceae). *Econ. Bot.* 41:452–454.

Crawford, A. L. 1981. *Aida: Life and Ceremony of the Gogodola.* Sydney: Port Moresby, National Cultural Council of Papua New Guinea in Association with R. Brown and Associates.

Cuzent, G. 1856. Du kawa de Noukouhiva, Iles Marquises. *Revue Coloniale* 2ème série 15:582–583.

_____. 1860. Du kawa, kava ou ava de Tahiti et des îles Marquises. *Revue Coloniale* 2ème série 20:630–646.

Degener, 0. 1940. *Flora Hawaiiensis.* Vol. 4. Honolulu: O. Degener.

_____. 1945. *Plants of Hawaii National Park.* Vol. 2. Oahu, Hawaii: Wailalua ed.

De Lessert, B. 1837. *Icones Selectae Plantarum.* Vol. 3.

Duve, R. N. 1981. Gas-liquid chromatographic determination of major constituents of *Piper methysticum. Analyst* 106:160–165.

Duve, R. N., and J. Prasad. 1981. Quality Evaluation of Yaqona (*Piper methysticum*) in *Fiji. Agr. J.* (Suva) 43:1–8.

Ferdon, E. N. 1981. *Early Tahiti as the Explorers Saw It, 1767–1797.* Tucson: Univ. of Arizona Press.

Firth, R. 1954. Anuta and Tikopia: symbiotic elements in social organization. *J. Polynesian Society* 63:87–131.

Fornander, A. 1919. Hawaiian antiquities and folklore. Memoirs Bernice P. Bishop Mus. 6.

Forster, J. G. A. 1786. *De Plantis Esculentis Insularum Oceani Australis.* Berlin: n.p.

Gaillot, M. 1962. Le rite du kava Futunien. Etudes Mélanésiennes 4ème série 14:95–105.

Garanger, J. 1972. Archéologie des Nouvelles-Hébrides. Publication de la Société des Océanistes 30.

Gatty, R. 1956. Kava—Polynesian beverage shrub. *Econ. Bot.* 10:241–249.

Glassman, S. F. 1952. The Flora of Ponapé. Research reviews, Office of Naval Research, U.S. Navy Dept., July:16–18.

Guillaumin, A. 1938. A florula of the island of Esperitu Santo, one of the New Hebrides with a prefatory note by the leader of the Oxford University expedition to the New Hebrides, 1933–34, J. R. Baker. *J. Linn. Soc., Bot.* 51:547–566.

Handy, E. S. C. 1927. Polynesian religion. Bernice P. Bishop Mus. Bul. 34:327–328.

_____. 1940. The Hawaiian planter. Vol. 1, His plants, methods and areas of cultivation. Bernice P. Bishop Mus. Bul. 161.

Handy, E. S. C., M. K. Pukui, and K. Livermore. 1934. Outline of Hawaiian physical therapeutics. Bernice P. Bishop Mus. Bul. 126.

Hänsel, R. 1968. Characterization and physiological activity of some kava constituents. *Pac. Sci.* 22:293–313.

Hänsel R., Weiss D. and Schmidt B. 1966. Fungistatiche Wirkung der Kavadrogue und iwer Inhaltsstoffe. *Planta Medica* 14(1):1–9.

Hocart, A. M. 1952. The northern states of Fiji. Royal Anthr. Institute Occ. Publication 11.

Jössang, P., and D. Molho. 1967. Dihydrokavain has sedative properties as dihydromethysticin. *J. Chromatography* 31:375.

Keller, F., and M. W. Klohs. 1963. A review of the chemistry and pharmacology of the constituents of *Piper methysticum*. *Lloydia* 26:1–15.

Kirch, P. V., and D. E. Yen. 1982. Tikopia: the prehistory and ecology of a Polynesian outlier. Bernice P. Bishop Mus. Bul. 238.

Kramer, A. 1903. *Die Samoa-Inseln.* II Band. *Ethnographie.* Stuttgart: E. Nagele.

Kretszchmar, R. 1970. Kavain als. Pschopharmakon. Müchen Med. Wochenschr. 4ème année. 112:154–158.

Lawrence, P. 1984. *The Garia.* Melbourne: University Press.

Lebot, V., and P. Cabalion. 1986. Les kavas de Vanuatu (cultivars de *Piper methysticum* Forster). Collection Travaux et Documents de l'ORSTOM 205:1–234.

Lebot, V., P. Cabalion, and J. Lévesque. 1986. Le Kava des ancêtres est-il l'ancêtre du kava? *J. Vanuatu Natural Society* (Naika) 23:1–10.

Lebot, V., and J. Lévesque. 1989. The origin and distribution of kava (*Piper methysticum* Forst. f.): a phytochemical approach. *Allertonia* 5:223–280.

Lewin, L. 1886. *Über* Piper methysticum *(kawa-kawa).* Berlin: Medical Society.

Mathews, J. D., et al. 1988. Effects of the heavy usage of kava on physical health: summary of a pilot survey in an Aboriginal community. *Med. J. Australia* 148:548–555.

Mickloucho-Maclay, N. (Von). 1874. Ethnologische Bemerkungen über die Papuas der Maclay-Küste in Neu Guinea. Natuurkungig tidjschrift voor Nederlandsch Indies 35:71.

_____. 1886. List of plants in use by the natives of New Guinea. *Proc. Linn. Soc. New South Wales* 10:687–695.

Nevermann, H. 1938. Kawa auf Neu Guinea. *Ethnos* 3:179–192.

Parham, H. B. 1939. Fiji plants, their names and uses. *J. Polynesian Society* 48/50.

Parkinson, S. 1773. *A Journal of a Voyage to the South Seas in His Majesty's Ship the* Endeavour *(1768).* London: S. Parkinson.

Risenfield, A. 1950. *The Megalithic Culture of Melanesia.* Leiden: Brill.

Rivers, W. H. R. 1914. *The History of Melanesian Society.* 2 vols. Cambridge, Massachusetts: Harvard Univ. Press.

Safford, W. E. 1905. *The Useful Plants of the Island of Guam: With an Introductory Account of the Island Features and Natural History of the Island, of the Character and History of its People, and of Their Agriculture.* Washington, DC: Government Printing Office.

Saüer, H., and R. Hänsel. 1967. Kawalactone und Flavonoide aus einer endemischen iper-Art Neu Guineas. *Planta Medica* 15:443–458.

Schultes, R. E., and A. Hofmann. 1979. *Plants of the Gods.* New York: MacGraw Hill.

Sengupta, S., and A. B. Ray. 1987. The chemistry of *Piper* species: a review. *Fitoterapia* 58:147–166.

Serpenti, L. M. 1965. *Cultivators in the Swamps. A Social Structure and Horticulture in New Guinea Society (Frederik-Hendrik Island, West New Guinea).* Assen. Van Gorcum.

Shaw, R. D. 1985. Narcotics, vitality and honor, the use of narcotic drink among the Samo of Papua New Guinea. Unpublished m.s.

Smith, A. C. 1975. The genus *Macropiper* (Piperaceae). *J. Linn. Soc., Bot.* 71:1–38.

_____. 1981. *Flora Vitiensis Nova: A New Flora of Fiji.* Vol. 2. Lawai, Hawaii: Pac. Trop. Bot. Garden.

Smith, R. M. 1979. Pipermethystin, a novel pyridone alkaloid from *Piper methysticum* (cultivated in the South Pacific as a drug plant and beverage plant). *Tetrahedron* 5:437–439.

_____ . 1983. Kava lactones in *Piper methysticum* from Fiji. *Phytochemistry* 22:1055–1056.

Steinmetz, E. F. 1960. Piper methysticum *(kava)*. *Famous Drug Plant of the South Seas Island.* Amsterdam: E. F. Steinmetz.

Sterly, J. 1970. *Heilpflanzen der Einwohner Melanesiens. Beiträge zur Ethobotanik des Südwestlichen Pazifik.* Hamburger Reihe zur Kultur und Sprachwissenschaft 6.

Terrell, J. E. 1986. *Prehistory in the Pacific Islands. A Study of Variation in Language, Customs, and Human Biology.* Cambridge, Massachusetts: Harvard Univ. Press.

Thompson, B. 1908. *The Fijians: A Study of the Decay of Custom.* London:

Titcomb, M. 1948. Kava in Hawaii. *J. Polynesian Society* 57:105–201.

Whitmore, T. D. 1966. *A Guide to the Forests of the British Solomon Islands.* London: Oxford Univ. Press.

Williams, F. E. 1936. *Papuans of the Trans Fly.* Oxford: Clarendon Press.

_____ . 1940. *Drama of Orokolo: The Social and Ceremonial Life of the Elema.* Oxford: Clarendon Press.

Wodzicki, K. 1979. Relationships between rats and man in the central Pacific. *Ethnomed* 5:433–446.

Young, R. L., et al. 1966. Analysis of kava pyrones in extracts of *Piper methysticum. Phytochemistry* 5:795–798.

Yuncker, T. G. 1959. Piperaceae of Micronesia. Bernice P. Bishop Mus. Occ. Paper 22:88–89.

Zepernick, B. 1972. *Arzneipflanzen der Polynesier.* Berlin: Verlag Von Dietrich Reimer.

CHAPTER 10

Ethnobotany of Breadfruit in Polynesia

DIANE RAGONE

Department of Horticulture
University of Hawaii
3190 Maile Way
Honolulu, Hawaii 96822

Breadfruit was an important staple throughout Oceania. Primarily important as a carbohydrate food source, every portion of the tree yielded materials useful to islanders. This chapter details the distribution of breadfruit in Polynesia and describes the tree and the many materials provided by it. One section is devoted to a discussion of the long-term storage practices developed to preserve and extend the seasonal crop produced by the breadfruit tree. The cultural importance of breadfruit is attested by the many legends associated with this tree and the ceremonies that accompany the breadfruit season.

Description and Distribution of Breadfruit

Breadfruit has been an evocative symbol of Oceania since Europeans and other outsiders first wandered into the region. Much of our information about its distribution and uses comes to us from the journals and accounts of those early visitors. Since so many early voyagers were attracted to Tahiti, it is the island with which breadfruit is most closely associated. Its importance to all Polynesians can be inferred by its widespread distribution and the abundance and diversity of its cultivars, as well as the many and diverse uses to which it was put.

Breadfruit, *Artocarpus altilis* (Parkinson) Fosberg (Moraceae) thrives on high volcanic islands where there is an abundance of rainfall and well-drained soil (Fig. 1). It was widespread in Polynesia, being absent only on Easter Island and New Zealand which were too cold for this tropical tree. It is known as *mei* in the Marquesas, Tonga, and Gambier Islands, *uru* in the Society Islands, *ulu* in Hawaii and Samoa, and *kuru* in the Cook Islands (Turner 1861; Barrau 1961, 1963). Breadfruit is a stately and strikingly beautiful tree. It is straight-trunked with a wide,

Figure 1. Breadfruit, *Artocarpus altilis* (Parkinson) Fosberg (Moraceae).

spreading canopy, growing to a height of 15 to 20 meters. The smooth-barked trunk may reach a meter or more in diameter. The large leaves are glossy and dark green, with pale green or yellow veins. The leaf margins range from entire to deeply dissected, with seven to nine lobes most common. The trees are monoecious, with female and male inflorescences on the same tree. The club-shaped male inflorescences emerge first, followed by the female flowers, and then the fruits which occur singly or in clusters of two to three at the distal ends of branches. The fruits are round, oval, oblong, or asymmetrically shaped and weigh from 0.5 to 2 kg. The yellowish green skin is characterized by hexagonal markings and a smooth or slightly bumpy to spiny surface. When ripe, the flesh is white or pale yellow and contains none to many large, dark brown seeds.

Seeded types are most common in the western South Pacific; in Micronesia and the northern and eastern islands of Polynesia seedless cultivars predominate. A related species, *A. mariannensis* Trec., is found throughout Micronesia; it grows wild in Palau, Guam, and the Marianas Islands. It has small, asymmetrical, very seedy, yellow-fleshed fruits and small, entire, or shallowly lobed leaves. Many cultivars of breadfruit in Micronesia show characteristics of the two species, suggesting that they are hybrids (Fosberg 1960; Coenan and Barrau 1961; Ragone 1988).

The origin and distribution of breadfruit in Oceania has been discussed by many authors. The theorized Indo-Malaysian origin has been expanded to include western Melanesia and the Philippines (Barrau 1957, 1961, 1965; Jarrett 1959). It was carried by aboriginal peoples across the Pacific as far east as the Marshall Islands in Micronesia and the Society Islands in the South Pacific, and as far north as Hawaii. However, Wester (1924) disputes *A. altilis* being found in the Philippines prior to the seventeenth century. Early descriptions of Philippine plants suggested that both *A. altilis* and *A. mariannensis* were introduced from Guam.

The origin of seedless breadfruit is of special interest. Seedless clones originated from seeded breadfruit but how and where this occurred is disputed. Seeded breadfruit are common and widely distributed in New Guinea and some of the few-seeded or seedless cultivars may have developed there (Jarrett 1959). However, while few-seeded forms are known, the seedless and parthenocarpic breadfruit typical of eastern Polynesia do not occur. These were brought from Samoa by missionaries in the nineteenth century (Barrau 1957). It is known that the greatest selection and diversity of seedless clones occurred in eastern Polynesia and parts of the Caroline Islands (Wilder 1928; Barrau 1973).

It is difficult to ascertain how many cultivars were cultivated in Polynesia. The number of seedless cultivars increases from west to east with the greatest number found in the Marquesas and Society islands. Little information was published on Tongan cultivars. The earliest account (Wilkes 1845) mentions that nine were found but no other information is given. Names and brief descriptions of seven, including three found in Samoa by the same names, were provided by Yuncker (1959). Few Tongan cultivars are seeded. Wilkes (1845) listed twenty cultivars of Samoan breadfruit. Setchell (1924) provided a bit more information. He listed 10 names, but said there were many other cultivars. Names and descriptions of 13 were published by Buck (1930) while Christophersen (1935) listed the names of 30 and descriptions for 17 of these. Eight to ten Samoan cultivars are seeded.

Seven cultivars were indigenous to the southern Cook Islands; none were found in the northern atolls. An eighth was an introduction from Tahiti (Gill 1885). Cheeseman (1903) listed only the names of the four "best" cultivars and Buck (1927) gave the names of three cultivars; one of these is *kuru rotuma*, probably a recent introduction from Rotuma. Wilder (1931) listed the same names for four esteemed cultivars, and a fifth one is mentioned as an introduction from the Marquesas. Only two Cook Island cultivars are seeded.

The first visitors to Tahiti, on Captain Cook's *Endeavor*, were enchanted with the breadfruit and wrote about its uses and importance in the diet. Cook and King (1784) mentioned that the Tahitians had twenty names for breadfruit. Bligh subsequently sailed to Tahiti in H.M.S. *Bounty* specifically to collect breadfruit cultivars for the West Indies. As a consequence, he provided eight names and descriptions for some of these (Bligh 1792). In his second visit, in H.M.S. *Providence,* he amassed 2126 plants and ultimately delivered 678 to Trinidad and Jamaica (Bligh 1976). His log documents the careful attention given them:

> All the plants are now in charming order, speeding their leaves delight-
> fully. I have completed fine airy places for them on the quarter deck and
> galleries and shall sail with every inch of space filled up (Bligh 1976).

Unfortunately he was not so diligent in recording which cultivars were collected. The only specific mention is his log entry for 20 May 1792.

> Received a parcel of fine breadfruit plants from Tiarrabo which are reckoned vastly superior to any at this place, Matavai. I had heard of this kind, and had such reports confirmed to me by the chiefs that I employed two men to go for more.

Ellis (1967) was as remiss. He recorded that the first missionaries collected names of almost 50 cultivars, but wrote, "I have this list by me, but it is unnecessary to insert them here." However, he did provide the names of two cultivars. Later visitors did a much better job of providing names and descriptions, especially for Tahiti. Fourteen Raiatean and six Mangarevan cultivars were recorded (Huguenin 1902; Buck 1938). An annotated list of 24 Tahitian cultivars was compiled by Bennett (1860) and 52 names were published by Wester (1924). Tahitian breadfruit information was provided by Henry (1928) who gave uses, descriptions, and names for 40 and Wilder (1928) published photographs, botanical descriptions, and information on fruiting season, cooking quality, taste, and uses of 31 cultivars. A list of 27 additional names was included. Only one variety is seeded.

The Marquesas were renowned for their abundance and variety of breadfruit. Christian (1910) listed 34 cultivar names from the islands of Hiva Oa, Nuku Hiva, Tahuata and Ua Uka. Brown (1935) claimed that over 200 cultivars were found in the Marquesas, but gave no supporting evidence. Based on Brown's notes, Wester (1924) documented only 25. Only one was seeded.

The Hawaiian Islands had only one breadfruit cultivar, which is seedless, known by the general name of *ulu* (MacCaughey 1917; Handy 1940). It is the same as *ulu e'a* Samoa, *kuru maori* in the Cook Islands, *uru maohi* in the Society Islands, and *mei maoi* in the Marquesas (Ragone 1987). Each of these is recognized as one of the oldest cultivars of its respective islands.

How did the Polynesians spread breadfruit from island to island? Breadfruit seeds do not remain viable for long. It would be difficult, if not impossible, to germinate them after a long sea voyage. Breadfruit is readily propagated by root shoots or cuttings, and this is the traditional method throughout the Pacific. Shoots or sections of roots could be trimmed and carefully wrapped in leaves or tapa cloth. As long as the roots were kept moist, they could be transported across great distances, as evidenced by the introduction of a seedless variety to the Hawaiian Islands from the south.

Solander provided evidence for the occurrence of seeded forms in the Society Islands (Ellis 1775). During his visit with Captain Cook, he spoke to old people on Tahiti and nearby islands who told him that they remembered many seed-bearing types. These types disappeared due to preference for seedless ones. It is surprising that Barrau (1973) postulated that breadfruit seeds were carried from Melanesia into the eastern Pacific. He suggested that seedless clones were selected from these seedlings, resulting in many different seedless clones. Since seeded forms do exist in western Polynesia, it is more likely that these, as well as seedless clones, were taken to the eastern islands as root shoots. Subsequently, selections were made from these. Several Samoan cultivars which produce only a few seeds are known for their ability to produce numerous root shoots.

Storage and Preservation of Breadfruit

The Polynesians faced many constraints on food production in their island ecosystems. Few cultigens were successfully introduced and established. Limited arable land was available for cultivation, and droughts, storms, and warfare all affected food supplies (Barrau 1973; Yen 1976; Cox 1980a, 1980b). Breadfruit is a seasonal crop available for several months of the year in varying quantities; it does not keep for more than a few days once harvested. Methods had to be developed to deal with and utilize the seasonal surplus of fruit to provide food during the annual and often extended periods of scarcity. The method developed was that of fermentation and storage in pits, known as *ma* in the Marquesas, *mahi* in the Cook and Society islands, and *masi* in Samoa (Barrau 1961; Cox 1980a). It will be described later in this section. Here I would like to explore two factors, drought and warfare, which influenced the development of pit fermentation to preserve and conceal breadfruit.

Famine was a major concern due to frequent droughts. In the Marquesas large, communal storage pits were built in the village or near tribal assembly areas. Additional pits were built in secluded places high in the hills where they would be safe from enemies (Handy 1923). A huge circular pit, five- to eight-meters deep, was found several kilometers from the mouth of Taipivai Valley on Nuku Hiva (Linton 1925). This valley was renowned for its aggressive, warring inhabitants (Porter 1822; Melville 1924). *Ma* from these hidden storage pits could last indefinitely. It darkened with age and lost most nutritive value but was still edible after more than 50 years (Handy 1923). The main crop in December and January belonged entirely to the chief and was used to fill his private pits from which members of his household, guests, and workers were fed. The tribal pits were also filled during this harvest and each family would gather and contribute thousands of fruits. Each family had a pit to supply household needs and filled these with fruits gathered during the second harvest in April and May. If this harvest was large, surplus fruits were added to the communal pits. During times of drought or warfare, when the villagers were driven from the valleys, the communal pits were opened and the contents divided among the families.

Traditional legends and accounts by early visitors provide vivid descriptions of the destruction, famine, and suffering caused by frequent and violent warfare. Victors entered the cultivated lands of defeated peoples, stripped the trees of breadfruit and coconuts, and cut down and destroyed trees. In addition, huts were looted and *ma* pits dug out (Smith 1813; Porter 1822; Williams 1837). Pits were often concealed and in many cases, secretly opened at night to prevent their detection. The need for this secrecy was evident as raiding parties would search for *ma* pits. Warriors from Tongatapu would go to other Tongan islands to steal *ma* and other provisions when their food supplies were low (Mariner and Martin 1827). *Ma* was also a valuable survival food. When a group of young Tongan chiefs had to hide from the Tui Tonga, they prepared *ma* in pits hidden in a fortified area. They were able to survive solely on this for six months until it was safe to return to their village.

A Mangarevan legend recounts the story of a man who had a vision (Buck 1938). His grandfather on another island had been overwhelmed and his breadfruit trees torn down by his conquerors. The man set out with his family in a large canoe and when they arrived saw that his vision was true. His grandfather was dead and all plants destroyed except a breadfruit and a banana hidden in each ear. The legend continues with a magical account of how these fruits were planted and quickly grew.

Williams (1837) was struck by the devastation on Rarotonga. He noted there was an area of uncultivated land one-half mile wide between each district where battles were fought. Great effort was taken to prevent the opponents from entering into the adjacent cultivated lands. All the coconut trees on the northwest and south sides of the island had been destroyed. A few old breadfruit trees were found, but the bark was stripped off one and the others all had deep gashes in the trunk. When he asked the king the cause of these wounds, the king replied that "we were fools enough to fight with the trees as well as with men, some we cut down ourselves lest our enemies should eat the fruit, the others our conquerors destroyed" (Williams 1837).

With the impetus of droughts, warfare, and a seasonal food source to motivate them, pit fermentation was an elegantly simple solution to these problems. It overcame the constraints of no pottery for durable containers, and the high temperatures and humidity that make long-term storage difficult (Cox 1980b). Pit storage was used in all Polynesian islands where breadfruit was an important crop (Linton 1925; Massal and Barrau 1956; Barrau 1961). It was not made in Hawaii (Cook and King 1784; Krauss 1974). Pit storage is a semi-anaerobic fermentation process, involving intense acidification, which reduces fruit to a sour paste (Murai et al. 1958; Parker 1967; Yen 1976; Parkinson 1984). The process entails reducing mature and ripe fruit to a pulp and burying this in a well-covered, leaf-lined pit. The pit serves as both a fermentation chamber and storage area for the resulting *ma* (see Fig. 2).

Pits were best dug in soil with a high clay content to prevent water from seeping in. They were often lined with stones in the Marquesas to keep soil from falling in (Handy 1923; Linton 1925). Pit size depended on the number of fruit to

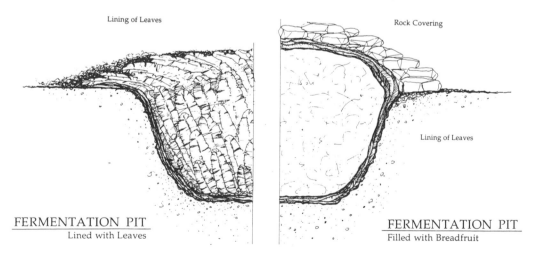

FERMENTATION PIT
Lined with Leaves

FERMENTATION PIT
Filled with Breadfruit

Figure 2. Fermentation pit.

be preserved. Family pits were usually one to two meters in diameter and up to one meter deep. The bottom and sides were lined with loose leaves or leaves woven into mats. Banana, breadfruit, coconut, *Barringtonia asiatica*, *Cordyline fruticosa*, and *Heliconia paka* leaves were all used. Ripe and mature fruits were gathered and allowed to ripen for a few days. When soft, the peel and core were removed. The softened fruits were piled on a layer of leaves or put into a suspended basket for several more days until fermentation had begun. If the fruits were carefully peeled before the softening process, the *ma* would be very white (Buck 1938). To utilize a full crop, unripe fruits were peeled, cored, sliced, and mixed into the already softened mass. In Samoa, *masi* was made from mature (i.e., green and ready for harvesting), but unripe fruits. They were quartered and put into the pit without peeling or removing the core and seeds (Buck 1930; Cox 1980b). The *ma* was put into a leaf-lined pit and trampled down to make a solid cake. A thick layer of leaves was placed on top and covered with large stones. The pit was periodically opened and the top layer of leaves and the hardened crust removed; *ma* was taken out as needed and the mound smoothed and covered with fresh leaves. It would keep in good condition in the pit for a year or more (Porter 1822; Gill 1885; Cheeseman 1903; Christian 1910; Handy 1923; Buck 1927; Barrau 1961).

The quality of *ma* depended on location and depth of the pit, type of leaves used, and careful filling and covering. Large storage pits ranged from three to nine meters deep and reportedly contained *ma* that was usable for years, even decades (Turner 1861; Gill 1885; Handy 1923; Cox 1980a, 1980b). In these deep pits, conditions would be more anaerobic and the fermentation process more complete. High temperatures were generated that would destroy bacteria, insects, and other organisms that affect *ma* quality. The type of leaves used was also an important consideration. Leaves rotted and crumbled over time; soil entered the pit and mixed with the *ma*, which darkened. *Cordyline* leaves lasted longer than most other leaves and were widely used. *Barringtonia* leaves were used in the Manua Islands, Samoa (Cox 1980a). The leaves were sewn together to make a tight lining for the pit; *masi* made in these lasted for three to four years (Gill 1885). Use of *Barringtonia* leaves to preserve *masi* for long periods was documented in the 1970s for these islands (Cox 1980a, 1980b). Cooked *masi* was put into tightly woven baskets of *Barringtonia* leaves. The baskets were placed in a deep hole and buried. These were never uncovered for food or ceremonial purposes but were saved for times of severe famine. Pits made generations ago were occasionally found when new pits were dug; the *masi* inside the baskets was purportedly edible (Cox 1980a, 1980b).

A Samoan legend tells the story of how *masi* was first made on Savaii in the village of Neiafu (Buck 1930):

> A crippled couple were unable to get breadfruit down from the trees. Their daughter, Sina, had the east and northeast trade winds blow the fruit down, but the couple were dissatisfied with the amount. They complained and Sina called in the boisterous west wind to blow down the rest of the fruit. The excess fruit was stored in a hole still seen in the rocks near Neiafu. The trade wind ushers in the good season in Samoa and brings gladness to all, except the old couple who complained because it did not serve their immediate need. The saying "Only Neiafu despises the trade wind" originated with this legend.

The development and use of pit storage had social ramifications beyond providing a stable food supply during the off-season and inclement periods. It was accompanied by increased social and ritual constraints on manufacture and distribution of *ma* (Yen 1976; Cox 1980a). In addition to being the mainstay of the daily diet, *ma* provided a portable, long-lasting food for journeys and sea voyages (Hawkesworth 1773; Buck 1930). When baked for a long time, it becomes hard and keeps for five to six weeks or longer. *Ma* was an essential item of tribute to chiefs and priests and it was a useful exchange commodity. Many of the inhabitants of Tetiaroa, an atoll 40 kilometers from Tahiti, traded fish for Tahitian breadfruit and *ma* (Smith 1813). The inhabitants of Mangareva in the Gambier group measured wealth by possession of land that produced food, especially breadfruit (Buck 1938). Land came into possession by inheritance, conquest, or gift. Those without land had to buy *ma* or concentrate on fishing to trade for ma. This sort of exchange was still practiced early in the twentieth century. A legend recorded by Buck attests to the antiquity of this practice: Toroga, a recent immigrant, was unable to acquire land or breadfruit trees. He became a fisherman and entered into an agreement with a chief's son named Uma to exchange fish for *ma*. He was gifted with a magical power over fish and caught so many that the exchange became a competition which the son lost: his *ma* pit was totally emptied while Toroga still had many fish.

Fermented and fresh breadfruit were the primary carbohydrate foods in the Marquesas, Society islands, and Gambier Islands. Its importance in the daily diet elsewhere in Polynesia varied with the availability of bananas, plantains, sweet potatoes, taro, and yams. Both forms of breadfruit are good sources of many essential dietary nutrients, but fermented breadfruit provides more carbohydrates, fat, protein, calcium, iron, and B vitamins than fresh fruit (Murai et al., 1958). *Ma* was never eaten directly from the pit. It was processed into a form known as *popoi* in the Marquesas and Society islands (Huguenin 1902; Handy 1923; Buck 1938; Ellis 1967). *Ma* was taken from the pit and placed in a wooden bowl or a trough made from a hollowed log. It was kneaded or pounded and water mixed in as needed; the older the *ma*, the longer it took to knead it into a soft, doughy mass. It was made into small cakes, wrapped in breadfruit leaves, and cooked in an earth oven (Handy 1923; Buck 1938; Barrau 1961). After cooking, it was again put in a trough, water added, and it was beaten to the desired consistency with a stone or wooden pounder. It was eaten warm or after it had cooled, and formed the basis of many dishes. Grated coconut or coconut cream was often added. Fresh, ripe breadfruit was mixed with *popoi* and made daily for infants in the Marquesas (Handy 1923). Women were fed heated *popoi* during a difficult childbirth (Handy 1930).

Western visitors to Polynesia were introduced to ma when islanders paddled out to the ships with this and other foods. Whether it was considered a delicacy or disgusting depended on the cultural bias of the individual. Polynesians esteemed it as a fine delicacy; many Westerners thought it foul, odorous, and unfit for human consumption. The unfavorable attitude of Beechey (1831) was typical. Upon his arrival in the Gambier Islands in 1825, the islanders sailed out and threw packages of *ma* aboard his ship; he caught one but quickly dropped it due to its overpowering odor. The natives made signs that it was to be eaten, and afterwards he found out that it was their main food, "the same as *mahie* in the Marquesas but with a high gout smell that I never heard that article possessed there." After being given bundles of this on a regular basis and seeing the natives eat with relish he commented,

> [T]hey possess the breadfruit, which in Otaheite is the staff of life, and the taro, a root which in utility corresponds with it in the Sandwich islands. Were they to pay but a due regard to the cultivation of last two an abundance of wholesome food might be substituted for nauseous mixture *mahie,* which, though it may, as indeed it does, support life, cannot be said to do more.

Turner (1861) found the odor of *masi* very offensive but noted that the older and more pungent it was the more it was relished by the natives.

In contrast, Captain King thought it remarkable that they (Hawaiians) don't have the art of preserving breadfruit and making the sour paste of it called *mahee* as in the Society Islands. It was some satisfaction to us in return of their great kindness and hospitality to have it in our power to teach them this useful habit (Cook and King 1784).

Celebration of the Breadfruit Season

The rituals associated with the breadfruit harvest and production of *mahi* were an important aspect of Polynesian life. The very method of determining time was delineated by the breadfruit season. Two seasons were recognized: summer, the season of breadfruit and plenty, and winter or scarcity. The main harvest season lasted three to four months, and the trees bore three, occasionally four, crops a year. Some cultivars matured at different times so fruit was available for nine months of the year (Henry 1928; Buck 1930; Christophersen 1935; Ellis 1969). Bligh (1792) noted that the year in Tahiti was divided into six parts distinguished by the kind of breadfruit then in season.

The principal crop occurred in January, February, and March in the Cook Islands, with a smaller one in May, and again in September and October. The period from June to September was a time of scarcity (Gill 1876; Buck 1927). The same pattern occurred in the Society Islands: the main harvest, *rehu,* in December, January, and February; scarcity and drought from July to September (Henry 1928; Ellis 1969).

The biggest harvest in the Marquesas was known as *ehua;* it occurred in December and January. The next largest, *mataiki,* was in April or May. Two smaller crops occurred between the main harvests (Handy 1923). An early visitor said that the breadfruit season was "a time of joy and festivity. It commences in December and lasts until September when the greatest abundance reigns. The breadfruit tree is everything to the natives" (Porter 1822). The breadfruit season in Hawaii was short when compared to that of the southern islands. There was only one variety and it produced its main crop in May or June to August (MacCaughey 1917; Handy 1940).

Time was also measured by lunar months and the associated cycles of constellations, marine and bird life, and the flowering and fruiting of plants, especially breadfruit. During the month of *ehua,* "the breadfruit grows large, it is warm, the sea runs high" (Handy 1923). *Iki'iki* was the month when the first breadfruit appeared in Kona, Hawaii. If there was no rain during this time, the fruit withered and fell (Beckwith 1932). In addition to the lunar month, the phases of the moon during each cycle were important for planting and other agricultural activities. Breadfruit planted during the full moon in the Marquesas would grow strong and the fruits would be plentiful and large (Handy 1923). *Olepau,* the tenth night, was very important. Hawaiian farmers planted their fields then to ensure good crops and the breadfruit put all its strength into bearing (Beckwith 1932).

In the Marquesas, parents dedicated a bearing breadfruit tree or planted a new one for each child's exclusive use. One to two trees would provide enough fruit to feed a person year round (Handy 1923). Captain Cook's assessment of the economic value of breadfruit trees was "if a man plants ten trees in his lifetime, which he may do in about an hour, he will completely fulfill his duty to future generations" (Hawkesworth 1773).

After the long period of scarcity, the breadfruit harvest was welcomed with ceremonies and festivities. Women were not allowed to harvest breadfruit, except in Mangareva, and there only when pregnant for the first time. It was believed that if a pregnant woman helped with the harvest, the trees would continue to be prolific and healthy (Buck 1938). Following the ritual offering of the first fruits to the gods, all the inhabitants in a district would gather for a feast of *opio.* Hundreds of breadfruit were picked while a huge oven seven to nine meters in circumference and two to three meters deep was prepared (Smith 1813; Henry 1928; Ellis 1967). A fire was built on top of the stones lining the bottom of the pit. When the fire had burned down, the embers were raked aside and whole, unpeeled fruits were placed in the pit. Leaves were placed on the fruit to keep them from being scorched by the embers raked over them. Additional leaves, grass, and a layer of soil up to one-half meter thick covered the embers. The oven was left for two to three days and, when ready, a hole was dug in one side. Breadfruit prepared this way could keep from several weeks to months (Buck 1927, Ellis 1967). The cooked fruit was removed as needed from the oven, which now served as a storage pit. As long as there was *opio* in the oven, there was great revelry and feasting, and little work was done (Ellis 1967).

Boys and young men of chiefly rank were sequestered during this period and fed huge quantities of *opio* to fatten them and to whiten their skin, which were much desired attributes (Cook and King 1784). "During this festive season, they seldom leave the house, and continue wrapped up in cloth. The use of this food for a month make them so fair and fat that they can scarcely breathe" (Smith 1813). A Tahitian king once died from eating too much breadfruit (Huguenin 1902). While the common people did not eat as much as the chiefly class, their diet of breadfruit made a difference. "The natives are very fond of it and their appearance improves a few weeks after the season starts" (Ellis 1967).

The early voyagers to Tahiti who arrived during the breadfruit season were fortunate in being able to witness and, perhaps, participate in these celebrations. Under the onslaught of Western goods, values, and belief systems brought by ever-increasing numbers of visitors, harvest celebrations became a thing of the past. They disappeared by the early 1820s (Ellis 1967).

Little is known about Marquesan harvest celebrations. As discussed in the preservation and storage section, the two main crops, *ehua* and *mataiki*, were used to fill the *ma* pits. The harvest festival, *ko'ina*, was celebrated after the pits had been filled. The preparation of *popoi* was deemed an important and even sacred responsibility. An elaborate ritual was employed to purify a person to allow them to make *popoi* (Handy 1923). The purification ritual took place when a child reached the age of ten. The maternal uncles and paternal aunts of the child would lie down and a *popoi* board would be placed on them. They would chant as *popoi* was beaten by the child with the father's help. Beating *popoi* on the bodies of relatives consecrated the child's first labor and consecrated the child's hands for future work. After the *popoi* was made, a feast was held and the family and relatives shared the newly made *popoi*. This ritual was so essential it was believed that a child would fall ill and possibly die if he or she made *popoi* before being purified.

Other Uses of Breadfruit

Primarily important as a carbohydrate food source, every portion of the breadfruit tree yielded useful materials. The tall-growing, straight-trunked trees were usually not used for timber until they were too old to produce large crops of fruit. The trees would be large and spreading, reaching heights of 15 to 20 meters with the first branches 5 to 6 meters from the ground. Timber from large trees was a valuable commodity because so many trees were destroyed as a result of warfare.

Breadfruit wood is light and durable, a golden yellow color that darkens with age. It was widely used for the construction of houses and canoes because of its resistance to termites and marine worms (Smith 1813; Gill 1885; MacCaughey 1917). It was also used to manufacture small items such as bowls, boxes, carved images, coffins, drums, fishing floats, surfboards, and tapa anvils (Smith 1813; Handy 1923, 1940; Henry 1928; Krauss 1974; Linton 1974). In Samoa, the best houses, especially the roofs, were made of durable breadfruit wood that could last for 50 years if protected from the rain (Turner 1861). Later in the century, houses with well-made roofs of breadfruit were considered valuable heirlooms (Gill 1885). Two cultivars were preferred for house building, *aveloloa* and *puou*, both very common and fast-growing trees (Christophersen 1935).

Small canoes were often made entirely from breadfruit wood, but the wood for the main hull of large canoes differed from island to island (see Banack, this volume). Deckhouses, gunwales, bow and stern pieces, and other parts of the canoe were made from breadfruit wood (Stewart 1831; Handy 1923, 1932; Buck 1927, 1930; Ellis 1969). Breadfruit gum was used to caulk canoes to make them watertight. The trunk produces a profuse sap, collected by cutting the bark in the early morning and scraping off the dried exudate later in the day (Gill 1885; Ellis 1967).

The gum had to be heated before it was used. In Tahiti, this was done by skewering candlenuts, *Aleurites moluccana*, with a coconut leaf midrib, and dipping these in the gum. The nuts were lit and as the gum melted the droplets fell into a bowl of water. The excess water was squeezed out and the gum was spread over the plank. Pieces of fine, shredded coconut husk were placed on top of the gum and smeared with more gum, and then the top plank was tightly lashed into place (Smith 1813). In Samoa, pieces of tapa were used instead of coconut husk, and the best sap came from the variety *ulu ea* (Buck 1930).

Breadfruit sap was commonly used throughout Polynesia to catch birds for food or their feathers. It was mixed with crushed, baked candlenuts and the resulting paste was smeared on the branches of trees where birds liked to roost (Gill 1885; Handy 1940). Birdlime was considered the most effective way to catch birds on the island of Hawaii. It was mainly used to catch the o'o bird for the few yellow feathers under its wings that were used for feather cloaks and other items (Fornander 1918–1919). In the Marquesas, the upper portion of a long pole would be smeared with birdlime and thrust into the roots and branches of a banyan. The wings and feet of roosting birds would stick to the pole (Handy 1923). A plague of small rats on the island of Nuku Hiva was dealt with by trapping them in birdlime (Porter 1822).

The adhesive properties of the gum made it useful for many things. Small, red seeds of *Abrus precatorius* were glued in decorative patterns to personal ornaments such as headdresses and breastplates. Bamboo handles were attached to shell trumpets with the sap, and arrows used for archery games were dipped into the gum to hold them tightly against the bow string. (Stewart 1831; Ellis 1969; Linton 1974). The sap was even used for personal adornment; Samoan women stiffened their hair with it, and Tahitians mixed it with pigment so the color would adhere to their skin (Turner 1861; Ellis 1969).

The sap had several medicinal uses. Huguenin (1902) saw it massaged into the skin to treat broken bones and sprains on Raiatea. In many islands it was used to treat skin ailments (Handy 1940). Other portions of the tree were also part of the native pharmacopoeia (see Cox, this volume). The root is astringent and was used as a purgative; when macerated it was used as a poultice for skin ailments (MacCaughey 1917).

The leaves of the breadfruit tree were widely used throughout Polynesia to wrap food for cooking. The dried leaves are rough. These and the encircling stipules were used to smooth bowls and candlenuts in Hawaii (Handy 1940). An unusual use of the leaves was seen in the Marquesas where they were strung together into long strips and used to thatch houses (Stewart 1831). This type of thatch was more durable and better than that of coconut leaves, the usual source of thatching material for most of Polynesia. The thatch became bleached from the sun and Stewart thought that the roofs gleaming in the sunlight among the dark foliage were very picturesque.

Tapa and Cordage

The breadfruit tree was an important source of bast used to manufacture cordage and bark cloth or tapa. *Broussonetia papyrifera* (Moraceae), the paper mulberry, and *Ficus prolixa* (Moraceae), or banyan, were also used (Koojiman 1972). In general, bark cloth is made by stripping out the soft, pliant, inner bark, which is soaked to soften and separate the fibers. Excess water is squeezed out and the bark is beaten with wooden implements on stones or wooden anvils to flatten and stretch it. When the cloth is the desired size, it is often dyed and decorated with vegetable colors. Tapa is made from the young branches or shoots of breadfruit. The bark on the trunk and older branches is coarse and dry and difficult to beat into cloth (Handy 1923; Buck 1930, 1938). Exceptionally large pieces of breadfruit tapa can be made. John Jenkins (1855) saw bales of tapa 150-meters long and one-meter wide during his visit to Tahiti.

Early accounts of the quality of breadfruit tapa vary. Tongan tapa was coarse, seldom worn, and used chiefly for funereal purposes (Mariner and Martin 1827). In contrast, a light and beautiful cloth was made from breadfruit on Rarotonga, Aitutaki, and Mauke in the Cook Islands (Gill 1892). Durable tapa was made from breadfruit in the Society Islands and this was often used to refurbish worn pieces of *Broussonetia* cloth. Newly made breadfruit cloth was beaten together with the worn-out pieces. The resulting mottled piece was often colored yellow with dye made from the root of *Morinda citrifolia* (Smith 1813). Breadfruit tapa was made even more durable and impervious to moisture by coating it with candlenut oil (Williams 1837).

Common Tahitian tapa was brown and made of banyan or breadfruit; several kinds of cloth were made from breadfruit (Henry 1928; Ellis 1967). Breadfruit tapa was often inferior in whiteness and softness to that of *Broussonetia* (Hawkesworth 1773). However, the choicest cloth was very fine and white, made from the bark of an uncommon variety of breadfruit known as *pu'upu'u*. Few visitors had the opportunity to see it as it was grown only on temple or *marae* grounds and the cloth was reserved for sacred and ritual purposes. It was worn by priests and workers at the *marae* while preparing for and during ceremonies. Novices in the *arioi* society wore robes and cloaks decorated with elaborate patterns during a performance welcoming them into the society. Hina, a mythological woman mentioned in many legends and myths, made her tapa from *pu'upu'u*.

Such fine tapa could be made from breadfruit that it was considered a worthy gift for the royal family of Tahiti. A single piece several hundred meters long was made by the women of Huahine in 1852 to welcome Queen Pomare to their island (Gill 1885). Gill recorded a fragment of an early chant composed by a woman of Mauke who made a beautiful piece of breadfruit tapa. She wanted a royal lover, the king of Tahiti, and believed that her gift of fine tapa would be irresistible to him. The large double canoe bearing her gift to Tahiti was driven back by a storm and the king never received her fine gift. While her gift did not succeed in gaining her a lover, her song helps document the fine quality of breadfruit tapa.

The art of making fine tapa quickly died out after the introduction of woven cloth. *Pu'upu'u* cloth was no longer made in the Society Islands. In the Marquesas, tapa was made on a regular basis only on the island of Fatu Hiva (Linton 1925). In the Cook Islands, tapa manufacture all but disappeared as the islanders stopped growing *Broussonetia*. When cloth was needed for rituals they had to resort to making common breadfruit or banyan cloth. Ethnographers visiting the Cook Islands, Mangareva, and the Marquesas in the 1920s saw little evidence of the fine tapa previously made. They only saw breadfruit tapa that was thick, coarse, and grayish brown (Buck 1944; Linton 1974).

In addition to its ceremonial and ritual uses, tapa was used for bedding and items of clothing such as cloaks, loincloths, robes, and turbans (Handy 1923). It was even used to make kites in the Cook Islands. Pieces of tapa were sewn or glued with breadfruit gum to a light wooden frame (Buck 1927).

Breadfruit bast was also used to make strong cordage. The cord was made by scraping and drying the inner bark which was then rolled and twisted into 2- or 3-ply cord. Large mesh nets for catching sharks were made in the Cook Islands and Samoa (Buck 1930). The cultivar *aveloloa* was preferred for making bast in Samoa, but others could be used.

Legends

Careful reading of legends can provide much information about the life-style, practices, and beliefs of a culture. All legends about the breadfruit tree are concerned with its origin: Was it introduced by people or supernatural events? One such legend from the Society Islands and Hawaii has several forms.

The earliest account of this legend is just a brief outline of the much longer version told by the natives of the Society Islands (Ellis 1967). Ellis emphasized that the events occurred during a time of famine, that the tree sprang up from the dismembered body of a man, and that the fruit was first offered to the chiefs and gods. A full version of this legend was written in 1887 from an oral account by the writer's grandfather on Raiatea (Henry 1928):

> During a time of famine long ago, red clay was the only food. A Raiatean man took his wife and four children into the mountains where they hid in a cave and ate ferns. He told his wife to go outside in the morning and she would see "my hands become leaves, the trunk and two branches my body and legs, and the round fruit my head and the core inside, my tongue." In the morning, a beautiful tree stood as her husband had foretold. That valley is now called Tuauru, the place of breadfruit. She roasted the fruit, soaked it in a nearby stream and peeled it. She fed her family, but did not first make a customary offering to the king. When she prepared the fruit, pieces of the core and peel washed downstream. Servants of the king were catching shrimp in the stream. They found and ate these pieces. They were curious about this strange food and searched until they found the tree. They asked the woman what it was, and she replied, "*uru*." She explained how it had arisen from the body of her husband who wanted to feed his family. The servants admired the tree which was covered with fruit of all the cultivars. The tree was taken down from the mountain and planted by her family's *marae*. A root was broken off and taken to the island of Tahaa where it grew. Ripe fruits were taken to the king and he liked it so much he ordered his servants to bring the tree and its owners to him. While they were transplanting the tree, a woman begged for some roots and planted them in a valley which became known as "*Maiore*." The family wept for their lost tree, but new trees soon arose from the roots left behind.

This legend provides some background on the usage of the terms *uru* and *maiore*. The original term for breadfruit was *uru* or head, but when a Raiatean king took this for his own name it could no longer be used. *Maiore* was then used for breadfruit and *upo'o* for the head. In later years, *maiore* was replaced by the old name, *uru*, but *upo'o* was retained for the head (Henry 1928). The legend also attests to the scarcity of food that forced the family to eat red earth and ferns. Famine was a frequent occurrence in ancient Polynesia due to the seasonal nature of the breadfruit crop, natural catastrophes, and destruction of crops and food supplies during war.

The same legend is known in Hawaii and is said to have been brought from Samoa or Tahiti along with the breadfruit (Pukui and Beckwith 1933). In the Hawaiian version, the god Ku married a Hawaiian woman and a breadfruit tree grew from his body after his death. Since Ku was a god with magical powers, the tree also was magical. It would run back into the ground if anyone not in the family tried to pick the fruit.

Fornander (1918–1919) gives a different version, from Kona, Hawaii, of this legend:

> The fruits were not the head but the testicles of the dead man. This new kind of tree attracted the attention of many of the lesser Hawaiian gods. They tried to eat it raw but it was unpalatable. It was delicious when roasted. Kane and Kanaloa, two important gods, were told about this wonderful new food. They replied that the gods were eating the testicles of a dead man. The gods were disgusted and began vomiting at Kona and continued through the mountains until they reached Waipio. Breadfruit trees sprang up from their vomit and this is why breadfruit trees are so plentiful on Hawaii.

Other legends stated that breadfruit was introduced to the southern coast of Oahu at Puuloa. There were two versions recorded by Fornander (1918–1919). Kaha'i, a chief, made a voyage to Kahiki and brought the breadfruit back from Upolu, an ancient place name in Samoa and the Society Islands. In the second version, two men out fishing were blown away by a storm. They landed on a mythical island, Kanehunamoku, and found the breadfruit. They took it with them and planted it at Puuloa. The goddess, Haumea, heard about this tree and came to see it. She saw that it was a new tree and took it and spread it throughout the islands.

The belief that breadfruit was introduced from Tahiti is supported by a Tahitian legend (Henry 1928). Tafi'a, a man with magical powers, drew the Hawaiian Islands out of the ocean. After this feat, he returned home to get people to move to these new islands. They took to Hawaii their gods, breadfruit, and other plants.

A Marquesan legend tells how breadfruit was taken to the Cook Islands (Handy 1930).

> Pepe'iu moved to Rarotonga from Nuku Hiva and married a chief. There was no breadfruit there, only taro. When she became pregnant she said that the newborn child had to be fed breadfruit. The chief's brother sailed to Nuku Hiva and collected branches from the trees. He planted these when he returned to Rarotonga, but they did not grow. Then the chief went to the valley of Hooumi, where breadfruit grew best on Nuku Hiva. He stole roots and young sprouts and successfully established these on Rarotonga. Pepe'iu needed breadfruit to feed her newborn baby because Marquesans thought that breast milk was poisonous for three days after the birth (Handy 1923).

Newborn babies were fed with breadfruit that had been ripened and slowly baked overnight. The tender part near the core was chewed by the mother and fed to the infant until it was safe to breast feed.

On Rarotonga the cultivar *kuru peka* is said to have come from the Marquesas (Wilder 1931). Another Cook Island cultivar was considered sacred as it was brought from Tahiti by Tangiia, the chief of one of the two original bands of settlers (Gill 1885). A Rarotongan named Tupa introduced breadfruit to the island of Mangareva in the Austral Group (Buck 1938).

"A'ohe 'ulu e loa'a i ka pokole o ka lou."
"No breadfruit can be reached when the picking stick is too short" (Pukui 1983).

This Hawaiian proverb means there is no success without preparation—and the Polynesians certainly had great success with breadfruit. With careful preparation and skill they transported it across the Pacific, spreading it throughout the Polynesian world. On reaching and settling new islands, the Polynesians nurtured and multiplied the few precious plants they were able to successfully transport and establish. Through careful observation and horticultural skill, they increased the number of cultivars by selecting seedlings and root shoots with characteristics different from the parent tree. Breadfruit grew and flourished in Polynesia, supporting and nourishing as it provided shelter, fabric, medicine, and food.

Literature Cited

Banack, S. A. 1991. Plants and Polynesian voyaging. In *Islands Plants, and Polynesians.* Eds. P. A. Cox and S. A. Banack. Portland, Oregon: Timber Press, Dioscorides Press.

Barrau J. 1957. L'arbre à pain en Océanie. *J. Agr. Trop. Bot. Appl.* 4:117–123.

———. 1961. Subsistence agriculture in Polynesia and Micronesia. Bernice P. Bishop Mus. Bul. 223:1–94.

———, ed. 1963. *Plants and the Migrations of Pacific Peoples.* Honolulu: Bishop Mus. Press.

———. 1965. Histoire et préhistoire horticoles de l'Océanie tropicale. *J. Sociéte i/ Océanistes* 21:55–78.

———. 1973. The Oceanians and their food plants. Trans. R. Roberts and C. Roberts. In *Man and His Foods.* Ed. C. E. Smith. University, Alabama: Univ. of Alabama Press. 87–117.

Beckwith, M. W., ed. 1932. Kepelino's traditions of Hawaii. Bernice P. Bishop Mus. Bul. 95:1–206.

Beechey, F. W. 1831. *Narrative of a Voyage to the Pacific and Berings Strait.* London: H. Colburn and R. Bentley.

Bennett, G. 1860. Gatherings of a Naturalist. Cited in The Seedless breadfruits of the Pacific archipelagoes. Ed. P. J. Wester. 1924. *Philippine Agr. Review* 17(1):24–39.

Bligh, W. 1792. *A Voyage to the South Sea. For A the Purpose of Conveying the Breadfruit Tree to the West Indies in H.M.S. Bounty.* London: George Nicol.

———. 1976. *The Log of H.M.S. Providence, 1791–1793.* Rpt. Surrey, England: Genesis Publications.

Brown, F. B. H. 1935. Flora of southeastern Polynesia. Bernice P. Bishop Mus. Bul. 130:1–386.

Buck, P. H. [Te Rangi Hiroa]. 1927. *The Material Culture of the Cook Islands (Aitutaki).*

Memoirs Board of Maori Ethnological Research. Vol. 1. New Plymouth, New Zealand: T. Avery and Sons.

_____ . 1930. Samoan material culture. Bernice P. Bishop Mus. Bul. 75.

_____ . 1938. Ethnology of Mangareva. Bernice P. Bishop Mus. Bul. 157:1–519.

_____ . 1944. Arts and crafts of the Cook Islands. Bernice P. Bishop Mus. Bul. 179:1–533.

Cheeseman, T. F. 1903. The Flora of Rarotonga. Trans. Linn. Soc. London Bot. Series 2d. 6:261–313.

Christian, F. W. 1910. *Eastern Pacific Lands, Tahiti and the Marquesas Islands.* London: Robert Scott.

Christophersen, E. 1935. Flowering plants of Samoa. Bernice P. Bishop Mus. Bul. 128:3–221.

Coenan, J., and J. Barrau. 1961. The breadfruit tree in Micronesia. S. Pac. Bul. 11(4):37–39, 65–67.

Cook, J., and J. King. 1784. *A Voyage to the Pacific Ocean. 1776–1780.* 3 vols. Dublin: H. Chamberlaine etc.

Cox, P. A. 1980a. Masi and tanu'eli: ancient Polynesian technologies for the preservation and concealment of food. Pac. Trop. Bot. Garden Bul. 10(4):81–93.

_____ . 1980b. Two Samoan technologies for breadfruit and banana preservation. *Econ. Bot.* 34(2):181–185.

_____ . 1991. Polynesian herbal medicine. In *Islands, Plants, and Polynesians.* Eds. P. A. Cox and S. A. Banack. Portland, Oregon: Timber Press, Dioscorides Press.

Ellis, J. 1775. A description of the mangosteen and the breadfruit. In *The Log of H.M.S.* Providence, *1791–1793.* Ed. W. Bligh. Rpt. Surrey, England: Genesis Publications, 1976. 35–87.

Ellis, W. 1967. *Polynesian Researches.* Rpt. London: Dawsons of Pall Mall.

_____ . 1969. *Polynesian Researches: Society Islands.* Rutland, Vermont: C. E. Tuttle Co.

Fornander, A. 1918–1919. Fornander Collection of Hawaiian Antiquities and Folklore. Ed. Thomas G. Thrum. Memoirs Bernice P. Bishop Mus. 4.

Fosberg, F. R. 1960. Introgression in *Artocarpus* in Micronesia. *Brittonia* 12:101–113.

Gill, William W. 1876. *Myths and Songs from the South Pacific.* London: Henry S. King and Co.

_____ . 1885. *Jottings from the Pacific.* New York: American Tract Society.

_____ . 1892. *The South Pacific and New Guinea: Past and Present.* Sydney: C. Potter.

Handy, E. S. C. 1923. Native culture in the Marquesas. Bernice P. Bishop Mus. Bul. 9.

_____ . 1930. Marquesan legends. Bernice P. Bishop Mus. Bul. 69.

_____ . 1932. Houses, boats and fishing in the Society Islands. Bernice P. Bishop Mus. Bul. 90.1–111.

_____ . 1940. The Hawaiian planter. Vol 1, His plants, methods and areas of cultivation. Bernice P. Bishop Mus. Bul. 161.

Hawkesworth, J. 1773. *An Account of the Voyages Undertaken for Making Discoveries in the Southern Hemisphere.* 3 vols. London: W. Strahan and T. Cadell.

Henry, T. 1928. Ancient Tahiti. Bernice P. Bishop Mus. Bul. 48:1–651.

Huguenin, P. 1902. *Raiatea la Sacrée.* Neuchatel: P. Attinger.

Jarrett, F. M. 1959. Studies in *Artocarpus* and allied genera. 3, A revision of *Artocarpus* subgenus *Artocarpus. J. Arnold Arbor.* 15:298–326.

Jenkins, J. S. 1855. *Voyage of the U.S. Exploring Squadron. 1838–1842.* New York: Alden and Beardsley.

Koojiman S. 1972. Tapa in Polynesia. Bernice P. Bishop Mus. Bul. 234: 1–498.

Krauss B. 1974. *Ethnobotany of Hawaii.* Honolulu: Univ. of Hawaii Press.

Linton, R. 1925. Archaeology of the Marquesas Islands. Bernice P. Bishop Mus. Bul. 23:1–187.

_____ . 1974. The material culture of the Marquesas Islands. Memoirs Bernice P. Bishop Mus. 8(5):1–211. New York: Krauss Reprint Co.

MacCaughey, V. 1917. The genus *Artocarpus* in the Hawaiian Islands. Torreya 17(2):33–49.

Mariner, W., and J. Martin. 1827. *An Account of the Natives of the Tonga Islands in the South Pacific Ocean.* Vol. 1. 3rd ed. Edinburgh: Constable and Co.

Massal, E., and J. Barrau. 1956. Food plants of South Seas islands. S. Pac. Comm. Tech. Paper 94.

Melville, H. 1924. *Typee*. London: Oxford Univ.

Murai, M., P. Pen, and C. D. Miller. 1958. *Some Tropical Pacific Foods*. Honolulu: Univ. of Hawaii.

Parker, R. D. R. 1967. *A Field and Laboratory Study of the Storage and Preservation of Breadfruit as Practiced in the South Pacific Islands*. M.S. Thesis, Univ. of Hawaii, Honolulu.

Parkinson, S. 1984. The preservation and preparation of rootcrops and some other traditional foods in the South Pacific. RAS 83/001, Suva, FAO. Field Document 1.

Porter, D. 1822. *Journal of a Cruise Made to the Pacific Ocean*. 2nd ed. New York: Wiley and Halsted.

Pukui, M. K. 1983. 'Olelo No'eau. Hawaiian proverbs and poetical sayings. Bernice P. Bishop Mus. Special Publication 71:1–351.

Pukui, M. K., and M. Beckwith. 1933. Hawaiian Folktales. 3rd Series. Poughkeepsie, New York: Vassar College.

Ragone, D. 1987. Collecting breadfruit in the Central Pacific. Pac. Trop. Bot. Garden Bul. 17(2):37–41.

———. 1988. Breadfruit Varieties in the Pacific Atolls. Suva: UNDP Integrated Atoll Development Project.

Setchell, W. A. 1924. American Samoa. Part 1. Vegetation of Tutuila Island. Washington, DC: Department of Marine Biology, Carnegie Institute.

Smith, W. 1813. *Journal of a Voyage in the Missionary Ship* Duff. New York: Collins and Co.

Stewart, C. S. 1831. *A Visit to the South Seas in the U.S. Ship* Vincennes, *1829–1830*. New York: J. P. Haven.

Turner, G. 1861. *Nineteen Years in Polynesia*. London: John Snow.

Wester, P. J. 1924. The seedless breadfruits of the Pacific archipelagoes. *Philippine Agr. Review* 17(1):24–39.

Wilder, G. P. 1928. The breadfruit of Tahiti. Bernice P. Bishop Mus. Bul. 50:1–83.

———. 1931. Flora of Rarotonga. Bernice P. Bishop Mus. Bul. 86:1–113.

Wilkes, C. 1845. *Narrative of the United States Exploring Expedition During the Years 1838–1842*. Philadelphia: Lea and Blanchard.

Williams, J. 1837. *A Narrative of Missionary Enterprises in the South Sea Islands*. New York: D. Appleton and Co.

Yen, D. E. 1976. Indigenous food processing in Oceania. In *The Anthropology of Food and Food Habits*. Ed. Margaret L. Arnott. The Hague: Mouton Publishers. 147–168.

Yuncker, T. G. 1959. Plants of Tonga. Bernice P. Bishop Mus. Bul. 220.

Index of Scientific Names

Index of Polynesian Words